THE ASSASSINATION OF
ROBERT F. KENNEDY

THE ASSASSINATION OF ROBERT F. KENNEDY

CRIME, CONSPIRACY AND COVER-UP — A NEW INVESTIGATION

TIM TATE & BRAD JOHNSON

THISTLE
PUBLISHING

"What has violence ever accomplished?
What has it ever created?
No martyr's cause has ever been stilled
by an assassin's bullet."

Senator Robert F. Kennedy, April 5, 1968
Speech to Cleveland City Club,
one day after the assassination of Dr. Martin Luther King.

PRELUDE

Ambassador Hotel, Los Angeles
Wednesday, June 5, 1968: 12.00am, Pacific Daylight Time

"*We want Bobby! We want Bobby!*"

The Embassy Room ballroom is packed tight. Amid the traditional paraphernalia of American elections – balloons, placards, button badges and straw boaters – 1,800 excited campaign workers and supporters repeatedly chant the name of the winner of California's Democratic primary.

"*We want Bobby! We want Bobby!*"

The mood is ecstatic: the victory is a major boost for their candidate's hopes of being the Democratic Party's nominee in the 1968 Presidential election.

12.01am

Senator Robert Francis Kennedy enters the ballroom to wild cheering; he steps up on to a makeshift platform at the north end of the room, smiles and embarks on a victory speech in which he offers a promise to heal a nation torn apart by injustice, inequality and war.

"What I think is quite clear is that we can work together in the last analysis and that what has been going on within the United States over the period of the last three years, the divisions, the violence, the disenchantment with our society, the divisions whether it's between blacks and whites, between the poor and the more affluent or between age groups or on the war in Vietnam that we can start to work together."

12.14am

Kennedy wraps up his speech by exhorting his supporters to continue their efforts to help him win his party's presidential nomination at its national convention later that summer in Illinois: "Now it's on to Chicago and let's win there, thank you very much." With his right hand, he flashes a V for Victory sign.

12.15am

Flanked by his wife, aides and reporters, Kennedy leaves the speaker's platform and makes his way through an anteroom behind the stage curtains and into a narrow backstage corridor. Escorted by two hotel staff members, Karl Uecker and Edward Minasian, he heads toward the swinging double-doors of the Ambassador's kitchen service pantry.

12.16am

As Kennedy walks through the pantry a small, dark-haired young man climbs down from a tray stacker, steps forward and, raising his arm, fires a cheap, small-calibre revolver.

After the second shot, Uecker grabs the gunman's arm, pinning it down on a steam table. But the shooter continues firing wildly, emptying his revolver of all eight bullets in its chamber.

Twelve seconds after the first shots, a CBS TV cameraman captures the first images of the chaos inside the pantry. They show Kennedy spread-eagled on the floor, blood pumping from a lethal wound in his head, a hotel busboy kneeling beside him. As members of Kennedy's entourage struggle to disarm the shooter, the cameraman films the fallen candidate; audio recordings capture his sobs amid the screams and shouting of others – *"Christ no!" … "Get away from the barrel, get away from the barrel, man!"*

12.18am

"Is there a doctor?" The first call for medical help is made from the stage lectern in the Embassy Room. Scenes of confusion

in the ballroom are carried live, but unexplained, by two of the three television networks which had been running continuous primary election night coverage.

12.21am

ABC TV broadcasts the first nationwide news of the shooting. News Anchor Howard K. Smith announces: *"Ladies and Gentlemen, we've kept the air on because we've heard an alarming report that Robert Kennedy was shot..."*

12.25am

Robert Kennedy is lifted on to a gurney and rushed outside to an ambulance.

12.26am

Both CBS and NBC TV broadcast live pictures of Los Angeles Police bundling the suspected shooter through the hotel; moments later they push him into a squad car.

***

Five other people were hit by gunshots in the pantry: each was walking or standing behind Kennedy when the shooting began. They were treated in hospitals across Los Angeles: none had life-threatening injuries and all would all survive.

Outside the Good Samaritan Hospital large crowds gathered in an almost silent vigil. Inside, surgeons battled through the night to save Robert Kennedy's life.

Just over twenty-four hours later, at 1.44am, Thursday June 6, they had stopped fighting. Senator Robert Francis Kennedy, brother and heir apparent to a murdered President, was pronounced dead, killed by an assassin's bullet.

INTRODUCTION

It is a cliché that those of a certain age will always remember where they were when John F. Kennedy was assassinated. The shooting of America's 35th President flashed around the world on Friday, November 22, 1963. More than five decades later, it continues to exert an unremitting grip on international interest. More than two thousand books have been – and continue to be – published, dissecting every detail of what happened in Dealey Plaza, Dallas that autumn afternoon. Seemingly endless allegations and counter-claims, televised re-constructions and free-floating theories seek to solve a murder which, in the public mind at least, remains shrouded in inconsistencies and mystery – not least because the two official commissions of enquiry reached opposing conclusions on whether the murder was the act of a lone gunman or a sinister conspiracy.

By contrast, the second Kennedy assassination almost five years later has attracted much less scrutiny. Unlike the killing of JFK, the shooting of Robert Francis Kennedy in a hotel pantry in Los Angeles was not examined by a successor to the Presidential Warren Commission, nor even by the subsequent Congressional inquiry, the House Select Committee on Assassinations. And yet the scientific facts of the RFK assassination – logistical, pathological and ballistic – have always been much more problematic than those surrounding the killing of John Kennedy. So, too, the politics.

Bobby Kennedy was shot and mortally wounded minutes after winning a key race in the battle to be nominated as the Democratic Party's candidate to face the Republican Richard Nixon in the November 1968 Presidential election.

Victory in the California Primary did not guarantee RFK the nomination, but it went a very long way towards it. And, in that troubled and violent year, with America torn apart by race and poverty riots, and with public anger at the ever-more catastrophic Vietnam War exploding on to the streets, to his supporters and detractors alike Kennedy alone seemed to be the candidate promising radical change – at home and abroad.

He had run a breathless and insurgent campaign, talking openly about the need for "revolution". He energised the young, the dispossessed and those desperate for transformation. And they believed. To those who campaigned for him, it was an article of faith that a second President Kennedy in the White House would signal an end to the blight of urban poverty and racial inequality – twin scourges which had caused riots across America in the years since John Kennedy's assassination, and which also played a background role in the murder of Martin Luther King Jnr. in April 1968.

But more importantly even than that, Bobby's supporters believed he would halt the war in Vietnam; and since he had, however belatedly, appeared to signal publicly that he was unconvinced by the Warren Commission investigation of his brother's murder, they hoped, too, for a new enquiry into the troubling inconsistencies surrounding the official account of the events in Dallas.

But for as many who loved Robert Kennedy there seemed to be an equal number who despised him. His role as counsel to the Senate committee investigating labour racketeering had earned him the enmity of corrupt union officials, while the war he declared on organised crime as Attorney General in JFK's administration made him a hate figure for America's most powerful mob bosses, and contributed to his unending feud with FBI Director J. Edgar Hoover.

Following the Bay of Pigs debacle, Bobby also clashed with the CIA, and his refusal to accede to the demands of the President's more hawkish advisors during the tense 13 days of the Cuban Missile Crisis created deep resentment within the senior ranks of the military. Nor did he make many friends on Capitol Hill: his brusque and impatient manner was viewed with deep suspicion – at the very least – by Senators, Congressmen, and much of Washington DC's political elite. And his championing of civil rights, racial justice and the plight of America's farmworkers attracted the loathing of segregationists, white supremacists and some of the country's major agricultural leaders alike.

RFK heard this drumbeat and – particularly after John Kennedy's assassination – knew what it could mean. As he once remarked to a reporter, "You won't have any trouble finding my enemies. They're all over town."[1]

Robert Kennedy's removal from the political stage that night in June 1968 brought comfort to his enemies, just as it destroyed all the hopes of those who believed in him and the promise of change he represented.

For those *political* reasons the shooting in the Ambassador Hotel pantry was a crime which demanded a thorough and honest enquiry.

But beside that there was an unanswerable *scientific* case for a rigorous forensic investigation. Much more clearly than in the JFK assassination, the fundamental facts of RFK's killing simply did not fit the official conclusion – that the murder was carried out by a lone gunman, Sirhan Bishara Sirhan. Within minutes of

---

1   "The Number 2 Man in Washington" by Paul O'Neill. *Life* [magazine], January 26, 1962, p.90.

the shooting, evidence emerged which suggested that Sirhan had not acted alone; within weeks Los Angeles Police Department and the District Attorney's Office knew that they could not reconcile the findings of the official autopsy with the testimony of key eyewitness to the shooting. But although the police and prosecutors publicly promised a scrupulous and transparent enquiry, they did the precise opposite. For almost twenty years.

We came into the case as television producers, separately and a decade apart. We were not the first journalists to raise questions about the evidence: in the years immediately after RFK's murder a handful of courageous reporters and (sometimes eccentric) citizen-investigators began flagging up substantial inconsistencies in the claims made by Los Angeles Police Department and the District Attorney. But it appears that we are amongst the longest-lasting.

Tim's 1992 documentary for Channel 4 television in Britain, and A&E networks in the US, was the first to broadcast tape recordings made by LAPD which revealed it to have distorted, falsified and suppressed evidence which suggested that a second gunman had murdered Robert Kennedy.

Fifteen years later, Brad's documentary for the Discovery Times Channel presented scientific proof of that second gunman: forensic audio analysis of a tape Brad uncovered – the only recording to have captured the sounds of the shooting in the pantry – demonstrated unequivocally that at least 13 shots were fired; many more than could have come from Sirhan Sirhan's 8-shot revolver.

Since those films we have – individually and later in tandem – spent decades painstakingly examining all the evidence. At times it has seemed a herculean and never-ending task, involving years carefully examining and cross-referencing tens of thousands of original documents, conducting forensic analysis of rare audio, film footage, video tape and photographs, and tracking down crucial witnesses.

This book, then, is the product of more than a quarter of a century's patient investigative journalism. What is most striking about the Robert Kennedy assassination is that the fundamental evidence – eye-witness, ballistic, forensic and, above all, scientific – points unequivocally to the conclusion that Sirhan Sirhan did not fire the fatal bullets in the pantry. Which raises two more troublesome questions: who did – and why?

We realise that positing answers to these questions may lead to accusations of conspiracy theorising. But, although we have found clear evidence of genuine conspiracies, we are cautious about claiming that these alone offer a solution to the mystery. Our approach has always been to ascertain the facts and then to pursue them wherever they may lead, however uncomfortable that may be.

The murder of Robert F. Kennedy was the final American political assassination of a turbulent decade. It, more than any other single act, signalled the end of the optimism and idealism which briefly flourished in the 1960s. It changed the course of both the United States and much of the world beyond its shores. For those reasons – as well as for natural justice – the events of June 1968 demanded an honest, open and thorough investigation by police and prosecutors.

This book exists because that did not happen.

CHAPTER ONE:
SHADOWS

On Saturday, March 16, 1968, Robert Francis Kennedy, the 42-year-old junior Senator for New York, walked into the Caucus Room of the elegant old Senate office building on Constitution Avenue, Washington D.C.

Eight years earlier, John F. Kennedy had boldly declared his candidacy in the 1960 Presidential election in the same room. Now, in front of a phalanx of pressmen and television cameras, JFK's younger brother was noticeably more solemn as he read a statement announcing his own run for the White House.

"I do not run for the presidency merely to oppose any man, but to propose new policies. I run because I am convinced that this country is on a perilous course and because I have such strong feelings about what must be done, and I feel that I'm obliged to do all that I can.

"I run to seek new policies. Policies to end the bloodshed in Vietnam and in our cities; policies to close the gaps that now exist between black and white; between rich and poor, between young and old, in this country and around the rest of the world.

"I run for the Presidency because I want the Democratic Party and the United States of America to stand for hope instead of despair, for reconciliation of men instead of the growing risk of world war.

"I run because it is now unmistakably clear that we can change these disastrous, divisive policies only by changing the men who are now making them."

The statement was the product of a scripting session which had run into the early hours, and it marked the end of months of uncertainty and doubt about Bobby Kennedy's ambitions. Washington and its press corps had long expected him to throw his own hat into the ring. But for months Bobby dithered and equivocated, while his closest aides, advisors and family members debated the wisdom of entering what promised to be a bitter and acrimonious contest.

As the sitting President, Lyndon B. Johnson would normally have expected to be the Democratic Party's candidate, but at the end of November 1967 Minnesota Senator Eugene McCarthy had announced his intention to challenge the incumbent, blaming Johnson for what he termed "a deepening moral crisis" across the nation[2], and making a clear commitment to ending the war in Vietnam.

Bobby's politics were more in line with McCarthy's positions than with the policies Johnson had been pursuing. But although his wife, Ethel, wanted him to run, his younger brother was opposed to the idea: Teddy believed that LBJ had a lock on the nomination and that if Bobby waited until the next election in 1972 he would be guaranteed the Democratic Party's wholehearted support.[3]

Two months after McCarthy announced his candidacy there was still no decision from the Kennedy camp. For a man who had just published a book in which he warned against "timidity" as one of the major barriers to much-needed change[4], Bobby's hesitancy was much noticed.

---

2   *Time* Magazine, December 8, 1967
3   Arthur Schlesinger Jnr; Robert Kennedy and His Times, p.895.
4   *To Seek A Newer World*, Bantam Books, 1967

When, on January 30, he told a breakfast gathering of fifteen journalists at the National Press Club that he had no plans to run against Johnson and McCarthy "under any foreseeable circumstances"[5], he found himself accused of cowardice and savagely ridiculed on the two most politically-significant prime time comedy shows, *Rowan and Martin's Laugh-In* and the *Smothers Brothers Comedy Hour*[6].

But the following month the co-incidence of three events forced Kennedy to confront his conscience and finally take a position. The first was the Tet Offensive – a campaign of coordinated attacks by North Vietnamese forces against US military and civilian command centres across the South. The war was already increasingly unpopular with the US electorate: by December 1967 opinion polls showed that 45% of Americans believed it had been a mistake to send troops to Vietnam[7] – not because the war was wrong in principle, but because the mounting casualty figures and rising taxes were too high a price to pay to defeat communism on the other side of the world[8]. The Tet attacks struck more than 100 towns and cities, stunning the South Vietnamese Government and the Johnson White House: even the US Embassy in downtown Saigon came under sustained fire. The heavy loss of life and – temporarily at least – the humiliating loss of key cities, exposed the failure and evident futility of the war.

Bobby blamed himself for failing to speak out earlier. According to journalist Jack Newfield, then deeply immersed the Senator's inner circle, "Kennedy saw the magnitude of his

---

5   The meeting was officially off the record, but Kennedy authorized this statement for official attribution. Jack Newfield: *Robert F. Kennedy – A Memoir*; p.220. Berkley Publishing, 1969
6   Evan Thomas; Robert Kennedy – His Life, p.356
7   Clark Dougan and Stephen Weiss; *Tet: The Crucial year of 1968.* p. 68. Boston Publishing Company, 1983
8   Stanley Karnow; *Vietnam – A History* p. 545-546. Penguin, 1997

own blunder... He could almost visibly see millions of people, overnight, change their opinions about Vietnam, recoiling away from the President and his policy. And they were rallying not to him but to Eugene McCarthy."[9]

For a full week, Bobby pondered his response. In Chicago, on February 8, he delivered it, for the first time denouncing Vietnam as an unwinnable war.

"Our enemy, savagely striking at will across all of South Vietnam, has finally shattered the mask of official illusion with which we have concealed our true circumstances, even from ourselves... For the sake of those young Americans who are fighting today, if for no other reason, the time has come to take a new look at the war in Vietnam, not by cursing the past but by using it to illuminate the future. And the first and necessary step is to face the facts...

"They have demonstrated despite all our reports of progress, of government strength and enemy weakness, that half a million American soldiers with 700,000 Vietnamese allies, with total command of the air, total command of the sea, backed by huge resources and the most modern weapons, are unable to secure even a single city from the attacks of an enemy whose total strength is about 250,000...

"The best way to save our most precious stake in Vietnam— the lives of our soldiers—is to stop the enlargement of the war, and that the best way to end casualties is to end the war."[10]

But if the speech was Bobby's first overt criticism of Johnson and his policies, he was still undecided about whether to run against the President. Then, on the flight back from Chicago, he read a letter from his close friend, the journalist and writer Pete

---

9   Newfield, p.220. *Ibid.*
10 Speech at Book and Author Luncheon, Chicago, February 8, 1968. *UPI Archives.*

Hamill: it made an unashamedly emotional appeal for Kennedy to enter the race.

"If we have LBJ for another four years, there won't be much of a country left...I wanted to remind you that in Watts [the inner city Los Angeles neighbourhood devastated by race riots in 1965] I didn't see pictures of Malcolm X...on the walls. I saw pictures of JFK. That is your capital in the most cynical sense; it is your obligation in another, the obligation of staying true to whatever it was that put those pictures on those walls."[11]

That perceived burden grew heavier at the end of the month. On February 29, the Kerner Commission issued a detailed 429-page report on the racial unrest and riots which had set cities across America on fire over the previous two years.[12] Although Johnson had set up the Commission, when he read its conclusions – that "white racism" was a primary cause of the violence – his White House bluntly dismissed them. The reaction convinced Bobby that four more years of LBJ was an insupportably high price to pay for his own doubts.

He told his advisors that Johnson was "not going to do anything about the war and he's not going to do anything about the cities either."[13] Running was his duty as the keeper of his brother's legacy – the promise of the New Frontier JFK had held out to America. But it was also, in a way he had begun to realize, his obligation to the Kennedy family.

***

For much of his life Robert F. Kennedy had lived in shadows.

---

11 Letter to RFK from Pete Hamill, February 1968. Newfield, p.224

12 *Report of The National Advisory Committee on Civil Disorders.* Eisenhower Foundation: http://www.eisenhowerfoundation.org/docs/kerner.pdf

13 Arthur M. Schlesinger: *Robert Kennedy and His Times*, p. 908. Houghton Mifflin, 1978

He was the seventh child of Joe and Rose Kennedy but, crucially, the third brother. His father dominated his family, instilling in his children a belief in their own entitlement – Joe's much speculated-upon wealth provided a gilded upbringing – and (in the boys, at least) a sense of *noblesse oblige*. Bobby's elder brothers were – and were held out to him as – role models. Both Joe Kennedy Jnr. and Jack fought in World War Two, earning Purple Heart commendations for valour. Jack was wounded during a torpedo boat action in the South Pacific in August 1943; twelve months later, Joe was killed in what amounted to an Air Force suicide mission over the English Channel. Bobby, born in 1925, was too young to serve in combat: he joined the Navy six weeks shy of his 18th birthday, but to his intense frustration, never saw active service.

Joe Snr. had long-harboured ambitions to see a Kennedy in the White House. After Joe Jnr.'s death, he began grooming Jack as a future President, raising funds and forming alliances to back a post-war political career for his son.

In 1946 Jack stood for Congress and Bobby, on his discharge from the Navy, helped out with the campaign. But it was Joe's money, connections and wheeler-dealing that ensured Jack's victory in the November election. As Jack took his seat in the House of Representatives, Bobby quietly returned to Harvard.

He was a diligent but unremarkable student, notable chiefly for his profound Catholic faith and a fierce, sometimes foolhardy, determination to prove himself on the football field or in fights. All of his subsequent biographers suggest that the "tough guy persona" Bobby adopted was aimed at an audience of one: his father. If so, it was a performance given from his brother's shadow and one to which Joe Snr. seems to have been somewhat indifferent.

After three years at law school and less than a year working for the US Department of Justice, in June 1952, Bobby once again returned to politics, managing Jack's successful bid to win a seat in the Senate – the next vital step on his planned route to the White House. Bobby's handling of the campaign earned him a reputation for ruthlessness, and the belated respect of his father: the following year Joe Snr. engineered his appointment as assistant counsel to the Senate Permanent Sub-Committee on Investigations – or, as it was more widely and infamously known, Senator Joe McCarthy's anti-communist witch hunt. McCarthy, an old family friend despite being a Republican, believed that Soviet agents had infiltrated the US State Department; as sub-committee chairman he embarked on a succession of brutal hearings in which witnesses were attacked, bullied and browbeaten.

McCarthy's crude, fact-free smears – amplified by the committee's chief counsel, Roy Cohn, a vicious and unprincipled mob-connected attorney – appalled Bobby. He later complained that "no real research was ever done. Most of the investigations were instituted on the basis of some preconceived notion … and they were not going to allow the facts to interfere".[14] In July 1953 Bobby resigned.

But within six months he was back – though on the opposite side. In February 1954 he became chief counsel for the Democratic Party's minority representation, facing off against both McCarthy and Cohn. Over the next two years he challenged their actions and, when the Democrats became the majority party, he was a key figure in televised hearings examining McCarthy and Cohn's conduct. The sessions boosted Bobby's public reputation while destroying those of the Senator and his counsel. Cohn, in particular, nursed a violent loathing for his nemesis, once throwing a punch at Bobby in front of startled reporters.[15] He missed – but it mattered little: Cohn had powerful friends who shared his hatred for Bobby. One was the nation's

---

14   Robert Kennedy: *The Enemy Within*. Popular Library, 1960.
15   *Cohn, Kennedy Near Blows In 'Hate' Clash*: New York Times, June 12, 1954

Republican Vice-President, Richard Nixon; the other was John Edgar Hoover, the Machiavellian Director of the FBI. Both became lifelong enemies of Robert Kennedy. They were not to be alone.

Between 1957 and 1959 Bobby served as chief counsel for the Senate McClellan Committee investigating corruption and racketeering within America's unions. Under his direction the Committee issued 8,000 subpoenas and held 270 days of often-televised hearings involving 1,526 witnesses: they also exposed violent extortion and endemic corruption by union leaders, some of whom had skimmed millions from the pension funds of ordinary workers to support their extravagant lifestyles. But they also uncovered close links between union bosses and the Mafia: one name, in particular, was at the centre of what Kennedy would later call "a conspiracy of evil."

Jimmy Hoffa, President of the all-powerful Brotherhood of Teamsters – America's largest and richest union – was a rough, unapologetically violent former warehouse worker from Detroit, and the veteran of numerous bloody labour disputes. His police files included allegations of assault, extortion and conspiracy, though he had never been convicted of any crime. He made no secret of his association with the country's most notorious organized crime gangsters – some of whom Hoffa had appointed to key positions within the union.

In early February 1958, while the McClellan hearings examined other Teamsters officials, Hoffa paid a New York lawyer to infiltrate the Committee. The lawyer reported the attempt to Bobby, who with the backing of the FBI, set a trap for Hoffa. Outside a Washington DC hotel, and under the gaze of covert cameras, the Teamsters' boss handed over an envelope stuffed with a second instalment of $2,000: the police pounced and took him down to the court house – where Bobby was waiting to witness the arraignment.

Aided by a wily lawyer, Hoffa was acquitted of bribery (he subsequently also beat the rap in two attempted wiretapping trials). By the time he appeared before the McClellan Committee in August 1957 Bobby was convinced that behind his unsophisticated image, Hoffa was a serious criminal in charge of a powerful union: he later wrote that "there were times when his face seemed completely transfixed with this stare of absolute evilness."[16] Over days of angry cross-examination, Bobby accused Hoffa of collaboration with senior Mafia gangsters: Hoffa responded either by professing convenient lapses of memory or by attacking the Committee counsel. "You're sick – that's what's the matter with you – you are sick", he snarled at Bobby during one particularly feisty exchange.

But for all the sound and fury, the hearings never truly damaged Hoffa. When, on September 20, 1958 and after more than a year of attritional warfare, McClellan declared a ceasefire, Hoffa was able to walk out of the Senate Building in no greater danger than he had been at the start. For Bobby, however, the war was far from over. He put Hoffa on his mental back-burner and turned his full attention to the union leader's partners in organized crime.

The Sicilian Mafia had controlled much of America's criminal underworld since the 1920s: its businesses included prostitution, loan-sharking, extortion, illegal gambling, bootlegging and – by the 1950s – the growing market in narcotics.

Yet under Hoover's direction the FBI had avoided any real investigation of organized crime: when Bobby began asking the Bureau for its files on the country's 70 most powerful mobsters he was shocked to discover that "they didn't have any information, I think, on forty out of the seventy. Not even the slightest piece of information."[17] Aided by intelligence reports from the rival

---

16   Robert Kennedy: *The Enemy Within.* Popular Library, 1960.
17   Interviews with New York Times journalist Anthony Lewis, December 4 – 6, 1964; [in] *Robert Kennedy in His Own Words,* p.120. Bantam Books, 1988

Bureau of Narcotics, Bobby summoned a succession of gangsters to appear before the Committee.

The star witness proved to be Momo Salvatore "Sam" Giancana, Chicago's *"capo di capi"* who had risen through the Mafia's ranks by virtue of extreme violence – he was reputed to have hung several of his victims on meat hooks – and the astute cultivation of useful politicians and celebrities. On June 9, 1959, in front of a rapt television audience, Bobby accused the crime boss of murdering his enemies.

"Would you tell us, if you have any opposition from anybody, that you dispose of them by having them stuffed in a trunk? Is that what you do, Mr. Giancana?"

Giancana, like all the crime bosses subpoenaed to testify, pleaded the Fifth Amendment, repeatedly responding: "I decline to answer because I honestly believe my answer might tend to incriminate me."

The hearings did not lead directly to any indictments or criminal proceedings against corrupt union officials or Mafia bosses. Instead, they had three more long-lasting effects.

The first was to raise Bobby's profile. Millions had watched him goad and ridicule some of the most powerful underworld figures in America: "Will you just giggle every time I ask you a question? ... I thought only little girls giggled, Mr. Giancana". Although John Kennedy was the rising political star – and, indeed, sat on the McClellan Committee – Bobby's relentless pursuit of what he subsequently termed "the enemy within" both burnished the Kennedy brand and ensured that for the first time he began emerging from the shadow cast by his elder brother. A feature in the *Cleveland Press* noted that "even with a couple of [other] veteran inquisitors on hand, it is plain that this is Bob Kennedy's show."[18]

---

18   *Cleveland Press*, March 6, 1957

The second was to convince Bobby that he had found a cause worth fighting for – and one which he, rather than his brother or father, could own. He began work on a book about the threat facing America from the Mafia[19]. The evidence he garnered for it lit a fire within him which would, within less than a year, be fanned into an unprecedented "war on organized crime" by the US Government.

The third, though less easily calculated, was to stoke within the minds of Mafia dons and their allies a visceral and lifelong hatred of the man Hoffa called "an arrogant young whippersnapper". But, as Bobby's public profile rose and his public naming and shaming of organized crime set the course for his crusade against the Mob, he appears not to have appreciated how well-connected several of his declared enemies had become.

Nor was he then winning many friends in politics. Bobby resigned from the McClellan Committee to manage John Kennedy's campaign for the 1960 Presidential election and quickly earned a reputation for ruthlessness which would dog him for the next eight years. Some of this was undeserved – a 'hard man' act designed to be little more than a cover for the candidate's own cold-eyed political ambition: long-time JFK aide Kenny O'Donnell told a television interviewer that "Jack was the tough one, not Bobby. Jack would cut you off at the knees. Bobby would say 'Why are we doing that to this guy?'".[20] But it was also partly true: during the primaries race to secure the Democratic nomination for John, Bobby engineered a smear-campaign which branded his main rival, Hubert Humphrey, as a draft dodger during World War Two. Working in the shadows, Bobby's brusque, sometimes casually offensive disdain for

19   Robert Kennedy: *The Enemy Within*. Popular Library, 1960.
20   [Quoted in] Evan Thomas; *Robert Kennedy – A Life*. p.91. Simon & Schuster, 2000

the Party's traditional powerbrokers and methods of operation offended many of its senior figures and much of Washington's political class. As one of Richard Nixon's policy gurus subsequently noted: "He has all the patience of a vulture without any of the dripping sentimentality".[21]

He was, however, effective. In the closest election for almost half a century, and aided by Joe Kennedy Snr's money, John Kennedy defeated Nixon by two tenths of one per cent of the popular vote – a majority of just 112,827 from an overall total of almost 69 million votes cast. But in the Electoral College, Kennedy gained 303 votes to Nixon's 219: the era of Camelot on the Potomac was about to begin.

Bobby had intended to return to the law – though since he had never actually been in practice, he had no clear idea of where or how to go about it. But Joe Kennedy had other ideas: against Bobby's wishes – and the new President's deep reluctance – he insisted that John appoint his younger brother as Attorney General, the Government's most senior legal officer.

Under the outgoing Eisenhower administration the Justice Department had been cautious and slow-moving at a time when the country was facing severe internal problems: in addition to the threat from organized crime, many of the former Confederate states still practised brutal – often violent – racial segregation in open defiance of a landmark 1954 Supreme Court ruling that this was illegal. As an issue, civil rights had not unduly troubled the Kennedy clan: despite the abundant evidence that African-Americans were the victims of grotesque discrimination, JFK's inaugural address made no mention of this, or of the efforts of the growing Civil Rights movement for justice, and Bobby admitted that he, too, had paid too little attention. "I won't say

---

21   Ralph de Toledano: *RFK – The Man Who Would Be President*, p.169. New American Library, 1967

I lay awake at night worrying about civil rights before I became Attorney-General", he told *Life* magazine in 1961.[22] Nor did the movement entirely trust the young, privileged white lawyer from Massachusetts. Nonetheless, the plight of African-Americans in the southern states pricked at his conscience and, over the course of his first two years in office, Bobby forced at least some measure of equality on towns and cities below the Mason-Dixon line – sometimes by deploying federal troops. In doing so he added new foes to his growing list of enemies: the Ku Klux Klan, conservative southern Democrats and right-wing segregationists, including racist state governors like George Wallace of Alabama.

He also clashed with J. Edgar Hoover over civil rights. The FBI's veteran director was concerned with only one colour – red. Hoover viewed the civil rights movement as a de-facto communist front and demanded that the Attorney General authorize wiretaps on its most prominent leader, Dr. Martin Luther King; Bobby eventually – and shamefully – acquiesced[23].

But if he was a late-comer to the fight for civil rights and racial justice, the problem of organized crime – still a blind spot for Hoover – was a crusade closer to Bobby's heart. Two weeks after his appointment as Attorney General, he launched a "war on crime", transforming the Justice Department's previously moribund racketeering section – in January 1961 it employed just 17 people – into a relentless army of 60 prosecutors. Jimmy Hoffa was the first high-profile target: in October 1962, he was charged with demanding kickbacks from a trucking company, but although the trial ended with a hung jury acquittal, it yielded a valuable whistle-blower from within the Teamsters' ranks.

Edward Grady Partin told the Justice Department that Hoffa was "fixin'" to firebomb Bobby's family home at Hickory Hill

---

22   Peter Maas: *Robert Kennedy Speaks Out. Life*, March 28, 1961
23   He gave his approval on October 10, 1963.

outside Washington DC; if that failed, Hoffa planned to have the Attorney General assassinated by a sniper.[24] According to Partin – who passed an FBI polygraph test about the claims "with flying colours"[25] – Hoffa had told him "I've got to do something about that son of a bitch Bobby Kennedy. He's got to go."

But the Teamsters leader was just one of Bobby's targets. Over the next two years a total of 404 mafia gangsters were convicted for narcotics trafficking, corruption and illegal gambling – an increase of 800% on the previous Justice Department success rate.

Three leading gangsters, in particular, became the focus of the war on organized crime: Chicago's Sam Giancana, whom Bobby had ridiculed for giggling like "a little girl" in the McClellan hearings, Florida mob boss Santo Trafficante Jnr., and the head of organized crime in Louisiana, Carlos Marcello. All three were close Hoffa associates; all three developed an abiding hatred for both Kennedys; all three would – before long – be accused of conspiring to act on that hatred.

In April 1961, on Bobby's orders, Marcello, one of the most senior *Mafiosi* in America, was forcibly deported to Guatemala. He returned secretly to New Orleans two months later and for the next three years fought a succession of legal battles with the Justice Department. His lawyer, Frank Ragano, also represented both Hoffa and Trafficante, the *capo di capi* of organised crime in the Sunshine State. In the summer of 1963, Hoffa instructed Ragano to tell Trafficante and Marcello that it was time to kill John Kennedy. Nor was this the only alleged assassination plot involving the crime bosses. Around the same time, as Bobby led a second attempt to kick him out of the country, Marcello told Trafficante: "Bobby Kennedy is making life miserable for

24 *Hoffa 'Plot' to Kill R.F. Kennedy Alleged*: New York Times, April 12, 1962
25 Report of the United States House Select Committee on Assassinations, 1979; p.176. US National Archives

me and my friends. Someone ought to kill all those Kennedys." Trafficante re-assured his fellow-mobster: "You wait and see, somebody is going to kill those sons of bitches. It's just a matter of time."[26]

But it was Sam Giancana whose enmity – and associations – posed the greatest threat. In August 1960, during the dying days of the Eisenhower administration, the CIA had concocted an elaborate plan to employ Giancana (and later Trafficante) to assassinate Fidel Castro. According to a CIA memo the Agency budgeted "a figure of one hundred fifty thousand dollars" for the operation – an offer the mobsters turned down, volunteering to kill the Cuban dictator with "poison pills" free of charge.[27] Over the next six months, the *mafiosi* made a series of unsuccessful assassination attempts before the mission was aborted in favour of the long-planned the Bay of Pigs invasion.[28]

Neither Kennedy brother knew of the CIA-Mafia plan at the time. Bobby first learned that Giancana was part of a plot to assassinate Castro from a pre-election memo Hoover sent the CIA on October 18, 1960. But, crucially, this made no mention of any Agency involvement. Then, in May 1961, Hoover sent a memorandum to Bobby himself: this linked the mob boss to "a CIA operation against Cuba involving 'dirty business': there was no explanation of what such "business" might be, and Hoover did not mention assassination. [29]

26 *Robert Kennedy's Anti-Crime Time. Washington Post,* December 4, 1995
27 *CIA Memorandum for the Record*; Sheffield Edwards, May 14, 1962. Copy in authors' possession.
28 *CIA "Family Jewels" Memorandum, 16 May 1973;* de-classified June 25, 2007. CIA Library: https://www.cia.gov/library/readingroom/docs/DOC_0001451843.pdf
29 *Final Report of the Senate Select Committee (the Church Committee) To Study Government Operations With respect to Intelligence Activities; p.129. US Government Printing Office, April 1976*

Relations between the Kennedy brothers and the CIA were, by then, at freezing point. The previous month the Agency had dragged the President into its ill-conceived plans for invading Cuba with a rag-tag army of anti-Castro exiles. The attempt, centred on the Bay of Pigs, was a military and geo-political disaster. The CIA blamed Kennedy for failing to order air strikes when the paramilitaries got into trouble. The President believed – correctly – that the debacle showed the CIA to be hopelessly out of its depth and dangerously out of control, and he reportedly vowed "to splinter the CIA in a thousand pieces and scatter it to the winds"[30]. He did not do so – but he severely clipped its wings, prohibiting future political assassinations and installing Bobby as overlord of the Agency's continuing, if less military, attempts to dislodge Castro from power. The move was not received well at Langley: within the Agency's most senior ranks, resentment at the Kennedys grew deep and bitter. Within months, the antipathy between the Attorney General and the intelligence agency blew up completely: once again, organized crime was at the heart of the row.

In December 1961, Hoover had sent Bobby a personal memo about Sam Giancana. It was based on surveillance recordings which had captured the Chicago don denouncing the Justice Department's efforts to prosecute him.

"Information has been received that Giancana complained bitterly concerning the intensity of investigation being conducted of his activities, and that he made a donation to the campaign of President Kennedy but was not getting his money's worth[31]."

Giancana also complained to his friends at the CIA. Specifically, he wanted immunity from Bobby's attempts to

---

30　*CIA – Maker of Policy, or Tool?*; New York Times, April 26, 1966
31　*Gambling Activities, Las Vegas.* Memo from FBI Director to Attorney General, December 11, 1961.

prosecute him over a wire-tap the Agency had installed – as a favour – on a hotel room used by a man Giancana suspected of sleeping with one of his girlfriends.

Not only had the CIA installed the (illegal) bugging device, in early spring 1962 it attempted to stop the Justice Department pursuing Giancana and his associates for it, claiming "the national interest would preclude any prosecutions based on the tap".[32] Bobby demanded an explanation: on May 7 the Agency's attorney, Lawrence Houston, gave the Attorney General a full (if not entirely frank) account of the relationship between the CIA, Giancana and several other major gangsters and the employment of *Mafiosi* to murder Castro. Bobby was furious, telling Houston "I trust that if you ever try to do business with organized crime again, with gangsters, you will let the Attorney General know".[33]

The illegal wiretapping case was abandoned, but Bobby's anti-mob squad pursued organized crime bosses with unremitting zeal. FBI agents monitored Giancana's every move – following him from his home to his favourite bar and even on to the golf course, where they regularly jeered if he missed a put. (Giancana became so incensed that he sued the Justice Department in federal court: the judge allowed the FBI to continue close surveillance, but ordered its agents to drop back at least two four-ball games behind the mobster.)[34]

By the middle of November 1963 the battle with his expanding list of enemies was taking its toll. Bobby was close to exhaustion, worn down by a near-daily struggle with Hoover and the

---

32 *Final Report of the Senate Select Committee (the Church Committee) To Study Government Operations With respect to Intelligence Activities; p.79. US Government Printing Office, April 1976*

33 *Final Report of the Senate Select Committee (the Church Committee) To Study Government Operations With respect to Intelligence Activities; p.133. US Government Printing Office, April 1976*

34 Arthur M. Schlesinger: *Robert Kennedy and His Times*, p. 533. Houghton Mifflin, 1978

demands of his self-imposed mission to bring Mafia mobsters to justice.

Two cases in particular were then dominating his workload: the first was the latest attempt to prosecute Sam Giancana – this time on charges of political corruption. On November 22, as John Kennedy flew to Dallas, Bobby held a lunchtime meeting to discuss progress on the case, before heading home to Hickory Hill. He was expecting a phone call that afternoon from his prosecutors in Louisiana, who were in court on the second case – a new attempt to deport Carlos Marcello.

At 1.45pm the extension phone beside the swimming pool rang. But it was not news from New Orleans: it was the FBI Director, J. Edgar Hoover.

CHAPTER TWO: REVOLUTION

I t was an unseasonably warm afternoon. Making the most of the weather, Bobby had enjoyed a lunchtime swim and was enjoying clam chowder and tuna sandwiches on the patio when the phone rang.

Bluntly and brusquely, the FBI Director told the Attorney General that his brother had been shot. The call lasted no more than 15 seconds and, to Bobby, "Hoover had no more emotion in his voice than if he was telling him that they just discovered a communist on the faculty of Howard University in Washington".[35] Forty minutes later Hoover called back with the news that the President was dead.

Bobby had little time for his own grief. There were phone calls to make – to Jackie Kennedy and his brother, Ted, asking him to break the news to Joe Snr., by then paralysed from a stroke. Then Johnson called, seeking guidance on the legality of being sworn as President immediately, and speculating that the assassination was "part of a worldwide plot"[36].

---

35 RFK biographer Evan Thomas, ABC TV News interview, November 20, 2000 http://abcnews.go.com/WNT/story?id=131457&page=1

36 Arthur M. Schlesinger: *Robert Kennedy and His Times*, p. 656. Houghton Mifflin, 1978

The idea had also occurred to Bobby. Amid the flurry of calls and staff aides arriving at Hickory Hill, he phoned CIA Director John McCone, asking him to drive over from Langley straight away. When McCone arrived, Bobby asked him directly if the Agency was responsible for the murder. The two men shared a devout Catholic faith, so when the Director swore that the CIA had not been involved, Bobby believed him.

Next, his suspicions turned towards organised crime – in particular, Jimmy Hoffa and Sam Giancana. He put through a call to Walter Sheridan, head of the 'Get Hoffa Squad' who was then in Nashville prosecuting the Teamsters leader on charges of jury tampering, and asked him to make discreet enquiries. Sheridan reported back that "Hoffa was in Miami in some restaurant when the word came of the assassination, and he got up on the table and cheered.[37]"

After Sheridan, Bobby phoned Julius Draznin, a Chicago-based expert on union corruption who worked for the National Labor Relations Board, asking him to find out whether the mafia – which, under the circumstances, Draznin took to mean Sam Giancana – had played any part the murder. Draznin cast around, but eventually called back to say he had found nothing.[38] But whether or not Draznin was right, Bobby had already come to his own conclusion that the assassination was, in some way, connected to the Kennedys' domestic or foreign policies. Walking through Hickory Hill's extensive gardens, he told press secretary, Ed Guthman: "I thought they would get one of us. But I thought it would be me."[39]

At 3.34pm, Eastern Standard Time, Monday, November 25, 1963, Bobby stood, stony-faced, beside Jacqueline Kennedy, as the

37 *Walter Sheridan Oral History Interview RFK #5*, p. 2, May 1, 1970, Washington DC. John F. Kennedy Library, Boston, MA.
38 "RFK Saw Conspiracy in JFK's Assassination". *Boston Globe*, Nov 24 2013
39 Ed Guthman: *We Band of Brothers*. P244. Harper & Rowe, 1971

President's body was laid to rest at Arlington National Cemetery. Bobby had just turned 38: for most of his life he had been in the shadows – an efficient and loyal *consigliere* to the overarching Kennedy political project.

True, he had glimpsed his own potential power, during the Senate hearings and as Attorney General: but to a significant degree this had been *conditional* power – based on the strength of Joe Snr.'s influence, the licence given to him by McClellan, and ultimately on the patronage of the President, who had made him the second most influential figure in Washington. Now he was alone – cut off from the protection of his brother, but also lacking anyone to serve or protect.

The diminution of his authority came swiftly and from two entirely predictable sources. Hoover moved swiftly to cut Bobby out of the political food chain. Prior to John Kennedy's death, the FBI Director had no direct access to the President: all communication went through the Attorney General. According to Bobby's son, Robert Jnr, within days of Johnson's accession to the Oval Office, that changed.

"After President Kennedy's assassination, my father never spoke to Hoover again. Hoover had no contact with him and he went right to Johnson with whom he was very close. So literally half the Justice Department's employees – 30,000 employees of the FBI – now were no longer deployable by my father … And I think he recognized the limitations on his own power. He recognized that he would not be at the Justice Department for long."[40]

Although Johnson persuaded the Attorney General and the rest of John Kennedy's cabinet to stay in post, he and Bobby held each other in mutual contempt. LBJ dismissed RFK as "a

---

40   Robert Kennedy Jnr. interview with Brad Johnson and Rob Beemer, Interesting Stuff Entertainment, Malibu, October 13, 2016

little shit-ass" and "a grandstanding little runt"[41], while Bobby described the new President as "mean, bitter, vicious – an animal in many ways"[42]. Even when Johnson pushed through JFK's stalled civil rights legislation, Bobby complained that LBJ "was getting the credit for" vital reforms for which "President Kennedy was responsible"[43]. It was clear that the relationship was unworkable: in August 1964, nine months after JFK's murder, Bobby resigned from the administration to seek a seat in the Senate, representing New York.

It was the first time he had run for political office and from the outset his campaign was hampered by allegations of carpet bagging – he had little genuine connection with New York – and the burden of inheriting a national myth: the dream of change which John Kennedy had held out to America and the world. He found himself forced to tread a difficult path, upholding JFK's legacy while simultaneously seeking to forge a new identity for himself. "He didn't want to trade on being his brother's brother," aide and speechwriter Peter Edelman would later recall. "At the same time he didn't have a series of things that [he] would do for the State of New York.[44]"

Television news film showed all too plainly that Bobby was struggling to find his own voice – both physically and politically. Ultimately, only Johnson's very public support helped him win the November election.

But the Senate proved to be a frustrating place, its glacial pace a far cry from the hectic days of power as his brother's Attorney

---

41   Jeff Sheshol: Mutual Contempt, Lyndon Johnson, Robert Kennedy and the Feud That Defined A Decade, p.3. W.W. Norton, 1998

42   Interviews with John Bartlow Martin, March 1 – May 14, 1964; [in] *Robert Kennedy in His Own Words,* p.417. Bantam Books, 1988

43   *Ibid,* p.407

44   Interview in "RFK": American Experience, WGBH/PBS, 2004 (Dave Grubin Productions Inc)

General and closest advisor. And so, although he had pledged to "devote all of my efforts and whatever talents I possess to the State of New York"[45], Bobby would spend a substantial portion of the next three years travelling across America and through the world beyond its shores.

To some, this was perceived as Bobby's "wilderness period" – out of power and crippled by mourning for JFK. Yet whilst the grief was a real and ever-present companion, the years between 1964 and 1967 were the time in which he underwent a fundamental change, a metamorphosis from ruthless back room fixer to passionate revolutionary.

Revolution was certainly in the air. America's comfortable post-war era, with its idealised whiter-than-white self-image of soda pops, lindy hops and *Leave It To Beaver,* was over. The Civil Rights movement demanded that the country face up to the reality of institutionalised racial prejudice in states on both sides of the Mason-Dixon line, and Bobby stepped up the fight. "A motel will serve a Communist or a narcotics pusher but the Negro is refused … yet we ask the Negro to perform many services for the United States", he told an audience in Atlanta, Georgia, in May 1964. "Six Negroes have been killed recently in Vietnam. Yet if one of their families buried their loved one in Arlington Cemetery and started home to Alabama, the mother would not know the motel to use, what restaurant, what restroom for her children. Yet her husband was killed for all of us. It is a continuous insult."[46]

Yet underlying the cancer of racial prejudice and discrimination was a deeper uncomfortable truth: in many of the cities of the world's richest country, poverty flourished. In April 1965, Bobby warned the National Council of Christians and Jews:

45   Robert Kennedy: announcement of candidacy, August 22, 1964.
46   *"Kennedy's backing cheered"*, Al Kuettner, Atlanta Daily World, May 27, 1964

"I have been in the tenements of Harlem in the past several weeks, where the smell of rats was so strong that it was difficult to stay there for five minutes, and where children slept with lights turned on their feet to discourage attacks."[47]

Two months later, at a commencement address to students at Buffalo, New York State, he warned:

"A revolution is now in progress. It is a revolution for individual dignity... for economic freedom... for social reform and political freedom, for internal justice and international independence... This revolution is directed against *us* – against the one third of the world that diets while others starve; against a nation that buys eight million new cars a year while most of the world goes without shoes."[48]

The demand for economic as well as political justice, Bobby saw, was fuelling the spirit of revolution. And while followers of Dr. Martin Luther King clung to a policy of non-violence, others supported a more direct approach.

In August 1965, the first of a succession of urban riots exploded in the poor and predominantly African-American Los Angeles suburb of Watts; over five days and nights, thirty-four people were killed and more than a thousand were injured. Bobby would not publicly excuse the violence and disorder, but he did grasp its underlying causes.

"He bumped into some reporter who asked him what he thought," recalled his aide and speechwriter, Adam Walinsky; "you know – should these Negroes, as we called them then, be obeying the law? And he said 'well, what did the law ever do for the Negro?'"[49]

---

47 Speech to the National Council of Christians and Jews, April 28, 1965.
48 Commencement address at University College of Buffalo. June 5, 1965. RFK Senate Papers, Speeches & Press Releases, 1964–1968. JFK Library, Boston MA.
49 Interview in "RFK": American Experience, WGBH/PBS, 2004 (Dave Grubin Productions Inc)

Two days after mass arrests and the deployment of the National Guard restored order to the streets of Watts, Bobby made explicit the connection between poverty and civil disorder. "All these places – Harlem, Watts, Southside – are riots waiting to happen."[50]

He was to be proved right. Over the next twenty-four months Cleveland, Ohio, Omaha, Nebraska, Newark, New Jersey, Detroit Michigan, and Minneapolis-St. Paul all burned as African-Americans took to the streets demanding justice.

Nor was the problem of economic injustice confined to America's urban ghettoes. Bobby travelled across the country – from Native American reservations to the Mississippi Delta – seeing at first hand the vicious, merciless, poverty eating at America's very foundations.

In Cleveland, Mississippi, at the request of civil rights activists, he ventured into slums made up of sharecroppers' shotgun houses: there were gaping holes in the roofs, the floors were alive with rats and cockroaches while children sat covered in sores, their bellies bloated from hunger. "My God," he said, moved to tears, "How can a country like this allow it?"[51]

The answer was that much of white America, still clinging to the 1950s dream of prosperity and comfort, either didn't know or – more probably – didn't want to know. It was a complacency which, in 1965, was symbolised by something the affluent middle classes had come to take for granted: grapes.

In September that year, after a record harvest, thousands of migrant California farm workers went on strike demanding to be paid the federal minimum wage and the right to union representation. The grape pickers – mostly Latinos and

50 Speech to the Order of Odd Fellows, Spring Valley, New York, August 18, 1965

51 Arthur M. Schlesinger: *Robert Kennedy and His Times*, p. 855. Houghton Mifflin, 1978

Filipinos – were some of the nation's lowest-paid workers; for years their plight had been largely ignored by the union which notionally represented their interests – Bobby's old *bête noir,* the Teamsters.

Cesar Chavez, the charismatic Mexican-American farm workers' leader, committed to non-violence, turned the strike into a nationwide boycott; in response, some major agricultural companies responded by hiring often-violent strike-breakers. They were supported by local police and sheriffs' departments, which attacked peaceful demonstrations and arrested strikers on the picket lines.

Chavez by-passed the Teamsters and the AFL-CIO, the primary federation of American unions, reaching out instead to a politically well-connected labour organiser and activist, Paul Schrade, then an official of the United Auto Workers Union.

"We had a policy of building relationships with the wider working community, and Chavez called me saying 'We need political help, what can you do?' I led a delegation up to Delano, the California town at the centre of the grape pickers struggle, and took local media along with us. But Chavez knew that they needed more national attention."[52]

Schrade had worked with Bobby on JFK's 1960 Presidential campaign, and the two men had a warm and mutually-respectful relationship. But by 1966 Bobby was primarily focused on the plight of impoverished African-Americans and the war in Vietnam; when, in March that year, a U.S. Senate Sub-Committee agreed to hold hearings in Sacramento and Delano examining the grape pickers' cause, Bobby, although a member, was reluctant to leave Washington. "Bob wasn't going to come," Schrade recalled. "Chavez called me and asked if we could get him out

---

52   Paul Schrade, interviews with Tim Tate, 1991 & 2016.

there. I called Bob, and his initial response was 'why the hell do I want to go to California?' But he finally agreed to do it."[53]

Bobby arrived in time for the third day of the televised hearings and quickly clashed with local law enforcement. The sheriff of Kern County, Leroy Galyen, had spent the previous six months arresting striking farm workers for the non-existent offence of shouting *huelga,* the Spanish word for strike.

Bobby's questioning of Galyen was as aggressive as his interrogation of organised crime bosses in the McClellan Committee hearings.

"Galyen: If I have reason to believe that there's going to be a riot started, and somebody tells me that there's going to be trouble if you don't stop 'em, then it's my duty to stop 'em.

Kennedy: And then you go out and arrest them?

Galyen: Absolutely.

Kennedy: And charge them?

Galyen: Charge them.

Kennedy: What do you charge them with?

Galyen: For violating unlawful assembly.

Kennedy: I think that's most interesting. Who told you that they're going to riot?

Galyen: Well, the men right out in the field that they were talking to said 'if you don't get them out of here, we're going to cut their hearts out'. So rather than let them get cut, you remove the cause.

Kennedy: How can you go arrest somebody if they haven't violated the law?

Galyen: They're ready to violate the law."

The sheriff's statement was met by laughter from the thousand spectators crowded into the high school auditorium. As the subcommittee's chairman banged the table, Bobby leaned back

---

53   Ibid

in his chair with a look of astonishment then said: "Could I suggest in the interim period of time – in the luncheon period of time – that the sheriff and the district attorney read the constitution of the United States."[54]

That single exchange strengthened Bobby's growing reputation as a tribune of the poor and oppressed. It also thrust the grape pickers' cause into a national spotlight and established a deep and abiding friendship with Cesar Chavez and his deputy, Delores Huerta. But equally it created new enemies for Bobby.

"My father hated bullies," Robert Kennedy Jnr. recalled in 2016, "and he suddenly saw this struggle as a heroic struggle for the integrity of the American system, and that these people were heroes.

"He spoke out very strongly – so strongly for them, that day in 1966, that Dolores Huerta told me she was worried about him coming out too strongly, because she thought that it would put him in danger. Both politically and, I suppose, physically."[55]

After the hearings Chavez took Bobby to visit the farm workers and to see for himself the homes they lived in and the deprivation they endured. "And when he saw the conditions," Paul Schrade remembered, "Bobby said: 'This is just like Mississippi.'"[56]

"It's not just a question of wages," Bobby told news cameras covering the California hearings, "it's a question of housing, of education, of living conditions. It's basic question of hope for the future."

---

54   Senate Sub-Committee Hearing on Migratory Labor; Delano California, March 16, 1966

55   Robert Kennedy Jnr. interview with Brad Johnson and Rob Beemer, Interesting Stuff Entertainment, Malibu, October 13, 2016

56   Paul Schrade, interviews with Tim Tate, 1991 & 2016.

The nationwide blight of injustice – racial, economic and political – affected Bobby more deeply than other conventional politicians. As Jack Newfield later put it: "Kennedy took things personally. He saw somebody hurting and he hurt. He was so intense, so personal about somebody else's pain, and that's what made him a totally different kind of Senator."[57]

Although Capitol Hill was not his natural home, Bobby was quite prepared to use the bully pulpit of the Senate to warn about both the dangers and potential benefits of what he could sense in the winds of change blowing across the country.

"A revolution is coming—a revolution which will be peaceful if we are wise enough; compassionate if we care enough; successful if we are fortunate enough—but a revolution which is coming whether we will it or not. We can affect its character; we cannot alter its inevitability."[58]

If inequality, and the crime that too often accompanied it, angered Bobby, so too did America's dangerous complacency. "Let television show the sound, the feel, the hopelessness, and what it's like to think you'll never get out," he said just before Christmas 1967.

"Show a black teenager, told by some radio jingle to stay in school, looking at his older brother who stayed in school and who's out of a job. Show the Mafia pushing narcotics; put a *Candid Camera* team in a ghetto school and watch what a rotten system of education it really is. Film a mother staying up all night to keep the rats from her baby … I'd ask people to watch it and experience what it means to live in the most affluent society in history – without hope."[59]

57 Interview in "RFK": American Experience, WGBH/PBS, 2004 (Dave Grubin Productions Inc)
58 Speech in the US Senate, May 9 1966.
59 A Holiday Reflection For America, Citizens Union, New York, December 14, 1967.

By the close of 1967 Bobby Kennedy had travelled a long road and found a cause for which he was determined to fight. However unlikely, the rich and privileged son of Massachusetts aristocracy had become the most effective and publicly-visible champion of America's poor and dispossessed.

But it was not only domestic injustice which fuelled the fire inside him: in the three years since leaving Johnson's government he had spent months away from his New York constituency, visiting Europe, Latin America and South Africa – trips that, according to his son, began in JFK's shadow, but in time enabled Bobby to develop his own moral authority.

"My father was an idealist, and a pragmatist at the same time. The thing that drove him and his brothers was a vision, a very idealistic view of what America's role in the world should be. They saw America as a template for democracy, for civil rights, human rights. They tried to change what our role in the world was…

"I remember in 1965 when I went to Europe with my father and we went to Poland, France, Germany, Italy and Greece. And everywhere we went we were met by crowds – sometimes hundreds of thousands of people – who swarmed around my father and my mother because they represented something that was idealistic; people were looking to America for leadership and they knew the difference between leadership and bullying… and they really looked at the United States as a moral force in the world."[60]

There were two striking aspects to Bobby's travels. The first was the countries he chose to visit, in particular a three week tour, beginning in November 1965, of Peru, Chile, Brazil, Argentina and Venezuela, followed by South Africa the following summer. Going to these countries put him in danger – both political and physical.

---

60   Robert Kennedy Jnr. interview with Brad Johnson and Rob Beemer, Interesting Stuff Entertainment, Malibu, October 13, 2016

Peru had recently emerged from the grip of a military *junta* and, in common with neighbouring Chile, was plagued by tension between the ruling élite and a vigorous – sometimes violent – communist underclass. Brazil had been run by an increasingly reactionary military regime since a coup in 1964, and Argentina would shortly go the same way; Venezuela, meanwhile, was suffering terror attacks by armed guerrilla movements. In each country, local officials passed on warnings of anticipated violent protests: in Concepción, Chile's third largest city, Bobby was spat on and jostled as he argued with communist students protesting American foreign policy, who denounced him "as the representative of a government whose hands are stained with blood."[61]

Politically, the South American odyssey was also fraught with peril. Johnson's officials tried first to persuade him not to go, then attempted to ensure that Bobby said nothing which could be interpreted as an attack on the administration's policies in the region. By defying the President, Bobby added new levels of *froideur* to his already deep-frozen relations with the White House.

But it is what he said, as much as where he said it, that – even at a distance of more than half a century – is most striking. In speech after speech, Bobby proclaimed the need for revolution. "The responsibility of our times is nothing less than revolution," he told students in Lima, Santiago and Buenos Aires.[62] He hammered away at this message of revolution across the Continent, deploying the word itself more than a dozen times in Chile alone; and he made clear that the revolution he foresaw was needed at home as well as throughout America's southern neighbours.

"We have had other revolutions since our independence," he told his audience in Buenos Aires, "for mine is a revolutionary

---

61   Rush gets Spat At in Uruguay, and Robert Kennedy in Chile: New York Times, November 17, 1965

62   Robert Kennedy Ends Peru Tour, New York Times, November 14, 1965.

country". He cited the fights against slavery and the power of "the great corporations" and the New Deal of the 1930s whose revolution was in welding "the ideals of social justice to the ideals of liberty."[63]

In Rio de Janeiro, where the Brazilian *junta*'s prohibition of political opposition forced the cancellation of many of his scheduled meetings, Bobby visited the *favelas*, seeing in the Brazilian slums the same the deprivation he had witnessed in the Mississippi Delta or the fields of northern California. At the city's Catholic University he told four thousand students: "Though I come from the richest state in the most fortunate of nations there are still far too many families living in poverty and ignorance and filth". He then challenged his audience – and those at home following reports of his tour in the *New York Times* – to do something tangible before it became too late.

"If all we do is complain about the universities, criticise the government, carry signs [and] make speeches to one another...then we have not met our responsibility. It is not enough just to talk about it. Unless we do something, there is not going to be any Brazil – or any world."[64]

Nor was he averse to taking his own direct action. After witnessing a crowd of protestors beaten up by soldiers on Rio's streets, Bobby climbed on to the roof of a car shouting "Down with the government! On to the [Presidential] palace!" – an action which led Brazilian officials to plead with his staff "to do something about this young revolutionary".[65]

---

63 *Speech to students in Buenos Aires,* November 19, 1965. Box 1, Robert F. Kennedy Senate Papers: Speeches and Press Releases, 1964 – 1968; John F. Kennedy Library, Boston, MA.

64 *Speech to students at Catholic University, Rio de Janeiro,* November 25, 1965. Box 2, Robert F. Kennedy Senate Papers: Speeches and Press Releases, 1964 – 1968; John F. Kennedy Library, Boston, MA.

65 Tom Johnston, RFK aide, October 27, 1969. Robert F. Kennedy Oral History Project; John F. Kennedy Library, Boston, MA.

Six months later the "young revolutionary" (having now turned 40, Bobby would unquestionably not have qualified for that adjective in the minds of America's youth) arrived in Johannesburg for a speaking tour which would send ripples around the world.

South Africa was then under the rule of the repressive, vehemently anti-Communist Nationalist Party. Its system of institutionalised racial discrimination and segregation – apartheid – had attracted international opprobrium, which, coupled with its brutal suppression of dissent, ensured that few foreign politicians travelled there. Nor was Bobby's proposed trip universally welcomed by his domestic critics: William Loeb, publisher of the conservative *Manchester Union Leader*, thundered that "Bobby Kennedy is the most vicious and dangerous leader in the United States today. It would make no more sense to us for South Africa to admit Bobby Kennedy ... than it would to take a viper into one's bed."[66]

Prime Minister Hendrik Verwoerd's government evidently shared the newspaper's antipathy, holding up the required entry visa for five months before finally agreeing to a limited and closely-monitored visit. When he landed at Jan Smuts International Airport a little before midnight on June 4, 1966, Bobby was met with hostile crowds, yelling "Yankee go home" and "chuck him out". In the capital, Pretoria, he found that neither Verwoerd nor any other minister would meet him.

But arriving in Cape Town the next day, after flying over Robben Island – "home to 2,000 political prisoners ... because they believe in freedom", he reminded Americans later [67] – he found a crowd of three thousand supporters who had waited for two hours to greet his plane. Standing in the part of the terminal

---

66   Manchester Union-Leader, November 11, 1965.
67   Robert Kennedy: *Suppose God Is Black*. *Look* magazine, August 23, 1966

designated for "non-whites" he made a brief speech, quoting his favourite Greek poet, Aeschylus.

"I come here to hear from all segments of South African thought and opinion. I come here to learn what we can do together to meet the challenges of our time, to do as the Greeks once wrote: to tame the savageness of man, and make gentle the life of this world."

By the time he arrived to give the Day of Affirmation address to students at the University, that evening, the numbers had swelled to 18,000 – every one of them, he noted, white. Undeterred, he began by teasing his audience.

"I come here this evening because of my deep interest and affection for a land settled by the Dutch in the mid-seventeenth century, then taken over by the British, and at last independent; a land in which the native inhabitants were at first subdued, but relations with whom remain a problem to this day; a land which defined itself on a hostile frontier; a land which has tamed rich natural resources through the energetic application of modern technology. A land which was once the importer of slaves, and now must struggle to wipe out the last traces of that former bondage. I refer, of course, to the United States of America."[68]

He continued to hold up the United States as an example of what happened when a nation oppressed its people – "there are millions of Negroes untrained for the simplest of jobs, and thousands every day denied their full equal rights under the law; and the violence of the disinherited, the insulted and injured, looms over the streets of Harlem and Watts and South Side Chicago" – and warned that the necessary revolution would not come easily.

"The road toward equality of freedom is not easy, and great cost and danger march alongside us. We are committed to

---

68 Robert Kennedy: N.U.S.A.S. Day of Affirmation Speech, University of Cape Town, June 6, 1966.

peaceful and nonviolent change, and that is important for all to understand though all change is unsettling. Still, even in the turbulence of protest and struggle is greater hope for the future, as men learn to claim and achieve for themselves the rights formerly petitioned from others."[69]

Then, as he approached his peroration, he exhorted his listeners to stand up for the millions of black South Africans oppressed by their government.

"It is from numberless diverse acts of courage and belief that human history is shaped. Each time a man stands up for an ideal, or acts to improve the lot of others, or strikes out against injustice, he sends forth a tiny ripple of hope, and crossing each other from a million different centres of energy and daring those ripples build a current which can sweep down the mightiest walls of oppression and resistance."[70]

The "Ripple of Hope Speech" would be carried – and applauded – round the world: the London *Daily Telegraph* – itself a deeply conservative paper – called it "the most stirring and memorable address ever to come from a foreigner in South Africa." Inside the land of apartheid opinion was less favourable: as Bobby returned home, the Afrikaans-language *Die Transvaler* newspaper condemned him and offered its "deepest sympathy for the American people if Senator Kennedy becomes their future President."[71]

There were those in the United States who shared that view. Teamsters leader Jimmy Hoffa had denounced Bobby in very similar terms during a press conference in his lengthy and unsuccessful series of attempts to overturn convictions for jury tampering and fraud.

---

69   Ibid
70   Ibid.
71   Arthur M. Schlesinger: *Robert Kennedy and His Times*, p. 805. Houghton Mifflin, 1978

"He took an interest in me first to further his own ambitions and secondly because he is a spoiled brat, one who thinks he can dictate policy to everybody. He was not a good Attorney General and he'll probably make a worse Senator. I hate to think what he would be like as President. We'd probably have a fascist government."[72]

Hoffa had previously been accused by one of his own officials of plotting to assassinate Bobby. Nor was this a solitary threat: when Bobby went to speak in Billings, Montana, in 1966, the FBI warned his aides that it had received an anonymous message – "Kennedy dies at 4".[73] But one issue above all put Bobby in the cross-hairs: Vietnam.

He had never been an active supporter of the war. Throughout his presidency John Kennedy consistently resisted Pentagon demands for deploying ground troops, attracting the hostility of the bellicose Joint Chiefs of Staff and the CIA – an antagonism which grew more visceral as JFK began to contemplate a total withdrawal of all US personnel from South Vietnam. Bobby largely kept out of the public debate, but, as the President's most trusted *consigliere,* he was presumed to be either in agreement with, or even the architect of, JFK's dove-ish tendencies.

The assassination in Dallas ended the drift to disengagement: within two days of entering the Oval Office Lyndon Johnson told aides he was "not going to lose Vietnam".

In February 1965 he authorised *Operation Rolling Thunder* – a sustained campaign of aerial bombardment; the following month he ordered the first American troops – two battalions of Marines – into the fighting.

It was a decision to which Bobby was deeply opposed, but, anxious not to be seen attacking the President's agenda, he kept his disagreements private. But as he travelled across the country,

---

72   *"Hoffa Assails Kennedy"*, AP report in New York Times, December 15, 1964
73   Evan Thomas: *Robert Kennedy – His Life*, p.356. Simon & Schuster, 2000

in that year of anti-war protests and college sit-ins, he was continually pressed to articulate his views. In the autumn the dam burst.

On November 5, after touring the riot-scarred streets of Watts, he held a press conference at the University of Southern California and was challenged to either endorse or condemn students who had recently burned their draft cards. He dodged the political bullet by professing a personal disagreement with the tactic, but sympathising with those who adopted it. Then a reporter asked him if he was in favour of blood donations to North Vietnam. With the caveat that the needs of America's allies in the south should come first, Bobby said: "I'm in favour of giving [to] anybody who needs blood. I'm in favour of them having blood", confirming with a follow-up answer that, yes, he did mean "even the North Vietnamese".[74]

The remarks were greeted with howls of outrage. A cartoon in the *Chicago Tribune* depicted Bobby astride a coffin draped in the Stars and Stripes while holding a placard which read "I am willing to give my blood to the Communist enemy in Vietnam"[75], while the *New York Daily News* pointedly asked: "If you feel strongly enough for the enemy to give him a pint of your blood every 90 days or so, why not go the whole hog? Why not light out for the enemy country and join its armed forces?"[76]

There was political fall-out, too. Barry Goldwater, Republican candidate in the 1964 Presidential election, denounced Bobby's statement as "closer to treason than to academic freedom". [77] It would not be the last time that charge was levelled.

---

74   Press Conference, University of Southern California, Los Angeles. November 5, 1965.

75   *Chicago Tribune,* November 12, 1965

76   *New York Daily News*, November 10, 1965

77   Arthur M. Schlesinger: *Robert Kennedy and His Times*, p. 790. Houghton Mifflin, 1978

In February Bobby addressed the Senate Foreign Relations Committee Hearings, urging LBJ to open negotiations with the North Vietnamese government on the basis that that the US had only three options: "kill or repress them; turn the country over to them; or admit them to a share of the power and responsibility."

"If negotiation is our aim, as we have so clearly said it is, we must seek a middle ground. A negotiated settlement means that each side must concede matters that are important in order to preserve positions that are essential ...

"Any negotiated settlement must accept the fact that there are discontented elements in South Vietnam, Communist and non-Communist, who desire to change the existing political and economic system of the country."[78]

The speech proved deeply unpopular, seeming to confirm Bobby's old reputation as a ruthless and opportunistic politician seeking to take advantage of popular opposition to the rising body count, and unwilling to fight the perceived communist threat in south east Asia. An editorial in the *Chicago Tribune* – headlined "Ho Chi Kennedy" – bluntly accused him of treachery:

"Senator Kennedy, out of his ignorance and political ambition has compromised his loyalty to the United States when it is at war by subscribing to Communist myths and adopting them as his own, in opposition to a national policy which is supported by an overwhelming majority of American citizens.

"He is not the junior Senator from New York. He is the senior Senator from communist North Viet Nam – Ho Chi Minh's Trojan Horse in the United States Senate."[79]

He was no more successful in his private attempts to influence Johnson's increasingly entrenched position by suggesting a

---

78   Robert Kennedy speech to the Fulbright Hearings of the Foreign relations Committee on Vietnam, Senate Caucus Room February 19, 1966.
79   *"Ho Chi Kennedy"*, *Chicago Tribune*, February 21, 1966.

pause in the bombing to encourage peace talks with Hanoi. In February 1967 the President summoned him to the Oval Office to berate him over news reports that the North Vietnamese had sent Bobby a back channel 'peace-feeler'. The story was untrue and Bobby denied it, but Johnson refused to listen, furiously tearing in to his long-time enemy and threatening to "destroy you and every one of your dove friends".[80]

By the time he reached his belated decision to run for President the following year Bobby had surpassed his own 1962 assessment of having "enemies all over" Washington. They were now spread throughout the country. Small wonder, then, that at a New York dinner party a few days after the announcement, Jacqueline Kennedy confided to their mutual friend Arthur Schlesinger Jnr.: "Do you know what I think will happen to Bobby? The same thing that happened to Jack... There is so much hatred in this country, and more people hate Bobby than hated Jack".[81]

80   *No Vietnam Secrets between RFK, LBJ, Politico,* October 20, 2009
81   Arthur M. Schlesinger: *Robert Kennedy and His Times,* p. 921. Houghton Mifflin, 1978

CHAPTER THREE:
CALIFORNIA

June 4, 1968, Malibu.

Under a dull, sullen sky and stretched across a pair of poolside chairs at the beachside home of film director John Frankenheimer, Robert F. Kennedy slept. It was early afternoon on Election Day: the die was cast and, after two and a half months of constant campaigning, Bobby was completely exhausted.

It had been a turbulent ride, inspiring and terrifying in almost equal measure. In 80 days Bobby had criss-crossed the country, addressing rallies everywhere from the traditional Kennedy north-eastern heartlands to the Deep South, at Universities in the prairie states and in thronged streets the length and breadth of California. Crowds – some adoring, others hostile – flocked to see him everywhere he travelled: he had been mobbed by admirers in Kansas City, Missouri and Watts, but jostled and spat on by black power activists in San Francisco.

This was a new politics – the razzmatazz of the rock star draped in technicolour over the cigars and smoke-filled rooms of traditional Democratic Party king-making. And it was deliberate. Bobby was a late entrant to the race, running against both Eugene McCarthy's insurgency and the current occupant of the

Oval Office. He had neither McCarthy's army of young, middle-class supporters, nor the backing of the powerbrokers who controlled the Party machine.

Former President Harry Truman threw his weight behind Johnson, denouncing those who dared challenge him as "a damned bunch of smart alecks"[82], while Frank O'Connor, President of New York City Council, rumbled that Bobby "might well be endangering the future of the country."[83] There was only one other possible route to victory: as Bobby told Helen Dudar of the *New York Post* "I have to win through the people. Otherwise I'm not going to win."[84] On the day Bobby announced his candidacy, his speechwriter, Adam Walinksy, set out the plan: "Our strategy is to change the rules of nominating a President. We're going to do it a new way. In the street."[85]

On March 17 Bobby flew to Kansas, the first stop on a two-week tour of 15 separate states – from Alabama to California – where he would make his case at rallies attended by more than 250,000 people. Reporters covering the campaign were instantly struck by the frenzied atmosphere: changing planes that night in Kansas City, Missouri, crowds of waiting supporters pressed against the barriers. "They tore the buttons from his shirt cuffs ... they tore at his suit buttons," wrote Jimmy Breslin in the next day's *New York Post*. "They reached for his hair and his face. He went down the fence, hands out, his body swaying backwards so that they could not claw him in the face, and people on the other side of the fence grabbed his hands and tried to pull him to them."[86] It was a brief foretaste of the passions Bobby would

82   Sam Houston Johnson *My Brother Lyndon*, p.242. Cowles Publishing, 1969
83   Newfield p.246
84   Helen Dudar, The Perilous Campaign, New York Post, June 5 1968
85   Jack Newfield, *Robert Kennedy – A Memoir*, p.251. Berkley Publishing, 1969
86   Jimmy Breslin; With Kennedy in Kansas, New York Post, March 18, 1968

evoke in ordinary voters across the country – the poor, the disposed, the disenchanted; those whom he saw as his constituency.

But if the strategy of plunging into, not flying over, the American heartland was new, the candidate's message remained unswervingly focussed on the problems he had already identified: racial inequality, economic injustice and – always – Vietnam. Paul Schrade, the Auto and Aerospace Workers Union official who joined Bobby at events throughout the campaign, said that "he felt responsible for what was happening in Vietnam. And as a person who had been involved in the anti-war movement for several years, it was one of the reasons I supported him. I felt he was the only candidate who could end the war."[87]

At Kansas State University, in the very first speech of the campaign, Bobby jerked his affluent and almost-exclusively white audience out of their complacency.

"Too much and for too long, we seemed to have surrendered personal excellence and community values in the mere accumulation of material things. Our Gross National Product, now, is over $800 billion dollars a year, but that Gross National Product...counts air pollution and cigarette advertising, and ambulances to clear our highways of carnage. It counts special locks for our doors and the jails for the people who break them. It counts the destruction of the redwood and the loss of our natural wonder in chaotic sprawl. It counts napalm and counts nuclear warheads and armored cars for the police to fight the riots in our cities...and the television programs which glorify violence in order to sell toys to our children.

"Yet the gross national product does not allow for the health of our children, the quality of their education or the joy of their play. It does not include the beauty of our poetry or the strength

---

87   Paul Schrade: interviews with Tim Tate, 1991–2016

of our marriages, the intelligence of our public debate or the integrity of our public officials. It measures neither our wit nor our courage, neither our wisdom nor our learning, neither our compassion nor our devotion to our country.

"It measures everything in short, except that which makes life worthwhile. And it can tell us everything about America except why we are proud that we are Americans."[88]

Then, warning that "if this is true at home, so it is true elsewhere in the world", he made an impassioned attack on Johnson's determination to bomb Hanoi into submission.

"Can we ordain to ourselves the awful majesty of God, to decide what cities and villages are to be destroyed, who will live and who will die, and who will join the refugees wandering in a desert of our own creation? ... In these next eight months we are going to decide what this country will stand for, and what kind of men we are."[89]

Bobby's candidacy terrified the White House and McCarthy's supporters alike. Three days after the speech in Kansas, two eminent left-wing historians, Lee Benson and James Shenton, took out an advertisement in the *New York Times*, damning Bobby for ruthless opportunism.

"The movement that has made Senator McCarthy its symbol exemplifies rationality, courage, morality. The movement Senator Kennedy commands exemplifies irrationality, opportunism, amorality", the academics thundered, describing the election as a choice "between morality and immorality"[90]. It would not be the last such criticism.

After a speech on March 24 at the Greek Theater in LA's Griffith Park, in which Bobby warned that "the national

---

88   Robert Kennedy, Alfred M. Landon Lecture, Manhattan, Kansas, March 18 1969
89   Ibid.
90   *New York Times*, March 20, 1968

leadership is calling upon the darker impulses of the American spirit – not, perhaps, deliberately, but through its action and the example it sets", the *Washington Post* suggested that he was becoming a "demagogue" and that the wild crowds he drew were part of a deliberate "strategy of revolution, of a popular uprising of such intensity and scale" designed to sweep him to victory at the Convention.[91]

One week later that victory became more likely. At 9pm on March 31st Lyndon Johnson addressed the American people on national television.

"I have concluded that I should not permit the Presidency to become involved in the partisan divisions that are developing in this political year … Accordingly I shall not seek, and I will not accept, the nomination of my party for another term as your President."[92]

To all but Johnson's inner circle, the announcement was a complete surprise. "I was shocked when President Johnson dropped out of the race," Bobby's then 14-year-old son, Robert Jnr. later recalled. "At that time I was in boarding school: I was at a Jesuit prep outside of Washington DC. I remember being in the library and they had the TV on for Johnson's speech, and that was the first time I thought 'my God – my father's going to be President'."[93]

Whilst LBJ himself made no overt public reference to Bobby's candidacy as the cause of his decision, he would later tell his confidante and biographer, Doris Kearns, that "the thing that I feared from the first day of my Presidency was actually coming

---

91   Richard Harwood, Crowd Madness and Kennedy Strategy, Washington Post, March 28, 1968

92   President Lyndon Johnson, television address from the White House, March 31, 1968

93   Robert Kennedy Jnr. interview with Brad Johnson and Rob Beemer, Interesting Stuff Entertainment, Malibu, October 13, 2016

true. Robert Kennedy had openly announced his intention to reclaim the throne in the memory of his brother."[94]

For the next three weeks, the race for the nomination was a straight fight between Bobby and McCarthy; and since there was little in principle between them on Vietnam – both advocated peace talks and a swift end to the war – Bobby's campaign stressed his core message of the need for economic social and racial justice to heal the country. "We are," as he told NBC's weekly primetime show, *Meet The Press*, "more divided than perhaps we have been in a hundred years."

One figure above all was the embodiment of that message: Dr. Martin Luther King Jnr. The two men had not always been close – indeed, as Attorney General Bobby had acceded to Hoover's paranoia about King's supposed links with communists, and authorised wire-taps on his phone. But for several months they had been collaborating on a radical scheme to force law makers to address the problem of urban deprivation: a new march by the poor and dispossessed on Washington, led by King's Southern Christian Leadership Conference. Peter Edelman, Bobby's legislative assistant, was present when the idea was born.

"The Poor People's Campaign was Robert Kennedy's idea ... He said, the only way there's ever going to be any change is if it's more uncomfortable for the Congress not to act than it is for them to act. He said what really has to happen is that you've got to get ... a whole lot of poor people who just come to Washington and say they're going to stay here until something happens and it gets really unpleasant and there are some arrests and it's just a very nasty business and Congress gets really embarrassed and they have to act."[95]

---

94 Doris Kearns, *Lyndon Johnson and the American Dream*, p.342. Harper Rowe, 1976
95 *Peter Edelman Oral History Interview, RFK #3*, p.331; August 5, 1969, Washington D.C. John F. Kennedy Library, Boston, MA.

The march, scheduled for the height of the election campaign in May 1968, was a radical plan and one which, Edelman later recalled, posed "a threat to Washington and the Establishment".[96]

In February, SCLC's leaders travelled to Washington DC to prepare the ground for what they and Bobby hoped would be a nationally-televised peaceful occupation of the nation's capital. Two months later, at 6.01pm on Thursday April 4, King was shot dead at the Lorraine Motel in Memphis, Tennessee.

Bobby was given the news as he arrived in Indianapolis for a scheduled campaign event in one of the city's most violent black neighbourhoods. Fearing a new outbreak of rioting, the local police chief advised him to abandon the rally; when Bobby refused, he ordered his officers not to escort the campaign into the ghetto.

It was a cold and windy night, but a thousand-strong crowd was waiting for Bobby in good spirits: they had not heard the news from Memphis. Climbing on to the back of a flatbed truck, Bobby gave an improvised speech, imploring his listeners to refrain from violence.

"Martin Luther King dedicated his life to love and to justice between fellow human beings. He died in the cause of that effort. In this difficult day, in this difficult time for the United States, it's perhaps well to ask what kind of a nation we are and what direction we want to move in.

"For those of you who are black – considering the evidence ... is that there were white people who were responsible – you can be filled with bitterness, and with hatred, and a desire for revenge.

"We can move in that direction as a country, in greater polarization – black people amongst blacks, and white amongst whites, filled with hatred toward one another. Or we can make an effort, as Martin Luther King did, to understand, and to comprehend, and

---

96   Peter Edelman interview, quoted in Lynda Obst, *The Sixties*, p.232-236. Random House, 1978

replace that violence, that stain of bloodshed that has spread across our land, with an effort to understand, compassion and love.

"For those of you who are black and are tempted to be filled with hatred and mistrust of the injustice of such an act, against all white people, I would only say that I can also feel in my own heart the same kind of feeling. I had a member of my family killed, but he was killed by a white man."

It was one of the few times that Bobby had spoken in public – however obliquely – of John Kennedy's death. He was not yet ready to take a position on the claims of a possible conspiracy being championed by New Orleans District Attorney Jim Garrison, but, according to Robert Kennedy Jnr., had privately asked his aides to make discreet enquiries.

"My father was walking through National Airport with [press secretary] Frank Mankiewicz and they saw a news stand that was filled with articles and magazines that had pictures of Jim Garrison...my father asked Mankiewicz 'do you think there's anything to that?' Mankiewicz said that he didn't know and my father asked him to investigate it – quietly. Mankiewicz and Walter Sheridan went and did their own investigation and they came to the conclusion that Garrison was not entirely correct, but that he was on to something.

"One of the things they looked at was the phone records between Jack Ruby and a number of people that my father had investigated, in the days leading up to President Kennedy's assassination, that showed that Ruby had these relationships and entanglements with many of my father's worst and most violent enemies, and President Kennedy's most violent enemies. And that, I think, made my father think that this was something that needed to be looked into."[97]

---

97   Robert Kennedy Jnr. interview with Brad Johnson and Rob Beemer, Interesting Stuff Entertainment, Malibu, October 13, 2016

But on April 4, it was the assassination of King – and the likelihood of new riots – which was uppermost in Bobby's mind. His impromptu speech in Indianapolis helped calm the city's streets, but across the nation, the mood was angry and violent.

As news of King's murder spread that night, cities began to burn. In Washington D.C. crowds broke windows and looted shops: the following morning, militant black power leader Stokely Carmichael fanned the flames of African-American anger.

"White America killed Dr. King last night," he told a press conference outside his storefront headquarters on April 5. "She made it a whole lot easier for a whole lot of black people today. There no longer needs to be intellectual discussions, black people know that they have to get guns. White America will live to cry that she killed Dr. King last night."

By the time Bobby arrived in Cleveland, Ohio, that same day, protestors were rioting on the streets in New York City, Pittsburgh, Cincinnati, and Trenton, New Jersey – with other cities bracing themselves for unrest. At a long-planned lunchtime address to Cleveland's City Club, Bobby spoke out against the hatred and violence tearing America apart. "This is a time of shame and a time of sorrow. It is not a day for politics," he told his audience. "I have saved this one opportunity – my only event of today – to speak briefly to you about this mindless menace of violence in America which again stains our land and every one of our lives."

Bobby spoke quietly, but, thanks to live television coverage, his words carried beyond the 2,200 rich, white upper-class club members gathered in the Sheraton Hotel.

"It is not the concern of any one race. The victims of the violence are black and white, rich and poor, young and old, famous and unknown. They are, most important of all, human beings whom other human beings loved and needed. No one – no matter where he lives or what he does – can be certain who will suffer from some senseless act of bloodshed. And yet it goes on and on and on in this country of ours.

"Why? What has violence ever accomplished? What has it ever created? No martyr's cause has ever been stilled by an assassin's bullet. No wrongs have ever been righted by riots and civil disorders. The sniper is only a coward, not a hero; and an uncontrolled, or uncontrollable, mob is only the voice of madness, not the voice of the people.

"Whenever any American's life is taken by another American unnecessarily – whether it is done in the name of the law or in defiance of law, by one man or by a gang, in cold blood or in passion, in an attack of violence or in response to violence – whenever we tear at the fabric of lives which another man has painfully and clumsily woven for himself and his children, whenever we do this then the whole nation is degraded."[98]

Cleveland, like Indianapolis, did not burn – that day or in the weeks to come. But other places did: in the most widespread unrest since the Civil War a century before, more than 75,000 federal troops and National Guardsmen patrolled the streets of 110 American cities. The cost of damage exceeded $50 million but the human cost was worse: by the time the smoke cleared, 46 people – almost all African-American – had been killed, with another 2,500 injured.

Bobby travelled across the country condemning the violence, but always reminding his audiences of its underlying causes – poverty, racial discrimination and injustice. "I have seen families with a dozen fatherless children trying to exist on less than $100 a month," he told a crowd at Valparaiso University on April 29,

---

98   Robert Kennedy: *The Mindless Menace of Violence* speech; Cleveland City
      Club, April 5, 1968

"and I have seen people in America so hungry that they search the local garbage dump for food."[99]

But the national mood was ugly and for many Bobby was a lightning rod for their anger. James Reston, executive editor of the *New York Times*, warned his readers that "there is a very large body of anti-Kennedy voters in this country these days... You can't even ride with the Irish cabbies in Boston without hearing some vicious remark about Bobby's policies or his personality... The opposition to him is personal, almost chemical, and sometime borders on the irrational".[100]

As the campaign hurtled on, Bobby's aides became increasingly concerned about his safety. The Secret Service did not, then, provide protection to Presidential candidates, let alone those running in party primaries; his security was primarily provided by Bill Barry, a burly former FBI agent who had once played college football for Kent State University, together with whatever local bodyguards he could drum up. Nor did Bobby's insistence on plunging into the middle of often-hysterical crowds make Barry's life any easier.

"It was a real problem," Walter Sheridan recalled. "We knew it was a real problem. And we knew that, really, there wasn't anything you could do about it because he was uncontrollable, and if you tried to protect him he'd get mad as hell.

"But I think Bill Barry lived in constant fear that something like that would happen... he was just frustrated because he felt the situation was going to get more and more dangerous, that Bob wouldn't listen to him, that there was no real security, and he didn't know what to do about it."[101]

---

99 Schlesinger, p.948
100 *New York Times,* April 24, 1968
101 *Walter Sheridan Oral History Interview RFK #1,* p. 89-90, August 5, 1969, Washington DC. John F. Kennedy Library, Boston, MA.

Ethel Kennedy, then pregnant with the couple's eleventh child, shared Barry's fears, but both she and Bobby kept them from their family. "There wasn't ever any discussion of my father's safety," according to Robert Kennedy Jnr. "I know that the idea must have occurred to him, and it occurred to everybody around him, but … I doubt it if I even considered the risks – because we were raised in this milieu where you had to be willing to be brave and you had to be willing to make sacrifices for ideals, for principles and for your country.

"My uncle Joe Kennedy had died during the war; my uncle Jack had disappeared MIA during the war. My father had joined the service at the very end of the war, but had fought to get in earlier, to get in action. And I think we were all raised with this notion."[102]

In May, Bobby beat McCarthy in the Indiana and Nebraska primaries, then lost to him in Oregon. On May 30 he flew to California. This was his biggest and most important test: another loss would stop his campaign dead in its tracks, but victory would deliver him the 174 votes which the California delegation would take into the convention – vital to the strategy of persuading Democratic Party power brokers that Bobby was the only candidate who could beat Richard Nixon.

But 'The Golden State' was politically schizophrenic. Its 10 million population was the most ethnically and economically divided in America, and registered Democrats outnumbered Republicans by more than a million; yet two years earlier California had voted to put the deeply conservative Ronald Reagan in the Governor's mansion. Nor could Bobby rely on the local party hierarchy, whose officials were already committed to McCarthy or Vice President Hubert Humphrey, who

---

102 Robert Kennedy Jnr. interview with Brad Johnson and Rob Beemer, Interesting Stuff Entertainment, Malibu, October 13, 2016

had belatedly thrown his hat into the electoral ring. Both had strong backers and constituencies: Humphrey had the support of the White House and McCarthy was the candidate of comfortable middle-class suburban voters. From the outset, Bobby's campaign focussed on the state's minority populations – black, Asian and Hispanic – and low-income and working-class white voters, largely by-passing the Democratic Party machine and relying instead on the efforts of key unions and grass roots activists.

Paul Schrade, who had been a Kennedy family confidante since JFK Presidency, brought the backing of the Auto and Aerospace Workers Union and became one of Bobby's closest advisors, working tirelessly to connect the rich and privileged candidate with blue-collar working men and women.

In the Los Angeles ghettos of Watts and surrounding neighbourhoods, activist Booker Griffin saw Bobby as a politician who could restore hope for African-Americans. "I was losing faith in the American system, and I was losing faith in my white fellow Americans," he remembered 25 years later, "but when Bobby Kennedy came along, there was a white person who was sensitive to the problems of this nation in a manner that did not gloss over its inequities."[103]

But it was California's Mexican-American population – the state's largest single minority – which would be crucial. In March, Cesar Chavez had abandoned a nationally publicized hunger strike to put his 13,000 farm-workers organization behind the campaign, reminding his followers, in a bi-lingual poster, of Bobby's support at the Delano hearings two years earlier.

"Senator Kennedy came at a time when our cause was very hard pressed and we were surrounded by powerful enemies who did not hesitate to viciously attack anyone who was courageous

---

103 Booker Griffin interview with Tim Tate, 1992.

enough to help us. He did not stop to ask whether it would be politically wise for him to come ... nor did he stop to worry about the color of our skin, ... or what languages we speak. ... We know from our experience that he cares, he understands, and he acts with compassion and courage."[104]

By the first week of April, the Kennedy campaign headquarters on L.A.'s Wilshire Boulevard was receiving reports that thousands of Latino farmworkers were being added to the voter registration rolls.

Nor were young voters forgotten: Sandy Serrano, a 20-year-old Latina studying part-time at Pasadena City College, set up a Youth For Kennedy operation. "In those days, Americans under the age of 21 didn't have the right to vote," she recalled in 2016. "But the Kennedy name and legacy and the assassination of MLK motivated me to do something. I felt that the Kennedy family had more of a feeling for minorities than McCarthy: I thought he was what I called a 'white limousine liberal'. The race was tight, but I had confidence, and I believed that if Bobby won the California primary he would get the Democratic nomination. And I felt that if he had won, we would have gotten out of the war much sooner, and that there would be increased opportunities for people of colour."[105]

Within days, Serrano signed up 85 other young, mostly Mexican-American volunteers who went door-to-door canvassing support. They were not always well-received.

"One day we went up to a higher income area, knocking on doors and I remember one guy coming out – and this was a democratic household – with a shotgun and saying 'get off my lawn: if you don't get off my lawn I'm going to shoot you'."[106]

---

104 Robert Kennedy campaign poster, California, April 1968
105 Sandy Serrano-Sewell interview with Tim Tate, July 2016
106 *Ibid.*

The undercurrent of violence – even in minority areas – was ever-present: Bill Barry catalogued a steady stream of threats directed at Bobby.

"A week before the primary," Walter Sheridan remembered, "a guy went into one of the Mexican-American headquarters outside the Los Angeles area and said he was going to kill the Senator. We got his name, and we went and told the F.B.I. and we told the Los Angeles police. There were a lot of threats like that; Barry had a whole file of them."[107]

Reporters embedded with the campaign worried that Bobby would be assassinated before the election. John J. Lindsay, covering the race for *Newsweek*, was convinced that Bobby had "the stuff to go all the way, but he's not going to go all the way … Somebody is going to shoot him. He's out there now waiting for him."[108]

Bobby took the threats seriously, but refused to change his policy of immersing himself in the crowds which constantly surrounded him. Campaigning in the narrow streets of San Francisco's Chinatown, someone set off firecrackers: Ethel Kennedy thought they were gun shots and immediately slumped down in the seat of the car, but Bobby continued standing and waving. He told *Look* magazine's Warren Rogers: "If there is somebody out there who wants to get me, well, doing anything in public life today is Russian Roulette."[109]

But assassination *was* on his mind. In New Orleans, District Attorney Jim Garrison continued to make headlines with a grand jury investigation into allegations that a conspiracy involving the CIA and organised crime was involved in the murder of John Kennedy.

---

107 *Walter Sheridan Oral History Interview RFK #1*, p. 89, August 5, 1969, Washington DC. John F. Kennedy Library, Boston, MA.
108 Schlesinger, p.968
109 Warren Rogers and Stanley Trettick; *RFK, Look*, July 9, 1968

Bobby had always publicly supported the official Warren Commission version that no such conspiracy existed (although he had deliberately never read its report), but by 1968 he had severe doubts about its credibility.

"He felt that the Warren report was a shoddy piece of work," Robert Kennedy Junior said in 2016. "It was not an area – at the time – that he was going to get into … but at the beginning of the California campaign, one of his first speeches was at San Fernando College in front of 12,000 people. At the end of it he opened it for question and answer: there was a woman in the audience who kept shouting 'tell us – who killed JFK?'

"My father ignored her for a while, but then finally responded to her and said 'I have been in the archives: I know what's in there and I'm going to open the archives at the appropriate time'. He was clearly signalling to people at that time that he knew that this was something that required further investigation … He said subsequently to his friends that he would re-open the investigation but 'we need to have the White House in order to do that'".[110]

On June 3, the last day of campaigning, Bobby set out on a final, 1,200 mile tour of the state. He rode in an open-topped car through the crowded streets of Los Angeles, flew north to speak in San Francisco, then back down for another motorcade in San Diego. He was mobbed everywhere he went: by the end of the day his clothes were torn, his hands scabbed and painful from shaking thousands of outstretched hands.

Finally, late that night, he and Ethel, accompanied by six of their children, arrived at the Malibu beach house of John Frankenheimer: he was exhausted but confidant.

"I think he felt not only that he was going to win but he felt like a president, that he could be president of the United States,"

---

110 Robert Kennedy Jnr. interview with Brad Johnson and Rob Beemer, Interesting Stuff Entertainment, Malibu, October 13, 2016

was Walter Sheridan's assessment. "And he showed it, and it was contagious. I think he knew that last night that he was going to be president of the United States, and he was. I think he knew he could beat Humphrey, and I think he knew he could beat Nixon."[111]

Election Day dawned cold and foggy. But in the key minority neighbourhoods, campaign aides reported an extraordinary phenomenon. "For the first time ever," recalled Paul Schrade, "African Americans and Mexican Americans were lining up before the polls opened, just to be able to vote for Robert Kennedy"[112]

At 6.30pm Bobby and John Frankenheimer set off in the director's car for downtown L.A, where the campaign had taken suites in the Ambassador Hotel. Bobby slumped in the passenger seat as Frankenheimer drove fast down the Santa Monica Freeway. "Take it easy, John," Bobby said. "Life's too short."[113]

111 *Walter Sheridan Oral History Interview RFK #*, p. 86, August 13, 1969, Washington DC. John F. Kennedy Library, Boston, MA.
112 Paul Schrade: interviews with Tim Tate, 1991–2016
113 Robert Blair Kaiser: *R.F.K. Must Die!*, p.15. E.P. Dutton, 1970

CHAPTER FOUR:
ELECTION NIGHT

The Ambassador Hotel was packed.

The eight-storey building sat on an entire city block between Wilshire Boulevard and West Eighth Street in downtown Los Angeles. From its Jazz Age heyday through World War Two, the hotel had been the haunt of choice for Hollywood celebrities, and had hosted six Academy Awards ceremonies.

By 1968 it had lost some of that glamour, but remained a popular venue for big business seminars and political parties. On the evening of June 4, the Ambassador was hosting corporate functions for employees of General Electric, the Bulova Watch and Pacific Telephone companies and two election night parties for candidates running in state elections as well as the Kennedy campaign's victory celebrations; 514 guests occupied the hotel's 512 rooms, their needs catered for by 244 staff. But it was Bobby's party which drew the greatest numbers: several thousand people – campaign workers, supporters, members of the media as well as the plain curious – crowded into the bars and coffee shop on the ground floor and the hotel's main ballroom, the Embassy Room, one level above, where Bobby was due to give his anticipated victory speech.

Despite this, security was remarkably light. Prior to June 1968 the Secret Service had never provided protection to presidential election candidates, much less to those contesting primary races. Los Angeles Police Department would normally have assigned officers to the hotel since its protocols required it to offer security to visiting VIPs and politicians. But there was bad blood between the Department and the Kennedy team: many individual officers believed that Bobby was hostile to them and that his staff "didn't want him to be seen in the same photograph with uniformed police officers."[114]

The ostensible origin of this antipathy was typified by an altercation during a motorcade through the city earlier in the campaign, when a uniformed traffic division officer had purportedly tried to rescue Bobby from a crowd of enthusiastic supporters who had pulled him out of his car. "Kennedy and his aides berated the sergeant and told him that they had not asked for the assistance of the police," LAPD subsequently noted. "This conflict measurably affected the conditions which existed just prior to Senator Kennedy's assassination."[115]

LAPD also justified the absence of police officers in the Ambassador Hotel by claiming, correctly, that Bobby's campaign never requested them.[116] But in early May, a request for assistance had been made by a "town hall group" when Bobby was staying in the Biltmore Hotel. The campaign asked LAPD's Intelligence Division for security to "keep the press from Kennedy's bedroom while he slept".

When this was refused, the group complained that the police had provided officers to protect Senator McCarthy, and asked why Bobby was to be treated differently; LAPD's justification was

---

114 Former LAPD Patrol Bureau Inspector Bob Rock; interview with Dan Moldea, February 10, 1990. Robert F. Kennedy Assassination Archives, University of Massachusetts Dartmouth.

115 Summary report of the Los Angeles Police Department Investigation of the Senator Robert Kennedy Assassination, p.3. California State Archives.

116 *Ibid*, p.124

"that reliable information had been received regarding a threat on Senator McCarthy's life. Such a threat came within the policy of the Department to provide security for V.I.P.s, dignitaries and political officials."[117]

The most LAPD was prepared to provide on primary election night was a rotating pool of eight officers in four squad cars, patrolling the streets around the Ambassador. Inside the hotel itself, the safety of thousands of people spread over eight floors in a 25-acre plot of land with multiple entrances, was left to eleven of the hotel's permanent security staff, supplemented by six part time private 'rent a cops', hired from the local Ace Guard Service.

John Frankenheimer's Rolls Royce, with Bobby in the passenger seat, pulled in to the Ambassador parking lot at 8.10pm, ten minutes after polls closed across the state. Around the same time the first security scare of the night was reported at the hotel: a man and a woman were discovered in the first floor lobby area, handing out bumper stickers bearing the caption "Kill Kennedy". That these – in the words of an FBI report – "justified the killing of John F. Kennedy" rather than urging the murder of Bobby was not greatly reassuring.[118]

The campaign occupied three rooms on the fifth floor. By 9pm, as America's three national television networks broadcast mixed messages – CBS projecting a Kennedy victory but NBC and ABC offering no concrete predictions – Bobby was restless. Journalist Jack Newfield watched as he "prowled into the hallway and was besieged by a pack of radio, television and print reporters".[119]

Downstairs, television channels had set up large cameras at the back of the Embassy Room ballroom where Bobby would

---

117 *Ibid*, p.124-125
118 FBI File X-5, Vol.17, p.26. California State Archives.
119 Jack Newfield, Robert F. Kennedy – A Memoir, p.321

make either a victory speech or concede defeat. The cameras were heavy and immobile, linked to their network control rooms by large trailing cables: anticipating a possible fire hazard – as well as the likely safety code violations common to all crowded functions – six marshals from Los Angeles Fire Department patrolled the ballroom and its surrounding service areas. Nor were the networks alone in sending cameras and microphones: local television and radio stations also assigned crew to cover the event: as crowds gathered, Don Schulman, a film runner for KNXT TV, scoped the room, looking for the best place to act as a 'spotter', relaying information to his camera crew.

As the evening wore on, more Kennedy supporters and campaign workers arrived at the hotel. Lisa Urso, an 18-year-old student at Mesa Junior College and part-time volunteer in San Diego, drove 120 miles to join the party; Paul Schrade, who had been in San Francisco during the afternoon, planned to watch election night on TV at his home in Laurel Canyon, but on his way home from Los Angeles Airport he decided instead to spend the evening with the campaign. He went straight to Bobby's suite on the 5th floor and "hung around waiting for the results".[120]

Sandy Serrano arrived around 9pm, hotfooting across town from the Youth For Kennedy offices in Pasadena. She was immediately struck by the number of people thronging the hotel's bars, cafés and corridors. "It was packed down there, really packed. It was a party – packed with young people, a lot of them people of colour. But I wasn't aware of any security – that never really came into my mind."[121]

William F. Gardner, a former LAPD lieutenant who was the Ambassador's head of security, stationed his uniformed guards at the points where he expected the biggest crowds. He assigned five

120 Paul Schrade interviews with Tim Tate, 1991–2016
121 Sandy Serrano-Sewell, interviews with Tim Tate 1992–2016.

uniformed men to the ground floor, known as "the Casino Level", four to the first floor "Lobby Level", where the Embassy Ballroom was located, and sent one upstairs "with orders to restrict traffic into the Kennedy suites"[122]. Gardner himself – who had been on duty since eight o'clock that morning – patrolled the hotel with his deputy Fred Murphy; both were in plain clothes.

In theory, only accredited Kennedy staffers and working press were allowed into the Embassy Room through its main entrance doors. But the ballroom was surrounded by numerous corridors, adjoining rooms, the hotel's main kitchen and a service pantry: all had access doors into the ballroom and revellers were easily able to avoid Gardner's men. When a campaign worker warned one of them that "numerous persons [were] entering the Embassy Room via the pantry", the guard explained that security was "unable to do anything about it as they did not have enough men."[123]

At 9.30pm the Embassy Room was dangerously overcrowded; fire marshals ordered that only those wearing red Kennedy staff badges, and accredited journalists with green or yellow press passes would be allowed to enter – and then only on a 'one in, one out' basis. But it was not difficult for those without a pass to get into the ballroom and surrounding areas. Conrad Seim, a 50-year-old press photographer, was approached twice by a "very persistent" young woman wearing a white dress with blue polka dots, who asked to borrow his press badge[124]. He refused, but a little while later campaign worker Susanne Locke spotted what appears to have been the same woman, expressionless

---

122 Summary report of the Los Angeles Police Department Investigation of the Senator Robert Kennedy Assassination, p.133. California State Archives.

123 *Ibid,* p.1434

124 Interview with Conrad Scim; LAPD "Special Unit Senator" files, Volume 40; p.319. California State Archives.

and "somewhat out of place" amid the exultant mood inside the Embassy Room: she "observed that the girl was not wearing a yellow press badge and thought this to be very unusual since it was necessary to have such a badge to gain entry".[125]

Booker Griffin, wandering down from the ballroom to the Ambassador Room on the floor below, noticed a short, dark-skinned young man who seemed out of place: unlike most of the smartly-suited crowd, he was "shabbily dressed with baggy pants". Griffin also noticed that the man appeared to be "together with" a young woman standing next to him.[126] After exchanging stares with the man, Griffin, who wrote occasionally for the *Los Angeles Sentinel* community newspaper, went to collect a press pass. Between 10.45pm and11.30pm he moved easily between the Embassy Room – now made oppressively hot by the TV cameras and lights – and the nearby – and much cooler – Colonial Room.[127]

By 10.50 the Embassy Room was so overcrowded that the situation was becoming impossible to police. Thane Eugene Cesar, a 26-year-old plumber for the Lockheed Aircraft company guard who also worked part-time for Ace Security, was assigned to the kitchen area behind it with orders to stop unauthorised entry into the ballroom. By his own account, Cesar had not expected to be on duty that night: he had been at home in Simi Valley when summoned to supplement security at the Ambassador. Wearing his grey Ace uniform with, he later said, a .38 calibre revolver in a holster at his hip, he stationed himself inside the

125 Interview with Susan Locke, June 7, 1968. FBI Field Office files, Ser. 3002-3095; p.254-255. California State Archives.
126 Booker Griffin FBI interview, June 11, 1968. FBI Files Interviews 2, p.50. California State Archives.
127 Interview with Booker Griffin; LAPD "Special Unit Senator" files, Volume 51; p.17-18. California State Archives.

pantry, noticing that "false press badges and staff buttons were prevalent" on many of those already inside.[128]

Meanwhile the candidate himself was back in the suite after shuttling between the fourth and fifth floors for live interviews with NBC, CBS and ABC television, and a radio Q&A with Metromedia. The conversations had been good natured, some even jocular, and Bobby seemed confident that he had won the election. But by the time he returned to his suite there was still no clear-cut consensus among the networks. NBC eventually joined CBS in predicting victory, but ABC was uncertain.

The crowd in the Embassy Room was happy but now restless. The heat was stifling as 1,800 supporters began to chant "we want Bobby, we want Bobby".

Vincent di Pierro, a 19-year-old student and son of the hotel's head maître D, drove down to the Ambassador hoping to catch a glimpse of Bobby: as a part-time waiter at the hotel – he was off duty on June 4 – he had little trouble getting into the service areas behind the Embassy Room. As the clock ticked closer to midnight, he stood chatting with other kitchen workers just inside the double doors between the pantry and the corridor behind the ballroom.

Around 11.45pm, Bobby decided to head downstairs and claim victory in the California Democratic Primary. Surrounded by a group of journalists, aides and union officials, and protected by Bill Barry, Roosevelt Grier and Rafer Johnson, he and Ethel took a service elevator down to the Lobby Level. At 11.58pm ABC broadcast live pictures of their arrival in the main kitchen, following as they walked through into its adjacent pantry, then entered a hallway leading to the Embassy Room: Vincent Di Pierro got to shake the candidate's hand.

---

128 Report of interview with Thane Eugene Cesar, June 11, 1969. FBI Files – Interviews 2, p.15 California State Archives.

At 12.01am ABC and CBS TV broadcast live pictures of Bobby entering the Embassy Room ballroom to thunderous cheers; as he approached the lectern, set up on a makeshift platform, America's third national network, NBC, joined in the live coverage, showing its viewers pictures of more than 20 aides and reporters on the platform and the ecstatic crowd once more chanting "we want Kennedy".

After a brief tussle with the loudspeaker system, Bobby began his victory speech at 12.04am. He thanked his supporters, name checking Cesar Chavez, Paul Schrade, his wife, Ethel, and even his dog, Freckles. Then he moved on to the meaning and importance of the California victory.

"What I think is quite clear is that we can work together in the last analysis, and that what has been going on within the United States over the period of the last three years – the divisions, the violence, the disenchantment with our society...whether it's between blacks and whites, between the poor and the more affluent, or between age groups, or on the war in Vietnam – that we can start to work together.

"We are a great country, and a selfish country and a compassionate country...but what I think all of these primaries have indicated...was the people in the Democratic Party and the people in the United States wanted change...The country wants to move in a different direction. We want to deal with our own problems within our own country and we want peace in Vietnam..."[129]

Then, bowing to the lateness of the hour, he wrapped up with the words, "My thanks to all of you, and now it's on to Chicago and let's win there." As the crowd cheered, he flashed a V for Victory sign. The time was 12.14am.

---

129 Transcript of Robert Kennedy Primary Victory Speech, *New York Times,* June 6, 1968

Bobby was expected to go down to the Ambassador Room to greet supporters who had been unable to get in to the Embassy Room. But less than five minutes earlier, senior campaign aide Fred Dutton had decided the crowds were "too rowdy and congested"; instead Dutton gave instructions to direct Bobby to a hastily-arranged press conference for non-broadcast journalists in the Colonial Room.[130] Surrounded by reporters, photographers and aides, Bobby stepped through the platform's rear curtains and off the back of the stage, walked quickly through an anteroom to its back door, turned right, then walked down the incline through a vestibule and into the pantry.

Paul Schrade, following the candidate in the pantry, recalled: "Bob stopped to shake hands with a couple of kitchen workers. I can remember the joy I felt at that point: I felt this was symbolic of the campaign and that now we were going to have a President."[131]

The campaign's official bodyguard Bill Barry and one of his unofficial security recruits, Olympic gold medallist Rafer Johnson, had become separated from the candidate. Instead, hotel staffers Karl Uecker and Edward Minasian flanked Bobby, with Ambassador security officer Stanley Kawalec in front of them and Ace Guard Thane Cesar immediately behind. At 12.15am, with Uecker grasping Bobby's right wrist, the crowd pushed through the double swing doors into the pantry.

Vincent Di Pierro, was walking a few feet behind Bobby and his escorts. As they approached an ice-cube machine set against the right hand wall, Di Pierro saw a knot of people standing by a tray stacker several feet ahead at the far end of the ice-machine.

130 Transcript of interview with Fred Dutton, September 6, 1968. LAPD "Special Unit Senator" files, Volume 98; p.193-203. California State Archives.

131 Paul Schrade: interviews with Tim Tate, 1991–2016

He noticed that one of them – a young, slim man in a blue jacket and white shirt –was standing on the tray stacker, crouched in "kind of a funny position … kind of down, like if he were trying to protect himself from something."[132]

A second before 12.16am Lisa Urso saw, to her horror, that the man in the blue jacket was now standing upright next to a steam table and was pointing a revolver at the on-coming crowd: then two shots rang out in the pantry. Paul Schrade, a few feet behind Bobby, was hit in the head. "I thought I had been electrocuted. I just passed out."[133] Schrade's blood spattered over Vincent Di Pierro's face and glasses. Then, after a very brief pause, a rapid succession of further shots erupted.

Lisa Urso, standing near the track stacker, saw Bobby react. "The Senator move[d] his right hand in the vicinity of his right ear and … staggered.[134]" Thane Cesar was inches behind Bobby's right shoulder. "I threw myself off balance and fell back … and then the Senator fell right down in front of me, and then I turned and … seen blood coming from this side of his face[135]." Stanley Kawalec, who turned back towards Bobby, thought he felt shots flying past his ear from behind.[136]

Karl Uecker had been the first to react decisively, wrestling with the gunman at the steam table. "I heard a shot [and] a second shot … I was right in front of the man who had a gun in his hand. I started grabbing for the gun … I got my right arm

132 Transcript of interview with Vincent di Pierro, June 5, 1968. LAPD "Special Unit Senator" files, Volume 94; p.47-73. California State Archives.
133 Paul Schrade; interviews with Tim Tate 1991 – 2016
134 Interview with Lisa Lynn Urso, June 27, 1968. LAPD "Special Unit Senator" files, Volume 61, p.185-186. California State Archives
135 Transcript of recorded interview with Thane Eugene Cesar, June 5, 1968. LAPD "Special Unit Senator" files, Volume 94; p.34-44. California State Archives.
136 Report of interview with Stanley Kawalec, June 7, 1968. FBI files X-1, Vol.2, p.81-83

round his neck ... in a headlock and bent him over the steam table ..."[137]

But the gunman was unexpectedly strong and kept firing. All Uecker could do was to slam the shooter's arm against the steam table counter and re-direct his aim as the man kept pulling the trigger. For just over five seconds bullets flew around the pantry, striking more bodies. Bill Barry, frantically pushing towards the steam table, recalled what happened in the seconds before he got there and helped subdue the gunman.

"I saw the susp[ect] holding the gun in his right hand, his arm was extended and the gun was about 12 inches from the Senator's head ... I took the gun away from him and put the gun on the counter ... and then [Rafer] Johnson and Roosevelt [Grier] helped me subdue the susp[ect] again[138]".

Twelve seconds after the shooting began, CBS TV cameraman Jim Wilson – who had managed to barrel his way into the pantry upon hearing the first two shots – switched on his camera and began capturing the first film images of the carnage: first Paul Schrade, face up on the pantry floor, wounded in the forehead and deathly still, then Bobby, lying on his back, his arms stretched out wide, as if on a cross. Hotel busboy Juan Romero, kneeling beside him, said "'Come on Senator, you can make it"[139]. Bobby was able to respond, asking "Is everybody ok? Is Paul [Schrade] all right?"[140]

At the steam table Barry punched the shooter twice in the face: the man dropped the gun but, moments later, somehow grabbed it back. Fire Department photographer Harold Burba

---

137 People vs. Sirhan Sirhan: Trial testimony of Karl Uecker, February 14, 1969. California State Archives

138 Report of interview with Bill Barry, June 5, 1968. LAPD "Special Unit Senator" files, Volume 52; p.286. California State Archives.

139 Trial Testimony of Juan Romero: *People vs. Sirhan Sirhan*. February 13, 1969. California State Archives

140 Paul Schrade: interviews with Tim Tate, 1991 – 2016

shot still pictures as aides and onlookers piled on top of the gunman. At 12.17am Andrew West, a reporter for KRKD audio, recorded himself warning by-standers in the pantry "get away from the barrel, get away from the barrel, man!" Twenty seconds later, as Roosevelt Grier wrenched the revolver out of the shooter's hand for good, West gave the all-clear: "Ladies and gentlemen, they have the gun away from the man."

Looking back down the pantry Grier saw Bill Barry kneel beside Bobby on the floor: he could see "blood on the right side of [Bobby's] head.[141]" The Senator's left hand grasped a rosary – placed there by Juan Romero. Then, with the gunman subdued and disarmed, Ethel Kennedy was allowed into the pantry. When she arrived at her husband's side, Bobby was not only still awake but called out her name several times.

As the commotion spread out to the Embassy Room, KTLA TV microphones captured one of the station's newsmen shouting "Bobby's been shot". Moments later, live pictures showed two young men climbing on to the stage and appealing for a doctor. Radiologist Dr. Stanley Abo was among the first to respond: he identified himself to a staffer who "pushed him through the crowd and towards the kitchen area". Such was the panic and confusion that Dr. Abo's jacket "was ripped off by the time he reached the kitchen."[142] He first checked on Paul Schrade and found a glancing scalp wound; satisfied that this posed no imminent danger, he moved over to examine Bobby.

Pressing his ear to the candidate's chest he heard a strong heartbeat and found a decent pulse, registering between 50 and 60; but Bobby's breathing was shallow and while his left eye was closed,

---

141 Interview with Roosevelt Grier, June 12, 1968. FBI files, X-2, Vol 7, p.72-77

142 Summary report of the Los Angeles Police Department Investigation of the Senator Robert Kennedy Assassination, p.163. California State Archives.

the right was open and staring in a manner which indicated possible brain damage.[143]

Reaching gently behind Bobby's head Abo found "a small entry wound, just back of the right ear. There was a mass of clotted blood around the wound, with a small amount of blood oozing out of the back of the neck."[144]

Ambulance Unit G-18 arrived at the Ambassador at 12.23am: its two-man crew, driver Robert Hulsman and attendant Max Behrman, forced their way into the pantry and lifted Bobby on to a gurney. "As they did this," Abo reported, "the Senator ... moaned loudly 'no, no, no'[145]"

At 12.26am CBS and NBC TV broadcast live pictures of uniformed LAPD officers rushing the suspect through the hotel. A few minutes later, away from live television cameras, Bobby was lifted into G-18. The police described the scene as "chaotic, as individuals attempted to board the ambulance."[146] Hulsman himself recalled the vehicle being surrounded and having to get out of the cab, twice, to re-lock its doors which people had opened.

As the ambulance sped away towards Los Angeles Central Receiving Hospital, writer Pete Hamill – who less than six months earlier had told Bobby to run for President in memory of his murdered brother – checked his watch. It was 12.32am[147].

143 Interview with Dr. Stanley Abo, July 11, 1968. FBI files X-4, Vol.12, p. 40-41

144 *Progress Report – Case Preparation for Trial*, August 1, 1968. . LAPD "Special Unit Senator" files, Volume 47; p.110. California State Archives.

145 Interview with Dr. Stanley Abo, July 11, 1968. FBI files X-4, Vol.12, p. 40-41

146 Summary report of the Los Angeles Police Department Investigation of the Senator Robert Kennedy Assassination, p.165. California State Archives.

147 Interview with Pete Hamill, August 6, 1968: FBI files X-5, Vol.17, p.70-71

CHAPTER FIVE:
24 HOURS

Major crime investigations and emergency surgery share a common truth: the first 24 hours are critical. The period is known to detectives and trauma surgeons alike as "the golden hours", because what happens during them usually dictates the prospects either of survival or of solving the crime.

At 12.27am Officers Arthur J. Placentia and Travis R. White pushed the suspected shooter into the back of LAPD patrol car 48 outside the Ambassador. They had been followed from the hotel by an angry crowd, yelling "kill the bastard, kill him."[148] As Placentia sat beside the suspect in the back and White fired up the engine, Jesse Unruh climbed into the front passenger seat. In the immediate aftermath of the shooting, Unruh, Speaker of the California State Assembly and chairman of the state's Democratic Delegation, had assumed responsibility for protecting the gunman: "this one is going to face trial," he shouted at the mob. "Nothing is going to happen to him ... We aren't going to have another Dallas."[149] The crowd surrounding the patrol car

---

148 Interview with Officer Arthur J. Placentia, August 27, 1968. LAPD "Special Unit Senator" files, Volume 102; p.117. California State Archives.
149 Summary report of the Los Angeles Police Department Investigation of the Senator Robert Kennedy Assassination, p.306. California State Archives.

had other ideas: it "surged forward towards the officers and completely surrounded them ... and began striking at the officers and Sirhan."[150]

White sped towards the nearest LAPD precinct, Rampart Division Police Station, two miles away on West Temple Street. He was alert to the very real possibility of attack and avoided main routes in favour of dark side streets while "constantly checking for possible pursuit from the crowd".[151] Inside the car, Placentia read the suspect his rights and asked if he understood: the suspect said 'yes' but did not respond when Placentia asked his name. Unruh leaned back to look at the man and asked why he had shot Bobby: "I did it for my country," the gunman answered, then – in reply to the question "why him?" – said "it's too late".[152] For the rest of the journey, the man said nothing at all[153]. En route, Placentia examined the suspect's eyes with a flashlight: from their reaction to the beam he suspected that the man "was under the influence of something".[154] A few minutes later Car 48 arrived at Rampart.

Almost two miles away Ambulance Unit G-18 pulled into the Central Receiving Hospital, a small trauma centre on West 6th Street. Bobby was rushed through to the emergency room

---

150 *Ibid*, p.193
151 Interview with Officer Arthur J. Placentia, August 27, 1968. LAPD "Special Unit Senator" files, Volume 102; p.118. California State Archives.
152 Interview with Jesse M. Unruh, July 21, 1968. LAPD "Special Unit Senator" files, Volume 63; p.286. California State Archives.
153 An internal LAPD report later claimed that the suspect also answered Unruh's "why him?" question by saying "You think I'm crazy, so you can use it as evidence against me." However, none of the witness statements by Placentia, White or Unruh contain any reference to this apparently self-aware remark. *Sirhan's Arrest & Arraignment*", report dated October 9, 1969. LAPD "Special Unit Senator" files, Volume 48; p.23. California State Archives.
154 Summary report of the Los Angeles Police Department Investigation of the Senator Robert Kennedy Assassination, p.194. California State Archives.

for assessment: doctors noted his condition as "comatose, thready pulse in extremis, blood pressure zero over zero, heartbeat almost imperceptible ... blood coming from his right ear and his eyes were open, staring, dry and lustreless".[155] There was also evidence of bullet wounds to his back. The doctors administered oxygen and within minutes Bobby was able to breathe on his own; his pulse became stronger and his heartbeat sounded good.

But it was obvious that brain surgery was needed immediately. Bobby was loaded back into an ambulance and at 12.48am was rushed into the Good Samaritan Hospital, three blocks away at the end of Shatto Street.

At Rampart, the suspect was taken into the station through a basement door and led upstairs to the Division's breathalyser room on the first floor – standard LAPD procedure for detainees believed to be under the influence of drink or drugs. According to Los Angeles Attorney Marilyn Barrett (who was later involved in the case) the officers took a blood sample in the breathalyser room[156]: however, there is no surviving record of any medical tests, only of a repeat flashlight examination which now indicated that the man's eyes were "normal."[157] With Jesse Unruh still standing guard, White searched the suspect: he found four one hundred dollar bills, a single five dollar note, a handful of change totalling 66 cents, a comb, two .22 calibre cartridges, one .22 calibre bullet and three pieces of paper. One appeared to be a poem or song about Bobby; the second was a newspaper advertisement for a campaign rally at the Ambassador three days earlier; the third was clipping from the *Pasadena Independent*

---

155 *Ibid*, p.166.
156 Authors' interviews with Marilynn Barrett, lawyer, 1991 – 2016.
157 Summary report of the Los Angeles Police Department Investigation of the Senator Robert Kennedy Assassination, p.195. California State Archives.

Star News describing Bobby's support for the state of Israel and criticism of its Arab neighbours. But there was nothing to provide a clue as to his identity.[158]

Shortly before 1am the suspect was taken to interrogation room B, which was equipped with a tape recorder. Rampart Sgt. William Jordan, the ranking detective on duty, switched it on and began asking questions: the suspect answered none of them.

Instead, the recording captured a succession of long silences, punctuated by incoherent mumblings and rasping, erratic breaths. Only once did the man – name still unknown – say anything intelligible, asking Officer Fred Willoughby, standing guard in the room, for a sip of his hot chocolate drink: when Willoughby refused, the suspect "kicked out suddenly with his right foot, spilling hot chocolate on himself and Willoughby".[159] Jordan switched the tape off and left to make arrangements for sending the prisoner downtown to LAPD's Parker Center headquarters.

In the meantime, five other victims of the shooting in the pantry arrived for emergency assessment at Central Receiving. Thirty-year-old William Weisel, Associate News Director for ABC, had taken a bullet in the stomach as he followed the candidate into the pantry. Elizabeth Evans – a 42-year-old Californian artist – had been standing beside Weisel: she and Paul Schrade, 43, the United Auto Workers Union official who had been a few feet behind Bobby, both had gunshot wounds to the head. Irwin Stroll, a 17-year-old student campaign worker, and Ira Goldstein, a 19-year-old reporter for Continental News Service, had less serious wounds: Stroll had a bullet in his left calf, while Stroll – who had been behind him when the shooting started – had one in his

---

158 *Ibid.*
159 Sirhan B. Sirhan – 1st Interrogation Tape, People's Exhibit 93, California State Archives.

left buttock. By 1.30am each had been examined and transferred out for surgery at different hospitals across the city.

At the same time Dr. Henry Cuneo, a surgeon at the University of Southern California, arrived at Good Samaritan to take charge of the team fighting to save Bobby's life.

He gave instructions to place him on an ice bed in the hope of holding down a dangerous surge in temperature, but it was clear that the patient was barely clinging on. Two Catholic priests joined Ethel Kennedy at Bobby's bedside: Father Lawrence Joy administered the last rites before Monsignor Joseph J. Trauxanaw began saying the mass.

Across town, at Midway Hospital on San Vicente Boulevard, Dr. Nathan Cozen operated on Irwin Stroll, removing a small bullet from his lower leg. It was the first of the rounds fired in the pantry to be recovered, but its evidential value was limited: the doctor noted that the slug was "flattened, deformed and its calibre could not be determined" – possibly the result of having ricocheted off the pantry floor.[160]

Then, at 1.45am Rafer Johnson walked into Rampart station and handed over the gun seized from the suspect during the struggle in the pantry. It was a cheap .22 calibre, eight-shot Iver Johnson revolver – a junk weapon commonly used by low-rent criminals and which police referred to as "a Saturday Night Special": empty shell casings occupied all eight chambers in the cylinder. The gun bore the serial number H53725, enabling LAPD detectives to check firearms records for the registered owner. It would turn out to be a long and complicated search.

In a Homicide Division interrogation room at Parker Center, their colleagues were involved in a convoluted attempt

---

160 Summary report of the Los Angeles Police Department Investigation of the Senator Robert Kennedy Assassination, p.182. California State Archives.

to interview the suspected gunman. The man still refused to tell them his name, but in marked contrast to his earlier, near-catatonic demeanour, he was now remarkably composed and even friendly.

He was allowed to take a shower – which he took in a "deliberate and thorough manner"[161] – and was given clean clothes to replace the shirt and trousers stained with hot chocolate. He cheerfully remarked on the pants being too big for his slight frame.

The tape recording of the interviews with the detectives and Assistant Los Angeles County District Attorney John Howard, captured a bizarre conversation in which the suspect seemed relaxed, calmly discussing the officers' careers and home lives, their thoughts on capital punishment and a recently-concluded double-murder trial in the city. But each time the interrogators brought the subject back to his identity, the man demurred: "I think I shall remain incognito," he told Howard more than once as the recorder ran and the hours ticked on.[162]

At 2.15am, the officers walked their prisoner down the stairway directly connecting Homicide to the booking section of LA's Central Jail. Since he still had no name, they registered him as "John Doe" – standard law enforcement terminology for an unknown man. And once again, the suspect's demeanour was striking. Martin Dismukes, the civilian officer handling custodial duties at the jail, described him as "very casual" and told the

161 Summary report of the Los Angeles Police Department Investigation of the Senator Robert Kennedy Assassination, p.311. California State Archives.
162 Transcript of interviews with Sirhan B. Sirhan, Parker Centre, Los Angeles, June 5, 1968. LAPD "Special Unit Senator" files, Volume 100; p.216-390. California State Archives.

police "that he had seen visitors to the jail who were a lot more nervous" when they were booked[163].

At Good Samaritan, medical staff prepared Bobby for emergency surgery; at the same time, in hospitals across the city, doctors worked on three of the other shooting victims. At Kaiser Hospital, they pulled a .22 calibre bullet from William Weisel's abdomen, three inches above his waistline: the injury was not life-threatening and the slug was recovered undamaged. Ira Goldstein was also in good shape and, although the bullet removed from his buttock was deformed, Dr. Max Finkel recognised it as .22 calibre: he scratched an 'X' on the misshapen slug to mark it for evidence.

Paul Schrade's condition was more serious. The bullet which felled him had entered just below the hair line and shattered as it passed through his head. X-rays showed that fragments of the slug had lodged in the bone, and splinters had been forced into his skull. Dr. Kasper Fuchs performed delicate cranial surgery to extract them; he also managed to remove small pieces of the bullet. These brought the total number of slugs, or slug fragments, recovered from the victims to three.[164]

The bullets offered the best hope for LAPD's investigators to piece together what had happened in the pantry – not least because the suspected gunman continued to give them no assistance. The entire interrogation process – and particularly his new 'John Doe' identity – seemed to amuse him: back in the interrogation room, a detective tried once again to prise a name from him. "One of the interesting things is to find out exactly who John Doe is," the officer mused. "That's what I'm interested

163 Statement of Martin Dismukes, September 3, 1968: "Special Unit Senator" files, Volume 70, p.132 California State Archives.

164 Summary report of the Los Angeles Police Department Investigation of the Senator Robert Kennedy Assassination, p.177-183. California State Archives.

in." The suspect replied: "You know that's beautiful, beautiful. Maybe we should keep it interesting".[165]

By 3am television and newspaper reporters were clamouring for information. Los Angeles Chief of Police, Tom Reddin, held an impromptu press conference, but other than confirming that the suspect's .22 Iver Johnson had been seized, he had few hard facts to impart. The presumed gunman's identity was unknown and the best Reddin could offer was that the man had "a slight accent": he speculated that the suspect "might be Cuban or Jamaican".[166]

As Reddin was speaking, his officers woke up the registered purchasers of the .22 revolver. Albert Hertz had bought it three years earlier at a gun shop in Pasadena, but his wife told the police she had given it to her daughter, who lived some distance away in Marin County. The detectives sent an urgent request to the local Sheriff's Department to knock on the young woman's door.[167]

At 3.10am, surgeons at Good Samaritan began the long and difficult attempt to save Bobby's life. He was comatose and "so far down that he would not respond to any type of painful stimulus"; only a respirator kept him breathing. After shaving the right side of his head, Dr. Nat Reid used an air saw to cut away a section of scalp, allowing Dr. Cuneo gently to probe the wound: Cuneo discovered that a bullet had shattered inside the skull, forcing bone fragments deep into Bobby's brain. Working slowly and cautiously, the surgeons picked them out before moving on to

165 Transcript of interviews with Sirhan B. Sirhan, Parker Centre, Los Angeles, June 5, 1968. LAPD "Special Unit Senator" files, Volume 100; p.248. California State Archives.

166 *Senator Fails to Improve After Surgery, Los Angeles Times,* June 6, 1968

167 Summary report of the Los Angeles Police Department Investigation of the Senator Robert Kennedy Assassination, p.315. California State Archives.

locate and lift small pieces of bullet and metal fragments from the tissue.

Despite the damage, the doctors observed some hopeful signs. Although Bobby remained comatose, his blood pressure improved and occasionally his respiratory system fluttered into life, allowing the anaesthetist to disconnect him from the artificial breathing apparatus. But the respite was temporary and unpredictable: as the hours passed, Bobby was frequently reconnected to the respirator. At 6.20am, the surgeons had done everything possible: all they, and the Kennedy family, could now do was wait – and hope.[168]

LAPD's detectives had also reached a dead-end. The suspected gunman had been interviewed for almost two hours, seemingly cheerful and willing to discuss almost any subject they raised; but he still refused to answer their two most urgent questions – why he had opened fire in the pantry and who he was. Sgt. Jordan came to the conclusion that "he was playing a game and enjoying it ... He wanted to talk and was happy to talk about anything other than the Kennedy case ... He appeared less upset to me than individuals arrested for a traffic violation."[169]

At 6.45am the officers led the suspect down an internal stairway to the jail yard: from there, and surrounded by a phalanx of protective officers, determined that there would be no repeat of the murder of John Kennedy's alleged assassin in Dallas, he was rushed to the 7th floor of the Hall of Justice for an arraignment hearing. At 7.25am, under the name "John Doe" he was formally charged with six counts of assault with intent to commit murder.

---

168 Summary report of the Los Angeles Police Department Investigation of the Senator Robert Kennedy Assassination, p.171-172. California State Archives.

169 Summary report of the Los Angeles Police Department Investigation of the Senator Robert Kennedy Assassination, p.312. California State Archives.

Bail was set at $250,000, but since the suspect's public defender made no request for his client's release, this was purely notional. At 8am, "John Doe" was taken through an underground tunnel to the new Los Angeles County Jail and placed in cell number 7057.

At the same time, detectives pursuing the ownership of the suspect's revolver finally caught a break. Their search had led them across the greater Los Angeles area for the past five hours; Albert Hertz' daughter had been woken up in her home, but told the investigators that she had given the gun to an ex-neighbour six months earlier. The neighbour was traced and interviewed, but said that he had sold the gun to one of his co-workers – a man he knew only as "Joe" – at a store in Pasadena. The detectives trudged back to Pasadena.

There was no sign of "Joe" when they arrived at Nash's Department Store at 8am, but one of the staff said that a fellow-employee called Munir Sirhan had been in earlier that morning and had said that he believed his brother might be the man suspected of the pantry shooting. Then, as the detectives prepared for the next leg of this seemingly-endless search, Munir Sirhan (who was known to staff as "Joe") returned to the store: the detectives put him in the back of their squad car and set off for Pasadena Police station. In an extraordinary twist, their arrival coincided with that of Munir's elder brother, Adel: he had come to tell the police that he believed one of his other siblings had shot the Senator.

At 9.35am, Adel was shown a copy of that morning's *Herald Examiner* newspaper, which had published a photo of the suspect being held in the County Jail: he positively identified the man as his youngest brother, Sirhan Bishara Sirhan.[170]

---

170 Summary report of the Los Angeles Police Department Investigation of the Senator Robert Kennedy Assassination, p.316-317. California State Archives.

In the intensive care unit at Good Samaritan, the Kennedy family waited and prayed. Three of Bobby's children – Joe, Kathleen and Robert Jnr – had stayed on the east coast during the election campaign: in the early hours they were flown to Los Angeles on the Vice-President's official plane, Air Force Two, and rushed over to the hospital.

"The floor that my father was on had been cleared and there were US Marshalls there," Robert Jnr. recalled. "My mother was sitting beside him; my father's head was bandaged and he had bruising on his face, his eyes were black and there were respirators pumping that were keeping him alive.

"My mother was to one side of the bed, holding his hand, and we took turns – me and my brothers and sisters – sitting on the other side of the bed and holding his other hand. My father was 5'10, so he was short compared to all of his children [as adults], but he had huge hands: he had big, wrestler's hands – and that's one of the things I remember, holding that big hand."[171]

Kennedy campaign staff had asked Dr. James L. Poppen, a neurosurgeon at New England Deaconess Hospital and an old family friend, to fly out and act as a consultant to the Los Angeles medical team. At 10am he examined Bobby and knew immediately that, even if he survived, the brain damage was devastating and irreparable. Although Bobby had reflexes in both eyes, arms and legs Dr. Poppen noted that "the eye pupils were wide and did not react to light, which is pretty serious business."[172]

Fifteen miles away, Adel Sirhan led a team of officers from LAPD, the FBI and the Sheriff's Department to the family's single-storey home on East Howard Street, Pasadena. At 11.15am the detectives began methodically searching the house and

---

171 Robert Kennedy Jnr. interview with Brad Johnson and Rob Beemer, Interesting Stuff Entertainment, Malibu, October 13, 2016
172 *How RFK Died 7 Hours Before It Was Told*: *Chicago Tribune*, June 8, 1968

garage: on the garage workbench, the officers found three .22 bullets and two empty shell casings, and in Sirhan Sirhan's bedroom they located a further bullet and a box of gun cleaning patches. But it was evidence discovered in the drawer of his dresser which seemed, beyond all reasonable doubt, to confirm Sirhan as the shooter in the pantry. A cheap, green, wire-bound notebook and a used US Treasury Department envelope were the most damning: the envelope bore a handwritten statement – "RFK must be disposed of like his brother ... Reactionary", while, amid what appeared to be handwritten college homework, the notebook contained a handful of scrawled pages setting out the writer's intention to kill Bobby.

One, dated May 18, 1968, read: "My determination to eliminate RFK is becoming more the more of [sic] an unstoppable obsession". Below this incriminating declaration, was a bizarre jumble of unpunctuated sentences: "RFK must die. RFK must be killed. Robert F. Kennedy must be assassinated ..." The scribbles were repeated, over and over, down to the bottom of the page.[173]

The evidence against Sirhan Sirhan, aka "John Doe", now appeared overwhelming. He had been arrested in the pantry, minutes after the shooting, with – quite literally – a smoking gun, and eyewitnesses described restraining him as he fired the weapon. The gun itself, now in LAPD's possession, had been owned by his brother: it had evidently been recently fired and all eight chambers held spent shell casings. The case seemed open and shut.

At 1.10pm the next piece of evidence was added to the growing tally. Surgeons at Memorial Hospital removed a .22 calibre bullet from Elizabeth Evans' scalp, bringing the total of slugs, or

---

173 Summary report of the Los Angeles Police Department Investigation of the Senator Robert Kennedy Assassination, p.320-328. California State Archives.

slug fragments, recovered from the victim-bystanders to five.[174] Fragments of lead picked out of Bobby's brain suggested a further bullet: if two more were found in the wounds in his back – and if the slugs matched the gun's unique ballistic characteristics – all of the eight empty shell cases in the Iver Johnson revolver would be accounted for and the circle of evidence would be complete.

The only real uncertainty seemed to be what crime Sirhan would eventually be tried and convicted of. As the afternoon wore on, crowds gathered in a near-silent vigil outside Good Samaritan, praying for the man still clinging to life inside. The medical team warned Bobby's staff that his chances were slim, telling press secretary Frank Mankiewicz that "they took some pieces of bullet out of his brain, but they couldn't get it all. They were as gloomy as doctors can be."[175]

That evening, Dr. Poppen examined Bobby again. He noted that "electrical brain wave stopped at 6pm … The Senator was medically and legally dead when the brainwaves ceased"[176]. But still his heart continued to breathe. As the hours wore on Mankiewicz stopped issuing updates to the waiting reporters. Then, at 2am the following morning, he walked into the make-shift press room to make a final statement: it was carried live on television and radio networks.

"I have a short announcement … which I will read at this time. Senator Robert Francis Kennedy died at 1.44am today, June 6, 1968".

At the moment Bobby's death was officially pronounced it was 25 hours and 28 minutes since the shooting in the pantry. And now the charge was murder.

174　Summary report of the Los Angeles Police Department Investigation of the Senator Robert Kennedy Assassination, p.180-181. California State Archives.

175　David Talbot, *Brothers*, p.369; Simon & Schuster, 2007

176　*Chicago Tribune*: June 8, 1968

CHAPTER SIX:
INVESTIGATIONS

Murder is not a federal crime. Unless a homicide takes place on federal property, involves crossing state lines, or the victim is either a US government official or a foreign emissary, the burden of investigation and prosecution falls on the authorities in the place where the crime occurred.

But that general principle does not take account of the veritable alphabet soup of sometimes-rivalrous agencies which invariably become involved in high-profile cases. And so, whilst Los Angeles Police Department assumed primary responsibility for investigating Bobby's murder, and the Los Angeles County District Attorney's Office took the lead in prosecuting his suspected killer, Los Angeles County Sheriff's Department and the FBI also conducted their own enquiries, and (federal) US Attorneys monitored LAPD and LADA's progress. In addition, the autopsy would be performed by Los Angeles County Chief Medical Examiner-Coroner, Thomas Noguchi, who was employed by the independent Los Angeles County Board of Supervisors. This confusion of sometimes-conflicting responsibilities was a proven recipe for chaos: immediately after the assassination of John Kennedy, there had been an unseemly tussle between the Secret Service, Dallas Police and local pathologists for custody of the President's body – a fact which contributed in no small measure to subsequent speculation about the official verdict on the shooting. The phrase "Don't let Dallas happen again" was never far from the lips of those charged with investigating Bobby's murder.

Thomas Noguchi had watched the events of election night unfold on television. He arrived at Good Samaritan Hospital at 2.45am on June 6, an hour after Bobby's death was formally pronounced. As he was ushered through the hospital's front entrance he passed a large crowd standing in almost complete silence: some still carried home-made banners reading "Pray For Bobby".

Noguchi had arrived in the United States from his native Japan in 1952 and, as Deputy Los Angeles County Coroner, had worked on previous high-profile celebrity deaths, most notably the 1962 post-mortem examination of Marilyn Monroe. In 1967, the Board of Supervisors promoted him to the post of Chief Medical Examiner. A small, intense man, fascinated by the science of pathology, Noguchi was careful and quietly compassionate. "I admired Robert Kennedy very much: I remember thinking, as I went into the hospital, that just over 24 hours earlier I had watched him give a Victory wave to his supporters and now I was about to perform his autopsy. Of course, I felt some emotion, and before I began I ordered that his face should be covered. It was a mark of respect."[177]

It was not Noguchi's only precaution. In the hours during which Bobby hovered between life and death, the coroner had called in three of the country's most experienced experts from the Armed Forces Institute of Pathology: they, along with Dr. Henry Cuneo, would act as both advisors and witnesses throughout what promised to be a lengthy procedure.

"The doctors who conducted the investigation into the killing of President John Kennedy failed to follow basic procedures.

---

177 Thomas Noguchi, M.D. Interviews with Tim Tate, 1991–1992.

As a result there was considerable public suspicion. I said to myself from the very beginning, 'I cannot allow this to happen here: we must not have another Dallas'."[178]

Before Noguchi began work he bowed to the body and observed a minute's silence. He noticed that Bobby's head had been shaved but the clumps of hair appeared to be missing. Knowing that these could contain critical evidence, he sent one of his staff to find them; then, starting at the feet and slowly working his way up, he began the post-mortem surgery.

"I always believed that a coroner is like a medical detective" he recalled twenty-three years, and numerous other high-profile cases, later. "A case like this was a mystery which I would help to solve. It was my job to explore the body and find the evidence which explained exactly and scientifically how this person died."[179]

The first bullet wound he found was just underneath Bobby's right armpit. The slug had entered from the rear, travelling on a slight rising trajectory from right to left – indicating that the shooter was positioned behind his victim, his gun pointing upward. Because it had exited from the front of Bobby's shoulder – what pathologists term a "through and through" wound – there was no bullet to be recovered.

About an inch below the first entry wound, the coroner found a second; but strangely – Noguchi termed it "surprising"[180] – the bullet which caused it had taken a different path than the through and through. Instead of a "back to front" direction, this shot had travelled laterally across Bobby's back, entering from his right side and lodging several inches to the left in the spinal column at the base of the neck. Using his index finger and thumb,

---

178 Ibid.
179 Ibid.
180 Thomas Noguchi, MD: *Coroner*, p. 101; Pocket Books, 1983

Noguchi carefully extracted the slug: it was deformed, but clearly a .22 calibre. To mark it for ballistics examination, he scratched "TN 31" on its base – a combination of his initials and the last two digits of the formal case identifying number, 68-5731. He then handed the bullet to LAPD Sergeant Bill Jordan, who put it into an evidence envelope.

Neither of these two shoulder wounds had caused Bobby's death. The fatal shot had been fired into the back of his skull, an inch to the left of the right ear, shattering as it ploughed into his brain. Noguchi located a few slug fragments – not enough to be matched definitively with the suspected murder weapon – and noted that "the direction of the bullet was right to left, slightly to the front and upward", entering at a rising trajectory of 15 degrees, and a leftward angle of 30 degrees. It was further evidence that whoever shot and killed Bobby had fired from behind him.

The autopsy was careful and thorough: it was not until 9.15am – more than six hours after he began – that Noguchi stepped away from the operating table. Bobby's body was then released to the family, to be flown back to the east coast. "His coffin was in the stern of the plane, and everybody else was in the front – my family and his close friends," Robert Kennedy Jnr. – then 14 years old – recalled.

"We took turns sitting with him and I remember thinking that the coffin seemed so small, because he seemed like such a large man to me. And it was surprising that he could fit in that little box."[181]

As the Kennedy family made the long flight back to New York, Noguchi briefed the waiting press. He briefly outlined his initial findings, explained that after microscopic tests on brain tissue, examination of all Bobby's vital organs and a study of the

---

181 Robert Kennedy Jnr. interview with Brad Johnson and Rob Beemer, Interesting Stuff Entertainment, Malibu, October 13, 2016

cranial x-rays taken before and after the post-mortem, "a complete medical report would be available in a few weeks". [182]

But the most important evidence emerged within 24 hours. Tests on the hair shavings revealed the presence of gunshot residue: more revealing still, the residue contained metallic elements – tiny fragments of bullets – and carbon particles. As soon as he saw the results, Noguchi understood what they meant.

"When a gun is fired, a gas containing very many different types of substances shoots out of the end of the barrel with the bullet: carbon particles, or soot, are one of these elements. But the gas is very light: it can only travel a few inches before it falls away. So because we found carbon particles in the hair, this showed that the gun must have been very close to the back of Senator Kennedy's skull: I estimated a distance of perhaps one and half inches."[183] It was a crucial finding – and one which would cause LAPD severe problems in the weeks to come.

The police had already experienced a taste of the difficulties posed by competition between the overlapping authorities involved in the case. Within hours of the shooting Los Angeles Mayor Sam Yorty – historically no friend to any of the Kennedys – held a press conference in which he revealed some of the contents of Sirhan's notebooks before these had even reached the LAPD unit which would investigate the crime. The pages, Yorty asserted, showed that Sirhan had been in contact with Communists or Communist-dominated organisations. The implication that the alleged assassin had links to political organisations was both premature and in direct contrast to LAPD Chief Tom Reddin's more cautious press statement that "there appears to be no international conspiracy. On the basis of the

---

182 Death Theory Substantiated, Los Angeles Herald-Examiner, June 7, 1968. (File 91, p.323)
183 Thomas Noguchi, M.D. Interviews with Tim Tate, 1991–1992.

investigation up to the point, we still see no massive conspiracy, but we are not ruling out that more than one person may have been involved in the killing of Sen. Kennedy".[184] The California Attorney General, Thomas Lynch, swiftly warned the Mayor against making further allegations.

Yorty ignored this, telling another press conference on June 6 that "Evil Communist organisations played a part in inflaming the assassination of Kennedy", and adding that Bobby's known support for Israel had also motivated Sirhan. When reporters asked "how he thought Sirhan could have been 'inflamed' by both Arab nationalism and communism, Yorty replied 'Both the Communists and Arabs are anti-Israel'."[185]

In response, the Attorney General issued a statement reminding all public officials to "avoid the danger of prejudicing jurors and prospective jurors by giving material to news-disseminating agencies which may be inflammatory or may improperly prejudice the defendant's rights".[186] This, like the previous warnings, fell on deaf ears: Mayor Yorty felt able to ignore both the AG's strictures and a subsequent court order specifically "prohibiting him and certain other persons from publicly discussing the assassination."[187] In a subsequent interview published in the Manchester (New Hampshire) Union Leader, he repeated his contention that Sirhan "was strongly influenced by Communist ideology and was strongly pro-Communist"[188].

---

184 'We Have Killed Him!' A Brunette Screamed, New York Daily News, June 7, 1968
185 Yorty Claims Red Groups Inflamed Assassin, Washington Post, June 7, 1968
186 Ibid.
187 Office of the District Attorney, Weekly Summary Of Activities Re; The Assassination of Senator Robert F. Kennedy, #2, June 19, 1968. SUS file 88, p.284
188 Fifty-nine threats made against Sirhan's Life, UPI for The Jerusalem Post, June 23, 1968

By accident or design, Yorty's grand-standing highlighted a widespread assumption, held by both the authorities and the public, that Sirhan was undoubtedly the assassin: the questions being asked were how and why he had killed Bobby, not whether he had, in fact, fired the fatal shot.

LAPD had begun its investigations in the early hours of June 5. It established a Command Post at the Ambassador Hotel within seven minutes of the shooting, but it took two more hours to clear the crowds from the hotel and to secure the pantry area. During that time, its officers, accompanied by representatives from the LA Sheriff's Department, the Fire Department and FBI detectives searched for evidence. Then, at 2am the Police Department's chief criminalist, DeWayne Wolfer, accompanied by police surveyor Albert Lavallee and photographer Charles Collier, arrived to begin a formal examination of the crime scene.

The first order of business was to establish the number of bullets fired, and where they had ended up. Lavallee made a detailed diagram of the kitchen pantry while Collier shot "orientation" photos showing Wolfer examining the pantry ceiling and the double doors through which Kennedy had passed en route from the ballroom. One showed Wolfer pointing at an apparent bullet ricochet mark near one of the doorframe's upper hinges; others showed two bullet holes in another part of the doorframe and two more bullet holes in the doorframe's centre divider[189]. Wolfer also examined the ceiling, removing several of the tiles and taking them away for forensic testing.

Nor was the LAPD team alone: the FBI sent Special Agent William Bailey to the pantry where he observed "at least two small calibre bullet holes" in the same doorframe centre divider

---

189 LAPD photographs and schematic diagrams: California State Archives

that Wolfer's men photographed[190]. He would later testify that "I definitely recall closely examining those two holes and they definitely contained bullets"[191]. When an FBI photographer also took a series of pictures and captioned them "bullet holes"[192], Sheriff's Deputy Walter Tew drew a circle round them, inscribing his badge number inside the circles as confirmation[193].

Throughout June 5, press cameramen and interested bystanders were also allowed to walk in to the crime scene and take pictures. Amateur photographers John Shirley and John Clemente photographed the bullet holes in the centre divider, with Walter Tew's initialled circles around them. A photographer from the Associated Press also gained access and snapped pictures of two uniformed LAPD officers pointing at yet another bullet hole in the jamb of a different doorframe, located up the hall from the pantry at the backstage double doors of the anteroom: one of them, Patrolman Robert Rozzi, stated that he "observed [the] hole in the door jamb and the base of what appeared to be a small caliber bullet lodged in the hole"[194]. Added together, the photographs and evidence indicated the presence of at least 14 suspected bullets that struck the six victims and the crime scene woodwork, with the ceiling tiles still to be examined.

As head of LAPD's Scientific Investigation Division, Wolfer's primary task was to produce a trajectory study, tracing the paths of all the bullets fired in the pantry. Sirhan's revolver could hold

---

190 *Affidavit of William F. Bailey: November 14, 1976*. Robert F. Kennedy Assassination Archives, University of Massachusetts Dartmouth.

191 *Statement of William F. Bailey to LA Board of Supervisors, 1976*. Robert F. Kennedy Assassination Archives, University of Massachusetts Dartmouth.

192 Operation Kensalt: FBI Los Angeles Field Office Files: California State Archives.

193 *Interviews with LASO officers, 1989 – 91*: Robert F. Kennedy Assassination Archives, University of Massachusetts Dartmouth.

194 *Affidavit of Robert Rozzi*, November 15, 1976. Robert F. Kennedy Assassination Archives, University of Massachusetts Dartmouth.

a maximum of eight rounds and, since its chamber held eight spent shell casings, he appeared to have fired them all. Seven bullets, or bullet pieces, had been recovered from the six victim, five of whom had survived their wounds: entire slugs from Bobby, Ira Goldstein and William Weisel, as well as fragments from Bobby, Elizabeth Evans, Irwin Stroll and Paul Schrade. On June 11, accompanied by Coroner Noguchi, Wolfer returned to the pantry to recreate the trajectory of each shot.[195] Back in his office, he put together a report which sought to explain how the shooting in the pantry unfolded.

Wolfer could not be absolutely sure of "the exact order in which shot was fired"[196], but his report theorised that the first bullet hit Bobby in the head, while the second passed through his jacket and hit Paul Schrade; the third bullet lodged in Bobby's shoulder and the fourth passed through him and up into the ceiling, where it was presumed lost. Bullet Five hit Ira Goldstein; number Six ricocheted off the floor into Irwin Stroll; the seventh hit William Weisel and the eighth ricocheted downwards off the ceiling into Elizabeth Evans.[197] There were several flaws in this theory, not the least of which was an absence of any explanation for the bullets or bullet holes apparently found – and photographed – in the pantry woodwork. But no-one inside LAPD or the DA's office questioned them.

Wolfer's next task was to carry out experiments to identify the gun which had fired each of the recovered bullets. There were three key elements to those tests: the gun, the bullets and how

---

195 *Affidavit of Thomas T. Noguchi, December 1, 1975.* Robert F. Kennedy Assassination Archives, University of Massachusetts Dartmouth.

196 Summary report of the Los Angeles Police Department Investigation of the Senator Robert Kennedy Assassination, p.650. California State Archives.

197 People vs. Sirhan Sirhan: written evidence of DeWayne Wolfer, February 20, 1969. California State Archives.

close to Kennedy the fatal shot had been fired: he started with the gun and the bullets. Sirhan's revolver was a .22 calibre Iver Johnson, bearing the serial number H53725. It was handed over to Wolfer late on June 5. Sometime during the next day[198] he carried out a test firing of the weapon, shooting it eight times into a basket in a water tank at SID's laboratory. He recovered seven of these test slugs (the eighth "jumped the basket and the water") and put them in an evidence envelope for later comparison with those recovered from the victims. He wrote the gun's serial number on the envelope.[199].

At 8.30am on June 6 he examined the bullets recovered from Irwin Stroll and Ira Goldstein; at 3.15pm he was given what LAPD now termed "the Kennedy neck bullet". At 9pm he compared this with the Goldstein slug.

Eleven hours later, on the morning of June 7, he appeared before the Grand Jury, called to return a true bill of indictment against Sirhan. Sirhan's Iver Johnson, serial number H53725, was entered into evidence, and Wolfer testified on oath that the shot which killed Robert Kennedy had come from this gun "and no other in the world[200]". The indictment was duly issued later that afternoon.

The third set of forensic tests stemmed from Noguchi's discovery of gunshot residue in Bobby's hair. To establish a scientific basis for his belief that this indicated the fatal shot had been fired very close to Bobby's head, Noguchi ordered seven pigs' ears from a local farm. "Pig flesh is very similar to human skin," the coroner later explained. "I arranged for the ears to

---

198 One of the problems with DeWayne Wolfer's evidence was that he did not keep detailed – or accurate – records of the tests he carried out. His official log makes no mention of the test firing.
199 DeWayne Wolfer: Deposition under oath, September 20 – October 11, 1971.
200 *People vs. Sirhan Sirhan*: Grand Jury transcript, June 6, 1968. California State Archive.

be attached to moulds made of muslin, and for an officer at the Police Academy to shoot .22 calibre bullets into them from a series of precisely-measured distances."[201] On June 10 Noguchi and Wolfer watched as a policeman placed the gun firmly against the first pig's ear and fired; then, moving the end of the muzzle back in quarter inch increments, he completed six further test shootings; each bullet was marked and handed over to Wolfer for safe keeping.

When the experiment was over, each of the pigs' ears was examined for gunshot residue, providing Noguchi with irrefutable scientific evidence of the distance between the gun and the victim. "I now knew the precise location of the murder weapon at the moment it was fired," the coroner subsequently wrote: "One inch from the edge of [Bobby's] right ear, only three inches behind the head."[202] It was a finding which would, in time, pose difficult questions for LAPD. Nor was it the only problem which would emerge from the ballistic experiment.

Because Sirhan's Iver Johnson, serial number H53725, was now in the secure evidence locker, and because he did not want to risk using – and potentially damaging – the presumed murder weapon, Wolfer had drawn a similar revolver from LAPD's seized property division. It too was an Iver Johnson, and bore the serial number H18602. The criminalist's decision was good forensic practice: but both the serial number and what he did with the test slugs would come to cast doubt on the reliability of the evidence against Sirhan.

Ostensibly at least, Los Angeles Police Department was determined to carry out a thorough and honest investigation into Bobby's assassination. On June 10 Deputy Police Chief Robert Houghton, a 26-year LAPD veteran, set up a dedicated task force

---

201 Thomas Noguchi, M.D. Interviews with Tim Tate, 1991–1992.
202 Thomas Noguchi, MD: *Coroner*, p. 104; Pocket Books, 1983

to handle the case. Special Unit Senator was based inside secure offices on the eight floor of Parker Center: it had a staff of 37 officers, including three detective lieutenants, eight detective sergeants as well as a polygraph specialist[203], and was divided into three teams.

The first handled preparation for the trial, conducting interviews with every person known to have been in the Ambassador Hotel on the night of June 4/5. Many – though not all – of these interviews were recorded on audio tape. The team also compiled an archive of more than 3,400 photographs, some shot by its own photographers, others collected from news outlets, freelancers and bystanders. The second team put together a complete profile of Sirhan, including his family history, political beliefs and connections, and a detailed "time chart", showing where he had been in the days before the assassination.

But to Houghton, the third section had the most politically important task: the ever-present spectre of Dallas and Memphis made him determined to probe any possible conspiracy underlying Bobby's murder. "We were faced with a crime that would be examined everywhere in the world, possibly for decades to come," he wrote in his 1970 book on the case. "I was resolved to make certain that the investigation into the assassination would leave no questions unasked, no answers untested, no evidence unchecked, no possible conspiratorial doors unopened".[204] It was a noble, if herculean, ambition: under the day-to-day control of Lt. Manny Pena, a WW2 combat veteran who had recently worked with the intelligence services, SUS Team Three would shortly be faced with "a great number of allegations implicating

---

203 Summary report of the Los Angeles Police Department Investigation of the Senator Robert Kennedy Assassination, p.IV. California State Archives.

204 Robert A. Houghton: *Special Unit Senator: The Investigation of the Assassination of Robert F. Kennedy*; p.93. Random House, 1970

Sirhan and other individuals or groups in conspiracies to kill Robert Kennedy"[205] [and] "public suspicions about connections between this assassination and the assassinations of President John F. Kennedy and Dr. Martin Luther King"[206].

As LAPD's investigations began, Bobby was lying in St. Patrick's Cathedral in mid-town Manhattan. Between June 7 and June 8, mourners and well-wishers filed slowly past his closed casket, paying their final respects. "There were people lining the blocks, lining 5th Avenue for I don't know how long; they were eight deep and they waited all night," recalled Robert Kennedy Jnr. "I stood by his coffin as kind of an honour guard that night, and there were people coming in – thousands of people – all night long."[207]

At 10am on June 8, the cathedral doors were closed and, broadcast live on television, a high requiem mass began. As Ethel, draped in black and protected by a veil sat silent and grim-faced, Ted Kennedy, his voice breaking with emotion, spoke a moving eulogy.

"My brother need not be idealized, or enlarged in death beyond what he was in life; to be remembered simply as a good and decent man, who saw wrong and tried to right it, saw suffering and tried to heal it, saw war and tried to stop it.

"Those of us who loved him and who take him to his rest today, pray that what he was to us and what he wished for others will someday come to pass for all the world. As he said many times, in many parts of this nation, to those he touched and who

---

205 Summary report of the Los Angeles Police Department Investigation of the Senator Robert Kennedy Assassination, p.61. California State Archives.

206 Summary report of the Los Angeles Police Department Investigation of the Senator Robert Kennedy Assassination, p.111. California State Archives.

207 Robert Kennedy Jnr. interview with Brad Johnson and Rob Beemer, Interesting Stuff Entertainment, Malibu, October 13, 2016

sought to touch him: 'Some men see things as they are and say why. I dream things that never were and say why not.'"

Immediately after the mass, Bobby's coffin, draped in the Stars and Stripes, was transported by train to Washington, D.C. Robert Jnr. accompanied his father's body on the journey.

"That was a very memorable ride for me because my father was in the caboose but the train was loaded with all the people who would have been in his government – and it would have been one of the most unusual governments in American history, one of the most diverse. There were all the great leaders from the civil rights movement and from the farm workers' movement."[208]

It should have taken two and a half hours to cover the 200 miles between Penn Station, New York City and Union Station, Washington DC. That June morning the route was so heavily lined with mourners that it took the train more than seven hours to reach the nation's capital.

"There was a million people on the tracks. And it was a cross-section of the country; the same kind of groups that I had seen during the campaign. There were military uniforms, there were hippies, there were nuns and priests and rabbis. There were poor whites and there were lots of blacks and many of them were carrying flags and signs which said 'goodbye Bobby'; they were holding up their babies, and when we slowed down going through Newark and Trenton and through the Maryland countryside we could see that people were crying."[209]

The funeral train arrived at 9.10pm that evening. Bobby's casket was then driven slowly through the streets, passing thousands of men and women from the Poor Peoples' Campaign which he and Dr. Martin Luther King had called into being a

---

208 *Ibid.*
209 *Ibid.*

few short months earlier. As the procession wound past the Mall, the marchers, camped out in tents and plastic sheeting, silently removed their hats and bowed their heads.

Finally, at 10.30pm, Bobby's body was laid to rest near John Kennedy's grave in Arlington National Cemetery. Camelot – the dream of, and for, a better America – was over. All that now remained was to ask 'why'.

CHAPTER SEVEN:
SIRHAN

The defendant in Case No: A-233-421, *People vs. Sirhan Bishara Sirhan*, was held in an isolated section of Los Angeles' County Jail for men. On the orders of LA County Sheriff Peter J. Pitchess, he was kept under constant observation, completely apart from other inmates. His food was prepared in a separate kitchen and he took daily exercise alone in a 30-foot internal corridor.[210]

Since Sirhan did not have the funds to hire a private attorney, at his arraignment the court had assigned a lawyer from the Public Defender's office to represent him. But on the same day an award-winning journalist began working with the American Civil Liberties Union to find him more powerful counsel. Robert Blair Kaiser was a devout Catholic who had trained as Jesuit before abandoning the order in order to marry. As a correspondent for *Time* magazine he had won plaudits for his reporting on the Second Vatican Council in 1962: now, in the aftermath of Bobby's murder, he wanted to write a book exploring the accused killer's motives. "I felt," he subsequently wrote in that book, "that no-one could hope to write the story of this

---

210 Sheriff Peter J. Pitchess, Press statement, June 20, 1968: LAPD "Special Unit Senator" files, Volume 88; p.312-313. California State Archives.

assassination unless he talked – and talked at great length – with Sirhan Sirhan".[211]

Access to the county jail was, however, tightly restricted. In the hope of getting a pass, Kaiser telephoned A.L. Wirrin, Chief Counsel for the ACLU in Southern California, who had volunteered his support to Sirhan. Together, the two men spent the fortnight following the arraignment trying to find a private attorney to take the case.

The man they wanted was one of America's leading criminal defence attorneys. Grant Cooper, a former president of the American College of Trial Lawyers and the Los Angeles County Bar Association, was a formidable veteran from both sides of the court aisle: now, 65, he had been a successful prosecutor in LA County District Attorney's Office, securing the death penalty in several murder cases, before setting up in private practice as an equally successful defence lawyer.

Cooper, though, was fully booked: in the summer of 1968 he was lead defence counsel for group of casino operatives charged with a five-year conspiracy to cheat gamblers by fixing card games at the Friars Club in Beverly Hills. One of the defendants was the notorious mobster Johnny Roselli – a close friend of Sam Giancana, and who had been recruited into the CIA's plots to assassinate Fidel Castro. Pressed by Kaiser, Cooper agreed to take on Sirhan's case on condition that he finished the Friars Club case first. It was a decision which would come to haunt him, and lead to accusations about his conduct of Sirhan's defence.

To cover for the months he would be unavailable, Cooper took on outside associate counsel. Russell Parsons was 69 years old and, like Cooper, a veteran of LA County DA's office who had gone on to win acclaim as a defence attorney in private practice. Both men would be working, *pro bono*, on a lengthy and

---

211   Robert Blair Kaiser, *RFK Must Die!*, p. 79. Dutton & Co, 1970

politically-charged trial but, as Parsons explained to reporters, "I'm a lawyer and this man is in serious trouble. I felt... [he] was entitled to be represented".[212]

Without having met his client, Parsons also gave the first hint of the defence strategy: "Parsons... has indicated he may argue that Sirhan suffered from brain damage," the Los Angeles Herald-Examiner reported. "He said he will have a psychiatrist examine Sirhan 'from the tips of his toes to the top of his head'."[213]

Sirhan's new legal counsel hired three investigators: Kaiser, Ronald Allen and Michael McCowan. Both Allen and McCowan were former police officers – Allen with the US Army, McCowan with LAPD – who worked together as licensed private eyes[214]. McCowan had left the force in 1965 after being arrested, then convicted, for theft and mail tampering: he was on court-ordered probation when he joined the defence team[215]. He and Kaiser vied with each other for permission to write a book about the case. Kaiser won the battle, signing a contract with Sirhan in August. Over the next six months they interviewed their client in the county jail, met his family and dug into his background. But from the outset, McCowan appears to have been unsympathetic. According to Kaiser, when the investigator examined Sirhan's collection of books, he bluntly denounced him as "a fuckin' Communist."[216]

Communism – or at least the fear of it – also dominated LAPD's investigations. After the arraignment Special Unit Senator began a thorough investigation of Sirhan's life. The

---

212 *Sirhan Hires New Defense Attorney, Los Angeles Times,* June 20, 1968

213 *Sirhan's Defense? Brain Damage. Los Angeles Herald-Examiner,* June 20, 1968

214 LAPD "Special Unit Senator" files, Volume 67; p.210. California State Archives.

215 *Sirhan Bishara Sirhan vs. George Galaza, Warden: Reply Brief On The Issue of Actual Innocence;* filed November 20, 2011. US District Court, Central District of California.

216 Robert Blair Kaiser, *RFK Must Die!,* p. 108. Dutton & Co, 1970

resulting 62-page "Profile Analysis" report[217] began with an outline of his origins and how he came to be in Los Angeles.

Sirhan was born on March 19, 1944 in Jerusalem, Palestine, the sixth child of Bishara and Mary, a Christian Arab family who adhered to the Greek Orthodox faith. Between 1920 and 1948 "Palestine" was ruled by Britain under a mandate issued by the League of Nations, but for the last year of British rule the territory was ravaged by violence: Jewish terror groups attacked both the colonial rulers and the Arab population in support of their demand for a new homeland. By the time the State of Israel came into being in May, 1948, the situation in many towns and cities was "close to a state of anarchy". The Sirhans, like many other families, found themselves caught between the new nation's armed forces and Arab fighters who opposed their rule. LAPD's enquiries discovered that the Sirhans' house was destroyed in a bombing raid and that Sirhan himself "witnessed an Israeli soldier kill an Arab in front of his home".[218]

Finally, in 1956, the family, now living under Jordanian rule in East Jerusalem, applied to emigrate to America. Security checks showed that none had any criminal or political records and, as refugees, they qualified for "non-quota immigrant" status. On January 12, 1956, most of the family – Bishara and Mary, together with four of their children[219] – landed in New York, and moved immediately to Pasadena, California. Sirhan was 12 years old.

Sirhan's father didn't stay long: unable to adjust to life in the United States, in 1959 he returned to East Jerusalem[220]; the fol-

---

217 *Sirhan's Background (Profile Analysis)*: Special Unit Senator: Final Report, p. 338-400, April 4, 1969. California State Archives.

218 *Ibid.* p.341

219 Two of the eldest children remained in Jerusalem; a third had died two years after Sirhan's birth.

220 He returned, periodically, working for construction firms in New York City.

lowing year, his two sons who had remained there were granted US entry visas and moved into Mary's home in Pasadena.

For the next six years the family lived quietly and – apart from a two minor incidents in which they were victims of petty crime – uneventfully. None became US citizens. Sirhan went to local schools where his academic career was undistinguished: the most common description by teachers and classmates alike was of a "quiet, well-mannered" boy[221]. He graduated from John Muir High School in June 1963, ranked 558 out of a class of 829 students, and went on to Pasadena City College. He stayed for two years, but – partly because his sister, Ayda, developed terminal leukaemia[222] – he had a poor attendance record and generally achieved mediocre results in his studies. LAPD found nothing to shed light on what had prompted a young man "who left little or no impression on his instructors"[223] to open fire on a prospective candidate for the White House in the Ambassador Hotel pantry.

Nor did his employment career yield any clues. Sirhan had worked since he was 13, first as a delivery boy for the *Pasadena Star-News-Independent* paper, then for varying periods as a gardener, a service station attendant and a short-order cook in a local hamburger joint. None of his fellow employees in these casual jobs recalled "any political comments or observations being made by Sirhan"[224]. And detectives came up against the same puzzle when they moved on to investigating his full-time post-college work history.

Sirhan had long harboured dreams of becoming a jockey and, in October 1965 at the age of 21, his small, light frame seemed to

---

221 *Sirhan's Background (Profile Analysis)*: Special Unit Senator: Final Report, p. 353, April 4, 1969. California State Archives.

222 Ayda Sirhan died in March 1965.

223 *Sirhan's Background (Profile Analysis)*: Special Unit Senator: Final Report, p. 359, April 4, 1969. California State Archives.

224 *Ibid*. p.362

qualify him as a suitable candidate. He began by finding work as a stable hand and "hot walker" – a groom who walks race-horses to cool them down after running – at Santa Anita Race Track, while simultaneously learning to ride. He applied for, and received, a hot walker's licence from the California Horse Racing Board in January 1966.

His ambition to become a jockey was, though, hampered by a lack of natural aptitude: Sirhan was not a strong rider and repeatedly fell, or was thrown, from his mounts. In September 1966 he was hospitalized after falling from a horse at full gallop: he sustained minor injuries, but was kept in overnight and spent the next six days recuperating. A week later, he fell again, and returned to the hospital for injuries to his eyes and face. In November he quit his full-time job, and drifted into part-time work as an hourly-paid freelance exercise boy; then at the end of the year, he walked away completely from the race tracks and stables.

Around this time Sirhan's mood seemed to darken. Ivan Valladres Garcia was, by common consent, his closest friend: they had known each other for four years and Ivan was a regular dinner guest at the Sirhan family home on East Howard Street.

He told FBI agents that "he considered Sirhan to be extremely polite, sensitive and thoughtful" and that "Sirhan's generosity and unselfishness towards his friends was very unusual, as was his most outstanding virtue ... Sirhan would do everything to make a guest or friend comfortable and at ease, and usually insisted upon paying bills wherever he went with friends, although he did not have a particularly large sum of money at any time."[225]

But, Garcia said, "He had noticed a very definite change in Sirhan after his accidental fall from a horse. Sirhan had been much more jovial before the accident, and seemed to be more

---

225 FBI Files X-4, Vol.13, p. 206-208. California State Archives.

gloomy and pessimistic about his future afterwards".[226] A former schoolmate who kept in touch with Sirhan gave a similar assessment, telling the Bureau that Sirhan "seemed to brood and remarked that due to the damage to his eyes he could no longer be a jockey". She added that Sirhan "became interested in mysticism and expressed a desire to be able to control a person's mind through extra sensory perception."[227]

There was some truth in this. LAPD's detectives discovered that Sirhan developed an apparent interest in Rosicrucianism – a worldwide non-sectarian quasi-religious organization dedicated to understanding the "esoteric truths of the ancient past". He was a paid up member of the Rosicrucian Order, attended meetings of its Pasadena branch and owned several books on the theosophical writings of 19th century Russian occultist Helena Blavatsky. But they found no evidence that he was a particularly dedicated student of mysticism.

A far more plausible explanation for Sirhan's change in mood was the realization that his dream of a well-rewarded career in horse racing was over. Certainly, he was not prospering financially: between November 1966 and the night of the assassination eighteen months later, Sirhan's only employment was a six month stretch as a delivery driver for a Pasadena Health Food store, where he earned $2 an hour. He had no credit cards, no credit rating and only a $1,705 insurance pay-out for the injuries he sustained in the September fall provided any significant boost to his limited funds.

He somehow managed, however, to indulge in a new interest: target shooting. Although Ivan Garcia told LAPD that his friend never mentioned guns and he never saw Sirhan with a gun"[228],

226 *Ibid.*
227 FBI Files X-2, Vol. 7, p.211-212. California State Archives. The woman's name is redacted in the FBI interview report.
228 LAPD "Special Unit Senator" file 58, p. 31-32. California State Archives

by the spring of 1968 Sirhan appears to have acquired the Iver Johnson .22 calibre revolver from his brother, Munir, and his signature was to be found on the registers of at least two gun ranges in the Los Angeles area.

On June 1, he checked in at Corona Police Department range at 12.50pm and was taken to target position number one: he began firing a .22 calibre revolver he had brought with him, staying at the range until 3pm. There were two unusual aspects to the visit: the first was that Corona was around 50 miles from Sirhan's home – a long drive out of the city for someone with limited resources, especially since there were other ranges much closer to Pasadena. The second was that, according to rangemaster William Marks who assigned Sirhan his target position, he was accompanied by a man whom detectives were subsequently unable to trace from the register.

The man was evidently sufficiently distinctive for Marks – a serving officer with Corona Police Department – to provide a clear description: Caucasian but speaking with "an unknown foreign accent", 20 to 30 years old, between 5'5" and 5'7" tall and 130 to 140lbs in weight, brown hair and sporting a "pencil-type mustache and…horn-rimmed glasses."[229] It would not be the last sighting of unidentified men – and women – in Sirhan's company during the days leading up to the assassination.

At 3pm the same afternoon Sirhan turned up at the Lock Stock 'N Barrel Gun Shop, a 'Mom and Pop' store in a suburban shopping centre on Huntington Drive, San Gabriel. He bought two boxes of high velocity 'Mini-Mag' .22 hollow-nosed calibre bullets; each box contained 50 rounds. Sirhan paid for the ammunition in cash and was given a receipt by sales clerk Larry Arnot. That receipt – number 2372 – was found in Sirhan's car on June 5.

---

229 LAPD "Special Unit Senator" file 81, p. 22-24. California State Archives

But it wasn't the sale of high-powered bullets which most concerned LAPD. On June 15, Arnot was interviewed by LAPD. He told its officers that Sirhan had been accompanied by two other men; he recalled that all three "appeared to be rather dirty in their appearance". One of the men with Sirhan had also bought two boxes of Super- X brand .22 slugs, bringing the sales total to $3.99 which he recorded on a the receipt.

The detectives showed Arnot photographs of all the Sirhan brothers: he positively identified Sirhan himself and thought that the picture of Munir "possibly" resembled one of his companions.[230] LAPD affixed a file note – "Personal Observations of Larry Arnot" – to the report of his interview. "Mr. Arnot is a male Caucasian, aged 39. He is a retired Pasadena City fireman, retired on disability and works part-time at the gun shop ... and should probably make a good witness".[231]

Three days later the FBI arrived at Lock Stock 'N Barrel. Arnot told the Agents the same story, positively identifying Sirhan, but said that his companion bore "a strong resemblance" to a photo of Sirhan's elder brother, Sharif. He gave the Agents detailed descriptions of all three men.[232]

Neither LAPD nor the FBI ever identified either of Sirhan's two companions. Instead, on August 7, Larry Arnot was brought into SUS headquarters in Parker Center and subjected to a polygraph examination.

From its inception, Special Unit Senator had been assigned an experienced polygrapher, Sergeant – very shortly he would be promoted to the rank of Lieutenant – Enrique 'Hank' Hernandez. According to an internal memorandum, Hernandez said the purpose of the test in Scientific Investigation Room 423A, was

---

230 LAPD "Special Unit Senator" file 53, p. 70-72. California State Archives
231 LAPD "Special Unit Senator" file 53, p.73. California State Archives
232 FBI file X-3, Vol. 10, p.234-295

"to determine the truthfulness in Mr. Arnot's statement given to the F.B.I. ... that he had sold four boxes of ammunition to suspect Sirhan Sirhan and two other dark foreign-looking males who were present with Sirhan."[233]

After hooking Arnot up to the machine and determining that he was "a proper subject for polygraph testing", Hernandez asked a series of questions about the sale of ammunition on June 1. The answers – according to Hernandez – "suggest very strongly that Mr. Arnot was being untruthful ... that he does not remember seeing anyone with Sirhan on that day ... [and that] it is the opinion of this examiner that Larry Arnot does not remember Sirhan or the business transaction that took place on June 1, 1968."

Hernandez then subjected Arnot to "a short period of interrogation", after which the clerk "admitted that the only logical explanation for his failing the test was that he lied." [234]

The problem with this was that the owners of Lock Stock 'N Barrel also claimed to have seen Sirhan previously, in the company of very similar-looking men to those whom Arnot described. On June 20 and 21 Ben and Donna Herrick told the FBI that Sirhan had come into the store early in April with two male companions: all were "of foreign extraction". The men asked for ".357 mag. tank piercing ammo, or words to that effect." [235] Ben Herrick told the Agents: "I do carry such ammunition which I sell to law enforcement officers. After observing that these men were not law enforcement officers, I said that we did not have such ammunition in stock. The men then left the store."[236]

The Herricks' statements show them to have been cautious in describing what they remembered without over-reaching.

233 LAPD "Special Unit Senator" file 53, p.74. California State Archives
234 *Ibid.*
235 Interview with Donna Herrick, June 21, 1968 FBI file X-3, Vol.10, p.225-230
236 Interview with Ben Herrick, June 20, 1968 FBI file X-3, Vol.10, p.231- 233

Donna was careful to point out that she had not been present on June 1 and therefore could not confirm that the men with Sirhan in April were the same as those described by Larry Arnot; Frank made clear that he was unwilling to absolutely guarantee that Sirhan was the customer on June 1 because "I have seen his photograph in the papers and on TV, and cannot now state that I am identifying him from being in my store or from seeing his picture in the news media." [237]

LAPD's response was to bring Donna Herrick in for a polygraph: on August 7, after he had "interrogated her for a period of approximately one hour"[238] Hernandez wired Donna up to his machine and asked her four questions about Sirhan and his visits to the store. "Upon conclusion of the polygraph examination" Hernandez recorded in a memo, "Mrs. Herrick was informed that her responses clearly indicated that she was either mistaken or that she was being deliberately untruthful, but that she could not honestly say that she remembered seeing Sirhan or talking to him in person. "Further, she was informed that her answers to the above questions were clearly indicative of deception". When Donna disputed this, Hernandez simply told her the machine proved she was being untruthful.[239]

Sirhan himself seemed to have made a point of conspicuous appearances in and around guns. At between 11 and 11.30am on June 4 – little over 12 hours before the shooting in the pantry – he arrived at the San Gabriel Valley Gun Club, in the small semi-rural city of Duarte.

He signed in as a non-member, taking up a position on the pistol range; other customers observed him rapid-firing more than 350 bullets from his .22 calibre Iver Johnson revolver over

---

237 *Ibid.*
238 LAPD "Special Unit Senator" file 47, p.208. California State Archives
239 LAPD "Special Unit Senator" file 34, p.160-161. California State Archives

a period of several hours. "Witnesses saw six boxes of Super-X long rifle shells at Sirhan's position and two boxes of Mini-Mag hollow point," LAPD's detectives noted. "Several witnesses stated that Sirhan discussed the hollow point as inflicting greater damage than the normal .22 caliber long rifle."[240] This, together with the witnesses' evaluation of Sirhan as "a good shot"[241] seemed to suggest an assassin practicing for his night's work.

But whilst the police were happy to log the witnesses as sufficiently reliable to testify in court, they were less sanguine about some of the evidence three of them provided. Everett Buckner was the club's Line Officer on duty throughout the day; over the course of two lengthy interviews, on June 8 and June 12, he told the FBI that a white couple – a slender man in his 30s, and a "husky build" blonde woman in her 20s and around between 5'6 and 5'8" tall – arrived at the range a little time after Sirhan. Buckner booked them in and they began shooting.

A little while later he overheard a heated exchange after Sirhan offered to help the blonde get her shots on target: "The woman said, 'Get away from me, you son of a bitch; they'll recognize you'. Buckner stated he was approximately five feet away from Sirhan and the woman during this conversation"[242]. The couple left the range shortly afterwards.

LAPD did not interview Buckner until June 17. By that point the SUS team was evidently irritated by the range master: a file note, dated June 12, 1968, reads: "Everett Buckner ... has been running off the mouth to *Time* magazine." In the "Action Taken" box an unnamed officer noted that the police "will send a team

---

240 Special Unit Senator: Final Report, p. 603, April 4, 1969. California State Archives.

241 *Ibid.*

242 Everett Buckner interview, June 8, 1968. FBI file X-2, Vol. 7, p.137-138. California State Archives.

out to tell him not to talk."[243] When the detectives from SUS did get round to recording his evidence, Buckner told them the same story he had given to the FBI. But unlike the federal agents, LAPD cast doubt on his credibility. The interviewing officer – again unnamed – reported: "It is my opinion that Buckner is a heavy drinker and is confused as to some facts."[244] On July 2 he was brought back into Parker Center for a second interrogation and a polygraph examination by Lt. Hernandez.

According to LAPD, Buckner failed the polygraph, and thereafter recanted his story. "After an extensive interview Buckner admitted he had been lying about the statement made by the blond directed at Sirhan. He stated he had seen a blond female Caucasian talk to Sirhan; however, he did not hear any conversation between the two. He would not give an explanation for his previous statement."[245]

In its running daily summary of activities SUS noted: "Buckner – out of picture – cop-out, phoney by polygraph"[246] (though not, apparently, too "phoney": Buckner would be called to testify, for the prosecution, at Sirhan's trial). Buckner's polygraph charts have – unusually for SUS – survived, but they are so faint and degraded that it is impossible to be sure what they revealed.

However, a transcript of the tape-recorded post-polygraph interview shows that the range master did not in any way admit "lying". As Hernandez pressured him to retract his account of Sirhan's interaction with the mystery blonde woman, the most Buckner would concede was that he "thought that's what she said". When the detective insisted "But you know that's not what

243 File 108, p.81
244 LAPD "Special Unit Senator" file 48, p.115-116. California State Archives
245 Intra-Departmental Correspondence, Sirhan Sirhan's activities at the San Gabriel Valley Gun Club, July 5, 1968. LAPD "Special Unit Senator" file 103, p.140. California State Archives.
246 LAPD "Special Unit Senator" file 25, p.164. California State Archives

she said; is that right?" Bucker responded cautiously: "I'm not sure that's what she said. I'm sorry"; he also carefully explained what he meant by this caveat – that he was only "ninety-eight, ninety-nine per cent sure" of his story.[247]

Everett Buckner was not the only witness to provide an account of events at the range which LAPD found awkward. Richard Grijalva and his sister, Roberta, arrived at San Gabriel Valley Gun Club at noon on June 4: they got a target from the office and walked over towards the rifle section. As they did, Richard noticed Sirhan on the pistol range: they stopped to watch "because the man was rapid firing which is unusual on the range"[248]. Twenty minutes later, when he went to get a new target, Richard saw the man still rapid-firing what looked and sounded like a .22 calibre revolver: he had two large cartons of ammunition stacked on a bench at his shooting position.

Around 2.30pm, as Richard and Roberta were coming towards the end of their session, the man moved from the pistol to the rifle range and began firing a .22 calibre bolt action rifle; Roberta noticed that he had "three boxes of ammo in a red, blue and white box with a big 'X' printed on the outside".[249] When the Grijalvas left the range at 3pm, the man was still shooting; both siblings positively identified him as Sirhan from police mugshots.

The Grijalvas' story posed LAPD a problem since, as detectives noted in a progress report on July 19, "no .22 calibre rifle was found at Sirhan's house or in his vehicle"[250]: this suggested

---

247 Everett Buckner, transcript of recorded interview, July 2, 1968. LAPD "Special Unit Senator" file 95, p.221-226. California State Archives

248 Interview with Richard Grijalva, July 2, 1968. LAPD "Special Unit Senator" file 48, p.234-235. California State Archives

249 Interview with Roberta Grijalva, July 5, 1968. LAPD "Special Unit Senator" file 48, p.236. California State Archives

250 *Investigation Progress, San Gabriel Valley Gun Club*, July 19, 1968. LAPD "Special Unit Senator" file 46, p.322. California State Archives

that someone else gave it to him. Troubled by the possibility of an accomplice, Richard Grijalva was summoned to Parker Center for a polygraph test: to Hernandez' evident surprise, he passed. If the machine's ability to detect false statements was as reliable as LAPD believed, the result should have led to a search for the rifle and the person who supplied it; instead SUS simply decided to dismiss the Grijalvas' evidence as "an honest mistake"[251].

Had the experiences of Larry Arnot, Ben and Donna Herrick, Everett Buckner and the Grijalva siblings been unique, LAPD's apparent determination to discredit their testimony might be understandable. They were not.

In the weeks following the assassination, Hernandez conducted fourteen polygraph examinations, two with Sirhan's brothers, Saidallah and Munir, the other twelve with people who all claimed to have seen Sirhan in the days before the shooting, or on the day itself, often in the company of unidentified men and women who were acting suspiciously. According to Hernandez' reports (which are not supported by any clear documentary evidence), eleven of these twelve witnesses failed the tests; only Richard Grijalva passed. On this somewhat questionable basis, SUS decided that Sirhan had acted as a lone assassin, without the assistance or involvement of any accomplices.

Instead, they pursued investigations into Sirhan's political beliefs and associations. Ostensibly, this made sense – Sirhan was, after all, a non-US citizen (and therefore not allowed to vote in elections), accused of assassinating a major political figure on the cusp of running for President. The notebooks found in his bedroom contained two pages in which Sirhan made apparent – if

---

251 *Progress Report – San Gabriel Valley Gun Club*, September 5, 1968. LAPD "Special Unit Senator" file 47, p.311. California State Archives

garbled – statements of intent to kill the candidate as well as five pages which suggested threats of violence to people other than Bobby; one referred to killing or removing "the 36th President"- Lyndon Johnson.[252]

In the same jotter, Sirhan had also written a two-page (and uncharacteristically coherent) discourse in which he looked forward to the day when "American capitalism will fall... to a worker's dictatorship."[253] But this was an isolated instance of left-wing beliefs: there were many more pages in which Sirhan made rambling references to – and demands for – money.

Taken as a whole, the notebooks hardly indicated a writer driven to murder by communist rhetoric. Despite this both LAPD and the FBI seem to have made a significant effort to tie him to communism.

In the weeks since Mayor Sam Yorty conflated communism and Arab nationalism at a press conference, the suspicion that Sirhan might either have been a member of the Communist Party, or was inflamed into an act of murder by those who were, had not receded; throughout June and July, detectives interrogated his links to two suspected communists, Walter Sherrill Crowe Jnr. and Tom Good. Both said that Sirhan had not been interested in their attempts to form left-wing student-based movements, but LAPD and the FBI decided that Crowe, an organizer for Students for a Democratic Society who had known Sirhan for two years, needed to be put under surveillance and interrogated at length.

According to a report of one of these sessions, on July 8, Crowe told Lt. Hernandez that Sirhan had "racist attitudes. He was strongly anti-Jewish and made statements about considering Hitler a hero. He started discussing politics, saying that politics was part of his whole commitment in life and explained

---

252 FBI files Sub File X-1 Volumes 5-6, p.13-78, California State Archives
253 *Ibid.*

that Israel could not be defeated militarily in the Middle East." Although some of this interview was recorded, there is no trace of any such statement by Crowe in the official transcript. Instead, it shows that Hernandez brought out his polygraph machine and asked: "When you talked with Sirhan, did he tell you he was planning to shoot Senator Kennedy?" Crowe replied 'No'. Two questions later Hernandez asked again: "Did Sirhan tell you he was planning to shoot Kennedy?" Again, Crowe answered "no".

Hernandez decided that these answers "emitted deceptive physiological responses" – though he conceded that whilst these responses were "consistent with deception" they "could also be attributed to the phychological [sic] involvement of the subject" – whatever that meant. But in the conclusions to his report, such ambiguity was dismissed: "Based on the available polygrams, the only sound conclusion is that Sirhan made some statement to Crowe regarding his intent to kill Senator Kennedy. Whether or not this was a causual [sic] statement or a detailed discussion cannot be ascertained from the test". [254]

By any reading of the report – the polygraph sheets them-selves have not survived – this was a gross overreach. The most Crowe admitted to Hernandez was that he was "afraid that you will ask me to what degree did I influence him'".[255] But LAPD was evidently persuaded that Crowe and Good were to blame for Bobby's murder. A July 19 internal Progress Report stated baldly that "Crowe indicated that he and Tom Goode were responsible for the assassination and when asked to elaborate on this he stated that he and Goode were responsible due to their frequent political conversations and close relationship while attending Pasadena City College during 1964-65."[256]

---

254 LAPD "Special Unit Senator" file 34, p.141-144. California State Archives
255 *Ibid.*
256 LAPD "Special Unit Senator" file 46, p.303. California State Archives

Then, two weeks later, Los Angeles commercial TV station KTLA broadcast a news story which fanned the flames of anti-communist paranoia. Robert Licher had been a US mailman for 9 years, before resigning in January 1968 to set himself up as a self-employed sign writer; for five years his daily beat had included the Sirhan family home on West Howard Street, Pasadena.

In his interview with KTLA, he claimed to have delivered "highly-inflammatory anti-American and pro-Communist mail" addressed personally to Sirhan. The story was quickly picked up by the rabidly right wing John Birch Society, which (without speaking to Licher) published a long and "hastily-compiled" account in its subscription-only weekly paper, *Review of The News*. It was enough to spur LAPD into action.[257]

Detectives from SUS interviewed Licher at his home in Sierra Madre on August 11. He repeated his allegation that Sirhan had regularly received communist literature, "mailed from the Mid-East under the return address of the Arab Students League". He was hazy on exact dates, but insisted that he had been so "highly incensed" about having to deliver this material that he had, on several occasions complained to his supervisor.[258]

Unfortunately, that supervisor – Lewis Peters – as well as two mailmen working the same beat, told LAPD a rather different story. None had ever seen any pro-communist literature addressed to Sirhan, and Peters said that whilst Licher had complained to him about the mail he was delivering to the family home, he "was positive it was American Nazi Party literature"[259] In his view, Licher was "a publicity hound".[260]

Instead of dismissing Licher's claims as a fantasy, LAPD simply entered them in the official record – unqualified by Peters'

---

257 LAPD "Special Unit Senator" file 47, p. 270-272. California State Archives
258 LAPD "Special Unit Senator" file 48, p. 304-306. California State Archives
259 *Ibid*, p.306-307
260 LAPD "Special Unit Senator" file 47, p. p.268. California State Archives.

rebuttal – as evidence of Sirhan's political motivation for murder.[261] (Fifty years on, right-wing writers continue to adduce the Licher story as evidence of Sirhan's pro-Arab, anti-Israel "terrorist" intentions[262].)

In truth, the detectives were drilling a dry hole. Sirhan's closest friend, Ivan Garcia, had explicitly told them that "Sirhan did not appear to be particularly aware of any political party, was not interested in groups or being a leader, and was not openly fanatical about politics." Nor could he understand the suggestion that a hatred of the Kennedys or anti-Israel fanaticism might have motivated him. "Sirhan never discussed Senator Kennedy, the Arab-Israeli dispute, or racial recriminations which might have arisen out of such a dispute."[263]

By the end of the summer, Special Unit Senator was no closer to understanding its chief suspect or his motivation. Sirhan had been caught, quite literally, with a smoking gun and his notebooks suggested that he had planned to assassinate Bobby. Yet all the investigations had truly revealed was that he had no criminal record, with just two minor traffic tickets on file; that he had a mild interest in Rosicrucianism, but no history of affiliation with political – much less with radical – organizations. LAPD's profile could not offer any clear motive for Sirhan's actions: it would be up to a succession of psychiatrists and psychologists to try and understand what inspired him to open fire in the Ambassador Hotel pantry.

261 Special Unit Senator: Final Report, p. 400-402, April 4, 1969. California State Archives.

262 Mel Ayton, *The Forgotten Terrorist – Sirhan Sirhan and the Assassination of Robert F. Kennedy*, p.255. Potomac Books, 2007

263 FBI Files X-4, Vol.13, p. 206-208. California State Archives.

CHAPTER EIGHT:
A MIND ON TRIAL

"There is no doubt," Emile Zola Berman told the jury in *People vs. Sirhan Sirhan,* "that he did in fact fire the fatal shot that killed Senator Kennedy".[264]

It was Friday, February 14, 1969; Berman was making his opening statement: an unequivocal assertion of Sirhan's responsibility for the assassination. This was standard court room procedure for a prosecutor setting out the case he would seek to prove over the coming weeks. But Berman was not representing the prosecution; a highly-experienced trial attorney, he had been brought in by Grant Cooper and Russell Parsons specifically to outline the thrust of the defence case – that although Sirhan had killed Bobby, he was legally innocent because he was suffering from "severe mental illness".

Three fundamental factors combined to steer the defence team towards this strategy. The first was that Sirhan had been caught, red-handed in the act of firing a gun, in the pantry; the second was additional pressure stemming from the decision by the lead prosecutor, Chief Deputy District Attorney Lynn D. Compton, to seek the death penalty.[265] "My job," Grant Cooper

---

264 *People vs. Sirhan Bishara Sirhan,* Certified trial transcript, Vol. 11, page 133-134; February 14, 1969. California State Archives.

265 *Prosecution to Ask Death [sic], Miami Herald* (UPI Report), July 17, 1968

admitted to his investigator, Robert Kaiser, "is to keep the kid out of the gas chamber."[266]

But what most heavily influenced Cooper's strategy was a combination of Sirhan's total amnesia about the shooting and the reports of nine psychiatrists and psychologists – two appointed by the court, one commissioned by the prosecution and six by the defence – on the suspect's mental state.

Between June and December 1968 they deployed an array of standard assessment techniques and more controversial methods in a bid to unlock Sirhan's apparently frozen mind. Ultimately, they all reached variations on the same diagnosis – Sirhan was mentally ill. Their differences were legal rather than medical: the defence experts argued he was suffering from paranoid schizophrenic psychosis and therefore, under California's law of diminished capacity, not legally responsible for his actions; the prosecution countered that the illness was not severe, and that Sirhan could distinguish between right and wrong – making him guilty of first degree murder.

On February 10, 1969 lawyers for both sides, accompanied by Los Angeles County District Attorney Evelle J. Younger, held a meeting in chambers with Judge Herbert V. Walker. The aim was to persuade the judge to sign off on a deal they had reached by which Sirhan would plead guilty to first degree murder in exchange for a guarantee that he would be sentenced to life in prison rather than face execution. Younger frankly admitted that, on the basis of the psychiatric reports, he could not "conscientiously urge the death penalty", and nor, since "the defendant is psychotic... would we get the death penalty even if we urged it." But uppermost in the D.A.'s mind was the question of cost.

"Are we justified in going through the motions of a trial, a very traumatic and expensive trial," he mused, "when we can't

---

266 Robert Blair Kaiser: *R.F.K. Must Die!*, p.165. E.P. Dutton & Co, 1970.

conscientiously ask for the death penalty anyway? We don't think we are."[267]

Cooper told the judge that the defence was torn between "our duty to our client to go forward with the trial" in the hope – only – of securing a conviction for second degree murder with a resulting minimum sentence of three and a half years, and the very real risk of a death penalty verdict.

"We have concluded that the odds were too strong... at least they were not in our favour, so we have concluded that the wise thing to do... would be to enter a plea of guilty to first degree murder with life imprisonment."[268]

Younger, an astute operator with political ambitions[269] was aware that the proposed plea bargain could, in a case so politically charged, lead to accusations of conspiracy or cover up.

"Your Honor, I am sure, doesn't want anybody to think that there was any hanky-panky going on if we do this, and if the recommendation is accepted, it would be our intention to... put into the record all pertinent materials, including statements of witnesses and... the psychiatrists' reports."[270]

Judge Walker, however, wasn't buying. "I appreciate the cost. I appreciate the sensation," he told the lawyers, "but I am sure it would be opening us up to a lot of criticism... by the people who think that the jury should decide this question." He ordered both sides to prepare for a full trial.[271]

But if the plea deal had failed, the substantial accord between prosecution and defence over the facts of the shooting ensured

267 *People vs. Sirhan Bishara Sirhan*, Certified trial transcript, Vol. 10, page 34-35; February 10, 1969. California State Archives.

268 *Ibid.*, p.38

269 In 1970 he was elected Attorney General for the State of California and eight years later would be the Republican nominee for Governor.

270 *People vs. Sirhan Bishara Sirhan*, Certified trial transcript, Vol. 10, page 40; February 10, 1969. California State Archives.

271 *Ibid.* p.41

that Sirhan's trial would not question or investigate the evidence suggesting he fired the fatal bullet. The court was told, from the outset that the defence accepted Sirhan had killed Bobby in the throes of mental illness. "The killing," Berman said in his opening statement, "was unplanned and undeliberate, impulsive and without premeditation or malice, totally a product of a sick, obsessed mind and personality."[272] As a result, throughout the trial's nine weeks, the defence attorneys would not challenge any of the prosecution's evidence about the events in the pantry.

On February 26, Coroner Thomas Noguchi testified that his autopsy and the subsequent gunshot residue tests showed that the fatal bullet had been fired from behind Bobby "very close to the edge of the right ear ... between one inch to one and a half inches from the edge". The other two wounds, on Bobby's back, were consistent with the same "close range" finding: the gun's muzzle had been no more than one inch away when it was fired.[273]

This conflicted with every statement, taken by LAPD, from eyewitnesses in the pantry: each had clearly placed Sirhan not behind but in front of Bobby – and at a distance of several feet. Yet, rather than examining the conflict between their testimony and Noguchi's forensic evidence, the defence team seemed anxious to get the coroner off the stand as fast as possible.

"Is all of this detail really necessary?" Cooper asked in one of his few challenges. "This witness may certainly testify to the cause of death, but I don't think it is necessary to go into the details. I think he can express an opinion that death was due to a gunshot wound."[274]

---

272 *People vs. Sirhan Bishara Sirhan*, Certified trial transcript, Vol. 11, page 133-134; February 14, 1969. California State Archives.
273 *People vs. Sirhan Bishara Sirhan*, Certified trial transcript, Vol. 16, page 87-119; February 26, 1969. California State Archives.
274 *People vs. Sirhan Bishara Sirhan*, Certified trial transcript, Vol. 16, page 99; February 26, 1969. California State Archives.

Nor was Cooper any more interested in the ballistic evidence. On February 21, during a meeting in Judge Walker's chambers, Deputy District Attorney David N. Fitts admitted that the DA's office did "not have adequate foundation" for some of LAPD criminalist DeWayne Wolfer's forthcoming testimony. Specifically, the prosecution could not provide proof supporting Wolfer's evidence about the bullets recovered from the shooting victims and those he test-fired. Cooper agreed to make a legal stipulation, accepting as true whatever the criminalist told the jury about the slugs. "There will be no question about that," he calmly assured Fitts.[275]

And so, *People vs. Sirhan Sirhan* would not be an enquiry into the facts of the assassination. The defence strategy was clear and unequivocal: to put Sirhan's mind on trial in the hope of saving his life.

The first psychological examinations had begun in June 1968 and followed a conventional approach. Dr. Martin Schorr, a clinical psychologist employed by San Diego County University Hospital, consultant for San Diego County DA's office and a regular lecturer at the Police Academy, visited Sirhan in his prison cell at the County Jail to administer a succession of "tests which are in use most commonly in all of the major hospitals in the United States and throughout psychiatric clinics"[276]. These included the Wechsler Adult Intelligence Test, which Schorr described it as being "like a mental X-ray. That is, what we try to find is not what an individual under the stress of a test thinks we want him to tell us, but we want to get behind the image of the personality and into the reality of the person".[277] The results

---

275 *People vs. Sirhan Bishara Sirhan*, Certified trial transcript, Vol. 14, page 162-163; February 21, 1969. California State Archives.

276 *People vs. Sirhan Bishara Sirhan*, Certified trial transcript Vol. 19, p.225. California State Archives

277 *Ibid.* p.226

showed a "patterning... typically consistent with schizophrenia" [278] – which Schorr defined as "mental illness where the individual is no longer responding to the world of reality".[279] A Rorschach test, in which Sirhan's perceptions of a series inkblots were analysed, reached much the same conclusion.

Schorr also delved into Sirhan's claim that he could not remember firing his gun in the pantry. He used the Minnesota Multiphasic Personality Inventory – a standard assessment based on 566 questions, designed to unearth genuine mental illness and expose anyone trying to fake amnesia. The results suggested "a paranoia scale and a hypomania scale well above the levels of significance" which re-enforced "the concept of a paranoid mechanism in this personality"[280]

Schorr's conclusions were supported by all the other defence psychiatrists and psychologists who examined the raw test data; the verdict of Dr. Orville Richardson, a highly-experienced clinical psychologist summed up the consensus. "The overall diagnostic impression," he told the court, "is a schizophrenic process, paranoid type, acute and chronic."[281] Even one of the prosecution's experts – Dr. Georgene Seward, Professor of Psychology at the University of Southern California – testified that on Rorschach test alone she would have no hesitation in diagnosing Sirhan as a paranoid schizophrenic.[282]

Sirhan's inability to recall the assassination was also found to be genuine. The tests, Dr. Schorr testified, showed that he "consciously does not remember" the shooting and that there

---

278 *Ibid.* p.253
279 *Ibid.* p.254
280 *People vs. Sirhan Bishara Sirhan,* Certified trial transcript Vol 22, p.120. California State Archives
281 *People vs. Sirhan Bishara Sirhan,* Certified trial transcript Vol. 22, p.169. California State Archives.
282 *People vs. Sirhan Bishara Sirhan,* Certified trial transcript Vol. 25, p.128. California State Archives.

was "nothing in any of the tests to indicate a malingering, socio-pathic or problem-denying personality of an individual who is trying to claim an amnesia that did not in fact exist."[283]

But despite this testimony, two weeks after the trial began the defence faced a major problem. On February 28, apparently angered by a procession of medical testimony about his limited intellectual abilities and damaged mental state, Sirhan inter-rupted the trial and demanded to change his plea.

"I withdraw my original plea of not guilty and say I am guilty on all counts," he told Judge Walker. For good measure he also insisted on firing his attorneys and demanded that the court sen-tence him to death.

"I request counsel to disassociate themselves with me. I will ask to be executed ... I believe it is in my best interests ... that is my prerogative". When Walker remonstrated with him, Sirhan shouted: "I killed Robert Kennedy wilfully, premeditatedly and with 20 years malice aforethought".

To his credit, the judge refused to accept the change of plea, telling Sirhan that he "was incapable of representing [himself]. I find you incompetent", and that if he caused any further disrup-tion he would be restrained. "You will be put in a face mask so that you cannot talk. Your arms will be strapped to a chair. Your trial will proceed. You will retain your counsel."[284]

Cooper tried to walk back the apparent confession, telling reporters that "the outburst was triggered by testimony showing Sirhan's poor school grades. He doesn't like to be demeaned. He doesn't consider himself to be of diminished capacity."[285] He also had Dr. Schorr testify that by asking to be put to death, Sirhan was eloquently proving his "paranoid state".

---

283 *Ibid.,*p.227
284 *People vs. Sirhan Bishara Sirhan,* Certified trial transcript Vol. 16, p.229-238. California State Archives.
285 *Lawyers Ask Sirhan Truce, Los Angeles Herald-Examiner, 1 March 1969.*

"It is highly consistent for the defendant, being in a paranoid state, psychotically disturbed, to take the position that he does; that he knows more than anybody else; that if he is not satisfied with the way the court is being conducted, he will not only dismiss his attorneys, but he, in effect, is telling the Judge, His Honor, that he is a higher authority than the Judge because he knows better than the Judge.

"This is consistent with his own grandiosity, as a person who believes himself superior to others, above all laws, because he is part of super-natural law."[286]

But the damage was done. Newspapers carried reports of the dramatic court room scenes:[287] Sirhan's eruption would damn him in the eyes of the jury, and haunt him for years to come.

Restored to the defence table, Cooper, Parsons and Berman hammered away at the thrust of their argument. They called to the witness stand Dr. Eric H. Marcus, a leading psychiatrist who had been appointed to assess Sirhan by the judge at his initial arraignment. Marcus was a member of a panel of experts in psychiatry regularly called on by Los Angeles County Superior Court to testify in court cases involving insanity, diminished capacity and fitness to plead; in 1968 alone he performed ninety examinations for the Superior Court and more than thirty for federal court hearings. He examined Sirhan in his jail cell on five occasions between June and the end of October 1968 and reached the same diagnosis as the other doctors. He had also been able to pinpoint when Sirhan's problems started.

"In my opinion," Marcus testified on March 20, "he started to show signs of mental illness at the very latest at the time following

---

286 *People vs. Sirhan Bishara Sirhan,* Certified trial transcript Vol.. 20, p.122 California State Archives.

287 *I withdraw My Plea of Not Guilty and Say Guilty on All Counts!, Los Angeles Herald-Examiner, 1 March 1969.*

his horse accident, and … his adjustment in mental state had deteriorated since then … in a rather slow, insidious way."[288]

But it was Marcus' evidence about some of the other tests he had administered which were more unusual – and, potentially at least, more revealing. Because Sirhan had apparently consumed several 'Tom Collins' cocktails in one of the Ambassador Hotel's bars, Marcus deliberately got him drunk in his jail cell and then administered an encephalograph test.

"Alcohol was given to determine whether or not he had any abnormal brain waves … with alcohol." If so, he explained, this would undermine a diagnosis of mental illness. Sirhan was duly given "six ounces of alcohol in the form of Tom Collins and then the brain wave test was done … The test took about twice as long as it would normally have taken. He was extremely irritated and restless during it, and he had to be restrained physically during many parts of the examination."[289]

The test showed Sirhan did not have "any type of electrical organic abnormality", and thus that the diagnosis of mental illness was not weakened. But the experiment yielded evidence of something unexpected. After the encephalogram was over Marcus discovered that Sirhan had fallen into some kind of trance in which he believed himself to be at the Ambassador on the night of the assassination.

"He was still quite intoxicated. He kept grabbing for his throat and he said 'What the hell is going on here?' And you would have thought we were choking him. He began some more name calling and he said 'I hate his guts' and later on he kept saying, repeating, 'I will get even with those Jews, God damn it' …

---

288 *People vs. Sirhan Bishara Sirhan*, Certified trial transcript Vol. 23, p.163. California State Archives.
289 *People vs. Sirhan Bishara Sirhan*, Certified trial transcript Vol. 24, p.20. California State Archives.

"There was a female technician there helping in the test and then at one time he said to her 'You are a hell of a waitress' and he thought, apparently, that he was back at the Ambassador Hotel... Then he talked about 20 years is long enough for the Jews; we have to have justice' and then mentioned some things about Kennedy. He was very hostile. He misidentified me. He thought I was his brother and he asked me to take him home. He thought he was back at the Ambassador Hotel and he had had too much to drink and he wanted me to drive him home...

"Then he looked around and there were about four or five deputy sheriffs guarding him... He thought, I recall, that the guards were Israeli soldiers. During this entire time he was trembling and irritated and he got very depressed. I asked him repeatedly... to describe killing Kennedy and he said that he never did. He kept talking about Kennedy as if Kennedy was alive. He kept saying 'That bastard isn't worth the bullets' and I constantly tried to get him to admit what happened and he never said that he committed the act."[290]

The combination of Sirhan's apparently genuine amnesia and his sudden, alcohol-induced trance, led the defence's chief psychological expert to conduct a series of increasingly bizarre experiments. Dr. Bernard Diamond was one of the most respected experts in California; a past Chairman of the American Psychiatric Association's Committee on Psychiatry and the Law, and a member of the California Commission on Insanity and Criminal Offenses, in 1968 he was Clinical Professor of Psychology at the University of California Medical School (San Francisco) as well as Professor of Law and Criminology at the University of California (Berkeley).

He examined Sirhan eight times, spending almost twenty-five hours with him in his cell; he also studied all the other

290 *Ibid*.p.19-22

doctors' reports, the post-arrest interrogation transcripts, and Sirhan's books and correspondence, as well as interviewing his family. His overall conclusion was that "Sirhan was suffering from a chronic paranoid schizophrenia, a major psychosis at the time of the shooting" – the product of his traumatic childhood in Palestine where he witnessed extreme violence and death. This explained the roots of the mental illness, and Diamond argued, led to Sirhan having been in a type of hypnotic trance on the night of the assassination – "a highly abnormal dissociated state of restrictive consciousness as a direct consequence of this psychotic condition."[291]

This "dissociated" state also explained Sirhan's inability to remember opening fire in the pantry. And since the amnesia was central to understanding how the trance came about, Diamond wanted to find a way to unlock Sirhan's frozen mind. Normally, as he told the court on March 21, he would have administered intravenous injections of the so-called 'truth drugs' Sodium Amytal or Sodium Pentothal. The prosecution had agreed to this, but there was a "remote possibility of risk" which required that the drugs be administered under hospital conditions – and the Sheriff refused to allow Sirhan to be moved from the County Jail.[292].

Instead, and with the agreement of all parties, Diamond decided to hypnotise Sirhan. It was a controversial technique and only the need to get results quickly justified its use.

"When we are confronted with the necessity of finding out more about what a defendant, a patient or a person is willing to tell you," Diamond testified, "I always prefer to ... simply wait and ... continue to talk and discuss the situation until the individual gains constant confidence in you and is willing to tell you

291 *People vs. Sirhan Bishara Sirhan,* Certified trial transcript Vol. 24, p.86. California State Archives.

292 *Ibid.* p.126-127

the whole story...I don't go around hypnotizing people every time I see them in my private clinical practice, but under special circumstances of which...this is a good example...you have to utilize some kind of short cuts."[293]

The advantage of hypnosis was that "it is possible to elicit from a hypnotised person, or in any other of these things like a truth serum, information which would not otherwise be available". But the disadvantage was that the information elicited might not, in fact, be true.

"I want to emphasise that these are not means of necessarily gaining the truth. Hypnosis is not a lie detector...It is a way, an instrument, that can be used for psychiatrists to gain access to the thoughts and feelings of a person who is resistant against his gaining access."[294]

Diamond first hypnotised Sirhan on January 4, finding it unexpectedly easy to put his patient into a trance. "Somewhat to my surprise he went to sleep fairly promptly; it took less than ten minutes...to put him to sleep."[295] His first question related to what he called Sirhan's "people" – Arabs – and what Sirhan intended to do about their plight. The result was immediate and disturbing.

"In the hypnotic state Sirhan went into a sort of convulsive rage, in which his fists clenched, his arms tightened up and he got a most dramatic contorted rage expression on his face and sobbed. The tears poured down his face. For the first time I had a glimpse or image of a completely different Sirhan than I had previously observed...This was repeated...and repeated again. And it comes out in two kinds of questioning. One, any kind of question, even just a hint is enough to trigger it off,

---

293 *Ibid.* p.123-124
294 *Ibid.* p.132
295 *Ibid.*

concerning his people, the Arabs, and their unfortunate plight and any talk about the Jews, the bombs and what has happened to Jerusalem."[296] But that rage was the limit of what the session revealed: it brought Diamond no closer to understanding what happened on primary election night – much less why Sirhan had opened fire in the pantry.

Diamond went on to hypnotise Sirhan on at least six occasions between January and February 1969. As the tests progressed the psychologist came to suspect that someone else had done so previously.

"One of the problems with Sirhan … is that Sirhan went into hypnosis very easily, but it was very difficult to get him to talk. He would mumble in a very soft tone and talk like someone who is profoundly asleep. Whenever you put any pressure on him, or tried to, you know, sort of push him where he was showing some sort of initial resistance, he would go off into a real deep sleep in which you couldn't get anything out of him at all. Now this is a kind of emotional resistance but it also indicated to me something peculiar about his hypnotic experience.

"At this time I did not know that Sirhan had been hypnotised before, but … if somebody has been hypnotised before they are quite placid in learning to talk under hypnosis. You learn that like you learn anything. He did go in very easily and he showed these other effects of the deep trance."[297]

Undeterred, Diamond tried again. On January 11, he put Sirhan into a hypnotic trance and, recording the session on tape, asked if he had been paid to shoot Bobby and, if "the Arab government [sic] have anything to do with it?" Sirhan answered no – promptly – to both questions. The responses changed, however, when Diamond asked "Did you think this all up by

---

296 *Ibid*. p.134-135
297 *Ibid*. p.141

yourself?" Sirhan answered "yes" – but only after pausing "for about four or five seconds". There was a similar lag in his reply to the question "Are you the only person involved in the Kennedy shooting?" Sirhan paused 'for a second or two" before answering "yes". These delays were unusual, seeming to indicate some sort of internal struggle, and when Diamond asked "Why did you shoot him, Sirhan?" there was no answer at all; only when he repeated the question did Sirhan mutter "the bombers". Diamond pressed him: "What are the bombers, you mean the bombers to Israel?" Sirhan responded with a monosyllabic "Yes". But however many times Diamond asked 'Why did you decide to shoot Kennedy?' Sirhan did not reply until – eventually – he said, 'I don't know'.[298]

Unable to break the mental log jam with regular hypnosis, Diamond decided to try a more extreme technique he referred to as "aberrations": it involved prompting the hypnotised patient to re-live an event which he could not clearly recall in a normal trance.

"It was something I had had a great deal of experience in," he explained to the jury, "because during the five years or so I was a psychiatrist in World War II I treated many, many hundreds, perhaps thousands, of cases of combat neurosis hysteria... and it was therapeutically very desirable to produce not only a recall of the experience but some re-living of the experience ... and he [the patient] observes everything as if he is right there and is almost at the original scene."[299]

But, he admitted, using "aberrations" carried two significant risks. The first was that there was "no absolute guarantee that what you see is the truth. It is quite possible that one recovers in such a state that what he sees is not the true event but a fantasy. You can

---

298 *Ibid.* p.141-143
299 *Ibid.* p.144-145

recall things that don't happen."[300] The second danger was the invasive nature of the technique: to prompt the release of what might – or might not – be genuine frozen memories, required the psychologist to implant information in the patient's mind.

"I want to emphasise that … you can't just hypnotize the person but you have got to feed him, you have to urge him … you have to sort of play into the individual's unconscious and make him believe you are suggesting that this happened right now and not just to recover it as a memory."[301]

On January 26, accompanied by Dr. Seymour Pollack, the prosecution's expert psychiatrist, Diamond put "aberrations" into action. He hypnotised Sirhan and then took him "step by step through all of the events at the Ambassador on the night of June 4 and 5."

Under hypnosis, Sirhan described having four Tom Collins drinks before going back to his car with the intention of driving home. But he realised that he was drunk. "He saw his gun lying on the seat of his car and his thought was that 'The Jews will steal my gun' … so he put the gun in his belt, or tucked it into his pants, with the intention of going back to the hotel and getting some coffee to sober up."[302]

In the Ambassador he met a girl who also wanted coffee. "He described this girl and he did not know who she was, Sirhan did not know her name and she never told him her name. I asked Sirhan what his thoughts were and his answers were that he was having sexy thoughts and he was really planning whether or not he could persuade the girl to leave the hotel with him …

"I questioned him at great length under hypnosis as to what his thoughts and his feelings were at this time, whether he was

---

300 *Ibid.* p.145
301 *Ibid.*
302 *Ibid.* p.147

thinking of the gun in relationship to Senator Kennedy with the thoughts of killing … and he was absolutely consistent as he has been under all of these hypnosis experiments in denying … that there was any thought of doing anything with the gun and that all he was thinking of was the girl and coffee."[303]

But still Diamond could not get Sirhan to recall shooting Bobby: he pushed further, ordering Sirhan to see himself opening fire in the pantry. "He did not re-enact or re-live the experience [so] … I gave him instructions. 'Do it over again. Now, I want you to be there. You are right in the kitchen now, Sirhan, look, Senator Kennedy is here, he's coming towards you'."

The psychologist was – unquestionably – stepping across a dangerous line: he was now implanting an image in the mind of his hypnotized patient. The results were startling.

"In response to these very strong suggestions on my part, Sirhan, who was sitting on his cell bed with me sitting beside him and Dr. Pollack, the prosecution psychiatrist whom I had invited to witness this, Sirhan simply pulled an imaginary gun out of the belt – this was the first absolute proof I had that it was in the belt. … and fired it convulsively over and over again and shouted out 'You son of a bitch'"[304]

Diamond testified that he believed this to be "the first indication, from any source, confirming what actually occurred at the time of the shooting". But any triumph was tempered by the evident pain caused to his patient.

"It was very dramatic and it was very real – the convulsive moments, the grabbing the gun and the expression on his face of the most violent contorted rage … then there was a momentary pause and he started to choke. He was actually re-experiencing the choking when they held him down and took away the gun.

303 *Ibid.* p.148
304 *Ibid.* p.150-151

He was gasping for breath, and actually turned blue a little bit, to the point where I became fearful ..." [305]

Despite this, Diamond continued to use his 'aberrations' technique: he wanted to explore the puzzle of Sirhan's notebooks and, specifically, the amnesia which seemed to surround them.

"I felt very dissatisfied with Sirhan's explanations which were essentially no explanation at all," the psychologist testified on March 24. "He denied the notebooks in a very odd, peculiar way. He admitted the notebooks were his, he admitted most of the time that the writing must be his, but he had no recollection about how it happened and couldn't give me an explanation as to how any part of the notebook came about." [306]

After putting Sirhan into a hypnotic trance, Diamond instructed him to write his name: he did so, over and over again "in a stiff mechanical way, his eyes fixed on the paper and writing mechanically." [307] Then Diamond told him to write about Bobby. "Sirhan is sitting back in his cell with his eyes closed, totally unresponsive to any questions ... I said 'Open your eyes. Write about Kennedy ... I want you to write about Kennedy' ... So he writes then, 'RFK, RFK, RFK', and he repeats it over and over again, and then I say 'Tell us more than his name, write more than his name', and he writes 'Robert F. Kennedy, Robert F. Kennedy, RFK, RFK, RFK, RFK must die, K must die, RFK must die, RFK must die, RFK must die, RFK must die, RFK must die, RFK must die, RFK must die, RFK must die.'" [308]

When Diamond asked why Bobby had to die he got no reply; then he queried whether Sirhan thought Bobby was dead: "no, no, no', was the response. To the question 'Who was with you when you shot Kennedy?' Sirhan wrote 'Girl, the girl, the girl' – but

---

305 *Ibid.* p.152
306 *Ibid.* p.156
307 *Ibid.* p.158
308 *Ibid.* p.165

when Diamond asked him to write down her name, there was no answer other than a groan.[309]

Once again Sirhan was becoming distressed. "There was considerable resistance and groaning and it is very hard for him ... when he experiences this kind of restlessness he squirms and he groans and he leans back and he seems to go into a coma, and you have to shake him again to get him started again."[310]

Evidently Diamond did just that, for soon Sirhan was back scribbling on the paper in front of him. When the psychologist asked him why he was "writing crazy", Sirhan wrote: 'Practice, practice, practice, practice, practice'. 'Practice for what?' Diamond asked. 'Mind control, mind control, mind control, mind control', Sirhan scrawled.[311]

Puzzled by Sirhan's "resistance" – the cause of his groans and evident distress – Diamond decided to expand his "aberrations" technique by using "post-hypnotic suggestion" to implant instructions in Sirhan's mind. What particularly baffled the psychologist was the fact that once awoken from his trance, Sirhan was genuinely unable to recall being hypnotised in the first place. On February 8, he set out to address this problem.

After putting Sirhan into a hypnotic trance in his cell, Diamond implanted the first of a series of post-hypnotic suggestions, instructing him that after he was awoken he would see the psychologist mopping his forehead with a handkerchief and was immediately to approach the guard and ask about the weather. The experiment worked exactly as Diamond had ordered.

Next he re-hypnotised Sirhan and gave a second post-hypnotic suggestion. "I said 'Sirhan, you are asleep now and when you wake up I am going to take my handkerchief out

---

309 *Ibid.* p.166-170
310 *Ibid.* p.171
311 *Ibid.* p.172

and wipe my forehead and you are going to feel that you are going to climb around the bars [of the cell] like a monkey'. And so in a little while when I took my handkerchief out ... he made faces at the guard and then started climbing up the bars of the cell all the way to the ceiling and perched himself up there". But despite a specific instruction that he would be able to recall this, when Diamond woke him up, Sirhan had no memory of being hypnotized – much less of performing like a monkey in a circus.[312] The strength and stubbornness of this blockage, together with the ease with which Sirhan could be put into a trance, suggested some pre-existing – and much deeper – hypno-programming.

Diamond eventually theorised that Sirhan had done this himself, using mirrors and candles, as part of his dabbling in Rosicrucianism; and that on the night of the assassination the camera lights and mirrors in the Ambassador Hotel had triggered a trance which allowed his pent up rage about the plight of Arabs in Palestine to emerge.

"With absolutely no knowledge or awareness of what was actually happening in his Rosicrucian and occult experiments, he was gradually programming himself – exactly like a computer is programmed by its magnetic tape – programming himself for the coming assassination.

"In his unconscious mind there existed a plan for the total fulfilment of his sick paranoid hatred of Kennedy and all those who might want to help the Jews. In his conscious mind there was no awareness of such a plan, or that he, Sirhan, was to be the instrument of assassination.

"He was confused, bewildered and partially intoxicated. The mirrors in the hotel lobby, the flashing lights, the general

---

312 *Ibid.* p.190-191

confusion – this was like pressing the button which starts the computer."[313]

Diamond was aware that the jury was likely to be sceptical of his diagnosis. "I agree that this is an absurd and preposterous story, unlikely and incredible," he said on March 24, the final day of his testimony. I doubt that Sirhan himself agrees with me as to how everything happened. Sirhan prefers to deny his mental illness, his psychological disintegration, his trances, his automatic writing and his automatic shooting. However...these are the psychiatric findings in this case. They are absurd, preposterous, unlikely and incredible because the crime itself was a tragically absurd and preposterous event, unlikely and incredible. But I am satisfied that this is how Sirhan Bishara Sirhan came to kill Senator Robert F. Kennedy on June 5, 1968."[314]

The jury evidently shared Diamond's pessimistic assessment of his own diagnosis. On April 17, 1969, after almost 17 hours of deliberation, it found Sirhan guilty of murder. Six days later it sentenced him to death.

Neither the jury members nor the psychologist knew then that halfway across the country a US government agency possessed evidence which would give credence to the "absurd and preposterous" hypno-programming theory. That evidence – along with unequivocal proof that Sirhan had not fired the fatal shot – would be suppressed for many years to come.

---

313 *Ibid.* p.205
314 *Ibid.* p.207-208

CHAPTER NINE:
CHARADES

O
n May 16, 1969, Judge Walker held a conference in his chambers with representatives of both legal teams and the Los Angeles County Clerk's Office. Walker, then in the process of deciding whether to affirm the jury's death sentence on Sirhan[315], wanted to ensure that all trial exhibits would be carefully preserved by the clerk's office. Over at Parker Center, LAPD's Chief of Detectives, Robert Houghton, was also concerned with the evidence his officers had assembled; at a news conference, he gave a clear and unequivocal commitment to full public disclosure. "The posture of the Los Angeles Police Department," he told the assembled journalists, "is that we think nothing in this case should be withheld from the public."[316]

Houghton's commitment was echoed and supported by Los Angeles District Attorney, Evelle J. Younger. On May 28, 1969, he told another press conference that "The Los Angeles Police Department has agreed without reservation that the interests of the public and law enforcement are best served by full disclosure of the results of the comprehensive investigation they

---

315 He did so on May 21, 1969.
316 *Request to The Los Angeles County Grand Jury, 1992*, p.14. Robert F. Kennedy Assassination Archives, University of Massachusetts Dartmouth.

have conducted"[317]. In a television interview eleven days later he promised that "there is tons of information over at LAPD that's going to be made public"[318].

But instead of that promised "full disclosure", the District Attorney, Los Angeles Police Department and the FBI did the polar opposite. Each locked all the material in their respective files and refused all requests to release it. For the next 18 years the only substantive information to emerge about the assassination stemmed from the determined efforts of a handful of citizen-investigators and a succession of public interest law suits.

Lillian Castellano and Floyd B. Nelson, founder members of a self-styled Kennedy Assassination Truth Committee, investigated the shooting for almost a year. In May 1969 they published a two-page story in the *Los Angeles Free Press*, an alternative weekly paper, which for the first time highlighted doubts about the official account. Under the headline "Ten Shots from an Eight-Shot Revolver", the article uncovered "photographic evidence that at least ten bullets were found" at the crime scene.

Nelson and Castellano's photographic evidence was the pictures shot on June 5, 1968 by John Clemente, showing what appeared to be bullet holes in the centre divider of the swinging doors at the west end of the pantry. Since LAPD's criminalist, DeWayne Wolfer, claimed to have accounted for all eight shots from Sirhan's revolver without mentioning these apparent bullet holes, the implication was clear – there must have been a second gunman who also fired his weapon.

The article was accompanied by an affidavit from John Shirley who had accompanied Clemente when he took the photo. "In the wooden jamb of the center divider were two bullet holes

---

317 Transcript of joint LA DA & LAPD press conference, May 28, 1969. Robert F. Kennedy Assassination Archives, University of Massachusetts Dartmouth.

318 Dan Moldea: *The Killing of Robert F. Kennedy*, p.132. Norton & Co., 1995

surrounded by inked circles which contained some numbers and letters …

"It appeared that an attempt had been made to dig the bullets out from the surface. However, the center divider jamb was loose, and it appeared to have been removed from the framework so that the bullets might be extracted from behind. It was then replaced but not firmly affixed."[319]

Nelson and Castellano also found a second photo, taken by an Associated Press cameraman in the hours following the shooting, in which an unnamed LAPD officer pointed to a hole in a separate door frame several yards up the hall from the pantry; the caption read "A police technician inspects a bullet hole discovered in a door frame in a kitchen corridor of the Ambassador Hotel in Los Angeles near where Sen. Robert F. Kennedy was shot and critically wounded early today". The AP photo brought the bullet count to eleven.

L.A. Free Press might have been an alternative paper, but it stuck to good journalistic practice. Nelson and Castellano took their evidence to the District Attorney's office, and published its response: according to Assistant D.A. John Howard the "bullet holes", were perfectly innocent "dents caused by kitchen carts".[320] The explanation, the photographs and – most particularly – the center divider would eventually come to haunt LAPD and the DA's office.

But, since Sirhan's own lawyers had failed to raise any of this in his trial, and with all the evidence under official lock and key, Nelson and Castellano's article drew little mainstream attention: that focussed instead on a semi-official book by LAPD Chief of Detectives Robert A. Houghton.

---

319 Floyd B. Nelson & Lillian Castellano: *Ten Shots from an Eight-Shot Revolver, L.A. Free Press*, May 23, 1969. Robert F. Kennedy Assassination Archives, University of Massachusetts Dartmouth.

320 *Ibid.*

"*Special Unit Senator*" was published in January 1970 and was written, according to Houghton's own foreword, "for the sole purpose of acquainting the American public with the facts of the investigation"; Houghton also specifically stated that "the material herein was drawn from the files of the Los Angeles Police Department, and particularly from the exhaustive work of Special Unit Senator."[321]

The book quickly garnered positive reviews. *Life* magazine called it "fine...in every way"[322], while *Library Journal* pronounced, "This fact-filled report ought to convince any open-minded reader that Sirhan acted entirely on his own."[323] But it also attracted litigation from an independent researcher.

Theodore 'Ted' Charach, a former bit-part actor in low budget Hollywood horror movies and TV comedies who re-invented himself as an "independent journalist", had been funding his own investigation into the assassination: in June he filed a law suit against LAPD, its senior officers and the District Attorney complaining that, since Houghton had been allowed access to the files, all of the evidence within them should be released to the general public.[324]

Charach was an eccentric and erratic figure, but his investigation had uncovered the biggest problem in the case against Sirhan – and one which the defence team had completely ignored – the conflict between the scientific evidence and the testimony of eyewitnesses.

Thomas Noguchi's 62-page post-mortem report had not been entered into evidence at the trial, and Grant Cooper had cut short his testimony on the witness stand. Charach filmed an

---

321 Robert A. Houghton: *Special Unit Senator*, Random House, 1970
322 *Life*, February 6, 1970
323 *Library Journal*, January 15, 1970
324 *Theodore Charach v. LAPD & Others, Los Angeles Superior Court Case No: 978371*, June 4, 1970. Robert F. Kennedy Assassination Archives, University of Massachusetts Dartmouth.

interview in which the coroner spelled out his key finding: that all four shots striking Bobby's body or clothing had been fired, at upward angles, from behind the Senator and at a distance of from contact to near-contact range.

Charach had also interviewed several of the prosecution's key eyewitnesses to the shooting, all of whom insisted that Sirhan had always been in front of Bobby and never closer than two or three feet. The testimony and the autopsy were in direct opposition to each other, and appeared to indicate that LAPD and the D.A.'s office had known of – and suppressed – evidence that Sirhan could not have fired bullets which hit Bobby.

What made the revelation more acute was that there had also been attempts by the Los Angeles authorities to silence the coroner. These began on the day of the Grand Jury indictment hearing with a warning from the D.A.'s office.

"I was advised not to have any information released as to the death of Senator Robert F. Kennedy," Noguchi recalled later. "I told them I cannot do that. I said that the cause of death and the circumstances surrounding it are like a jigsaw puzzle, and sometimes the puzzle is not complete. But I cannot adjust the circumstances or change the scientific facts."[325]

On March 4, 1969 – one week after his curtailed testimony in Sirhan's trial – Noguchi was suspended by the County of Los Angeles. Ten days later he was fired. The dismissal notice from the county's Board of Supervisors claimed – amongst a bizarre litany of sixty-four separate allegations – that "after Senator Robert Kennedy was shot but before the Senator actually died you expressed the belief that... his death would give you the chance to make a reputation for yourself".[326]

---

325 Thomas Noguchi, interviews with Tim Tate 1991–1992

326 Letter from Los Angeles County Board of Supervisors to Coroner Thomas Noguchi, March 14, 1969. Robert F. Kennedy Assassination Archives, University of Massachusetts Dartmouth.

The coroner hired a prominent trial attorney, Godfrey Isaac, to challenge the decision. Neither was in any doubt what lay behind the dismissal. "The problems were related to the Kennedy case," Noguchi said later. "Somebody decided that it was necessary to challenge my autopsy, to suggest that in some way I had botched it and that my findings could not be relied on. They did not, however, expect me to fight back in the way I did."[327]

Isaac filed an appeal and made clear that the post-mortem report – then still unpublished – would be at its heart. According to Isaac's account, lawyers for the county objected on the grounds that revealing its findings would cause "international repercussions".[328] For six weeks between June and July the Los Angeles County Civil Service Commissioners heard the case; on July 31 they issued a ruling that "not one single charge against Dr. Thomas T. Noguchi has been proven. He is re-instated forthwith."[329] It would not be the last time the coroner, and his autopsy, caused problems for the authorities.

Throughout 1970 Charach continued his investigations; in late summer he joined forces with a highly-respected independent authority on ballistics. Over a career spanning 35 years, William W. Harper had worked on more than 300 homicide cases involving firearms, had been a consulting criminalist with the Pasadena Police Department, and was a court-qualified expert witness in seven states.

In November, with the backing of Sirhan's legal team, he inspected the ballistic evidence, then held at the Los Angeles County Clerk's office. He brought with him a portable Balliscan camera to examine the bullets recovered from the victims and the test bullets which LAPD's criminalist DeWayne Wolfer used

327 Thomas Noguchi, interviews with Tim Tate 1991–1992
328 *Los Angeles Free Press: "Who Really Killed RFK?"*, June 12, 1970
329 Thomas T. Noguchi, *Coroner*, p. 124. Pocket Books 1983

for prove that Sirhan's gun had fired the fatal shot. By rotating a bullet in front of its high-powered lens, the Balliscan could photograph the unique lands, grooves and rifling patterns caused by a weapon's barrel.

Three slugs removed from three of the five victims were logged with their trial identifiers; People's Exhibit 47 was the bullet recovered from Bobby's neck, while numbers 52 and 54 were those taken from Ira Goldstein and William Weisel. On the witness stand Wolfer had testified that his tests proved that all three had been fired by Sirhan's gun. "Looking at the scratches under the comparison microscope," he told the court on February 24, 1969, "I can say that they were fired from this gun and no other gun".[330]

The three test bullets, which Wolfer had fired into a water tank and placed into an evidence envelope with the test weapon's serial number written on the label, were marked as People's Exhibit 55. He testified that when he compared them under a microscope with slugs taken from the victims, the lands, grooves and rifling were identical – thus proving that the crime scene bullets and the test bullets had all been fired from the same gun. Once again he spelled out the certainty of his conclusion: the test bullets came from Sirhan's gun "and no other gun".[331]

Harper's Balliscan examinations, however, found fundamental flaws in those claims: he recorded them in a sworn affidavit on December 28, 1970. The first problem was a significant difference between the slug removed from Bobby's neck (Exhibit 47) and the one recovered from William Weisel's stomach (Exhibit 54).

"My examinations disclosed no individual characteristics establishing that Exhibit 47 and Exhibit 54 had been fired by the same gun. In fact, my examinations disclosed that bullet

---

330 *People vs. Sirhan Bishara Sirhan*, Certified trial transcript, Vol. 15, page 42; February 24, 1969. California State Archives.
331 *Ibid.*

Exhibit 47 has a rifling angle approximately 23 minutes (14%) greater than the rifling angle of bullet exhibit 54. It is therefore my opinion that bullets 47 and 54 could not have been fired from the same gun."[332]

Worse, the supposed Kennedy neck bullet Wolfer claimed to have examined did not have the TN31 initials scratched on by Coroner Noguchi – suggesting that the criminalist could not have looked at it.

Nor did Wolfer's test bullet testimony hold up to scrutiny. The serial number of the test fire weapon, written on the front of the evidence envelope, showed it to have been H18602. But the revolver wrestled from Sirhan during the shooting bore the serial number – H53725: Wolfer had evidently used a different gun to fire the shots into the test tank, making his claim – "this gun and no other gun" – incorrect at best, or perjury at worst. Harper's inference was as logical as it was unequivocal.

"The only reasonable conclusion from the evidence developed by the police, in spite of their protestations to the contrary, is that two guns were being fired in the kitchen pantry of the Ambassador Hotel at the time of the shooting of Senator Kennedy."[333]

Harper's investigations overlapped with an appeal by Sirhan's new lawyers: their voluminous 740 page brief, filed on November 12, did not challenge the facts of the case against him, but instead sought to have his death sentence commuted to life in prison. The appeal was rejected, but within 18 months California's Supreme Court declared capital punishment unconstitutional, sparing the lives of 105 death row inmates including Sirhan.[334]

332 Affidavit of William W. Harper, Criminologist, December 28, 1970. Robert F. Kennedy Assassination Archives, University of Massachusetts Dartmouth.

333 *Ibid.*

334 *People vs. Anderson,* California Supreme Court, April 24, 1972.

Although Harper's forensic findings and analysis could not be ignored, the response by the Los Angeles authorities was not as the respected criminologist might have expected. Instead of ordering a review of Wolfer's claims, the Los Angeles District Attorney summoned a Grand Jury to accuse Harper of tampering with the bullets. There was not a shred of evidence to support this and the Grand Jury issued no indictments; but – for a time, at least – the tactic took media heat off the D.A.'s office.

In fact, rather than investigating Wolfer, the Los Angeles authorities endorsed him: on May 28, 1971 LAPD promoted him to the position of Chief Forensic Chemist. The move appalled lawyers and fellow criminalists alike, and later that same day Barbara Blehr, a prominent local attorney, filed a complaint with the city's Civil Service Commission, arguing that Wolfer was "completely unqualified" for his new role.[335] Her four-page letter alleged that he had "violated four separate precepts of investigative procedure in the Kennedy investigation", and was supported by statements from three notable ballistics experts, including William Harper.[336]

The official backing for Wolfer was particularly surprising given a warning, sent privately to Evelle J. Younger – the D.A. who had led Sirhan's prosecution and was now installed as California's Attorney General – from one of America's leading experts in criminology. Marshall Houts was a former FBI agent, judge and professor of law, who had also taught forensic pathology at the University of California Irvine Medical School, and in 1971 was Editor in Chief of the highly-respected *Trauma* journal.

"I have no personal interest in this matter," he wrote to Younger, "but [I] do have a deep academic and professional

---

335 Barbara Blehr: letter to Los Angeles Civil Service Commission, May 28, 1971. Robert F. Kennedy Assassination Archives, University of Massachusetts Dartmouth.
336 *Errors Charged In Kennedy Gun Probe; Los Angeles Times,* May 29, 1971.

concern over Wolfer's horrendous blunders in the past and those he will commit in the future if he continues on in his present assignment.... Wolfer suffers from a great inferiority complex for which he compensates by giving the police exactly what they need to obtain a conviction.

"He casts objectivity to the winds and violates every basic tenet of forensic science and proof by becoming a crusading advocate. This is rationalized as being entirely legitimate since the accused man is guilty anyway..."[337]

Wolfer responded to Blehr's charges by filing a $2 million libel suit. It was later dismissed by the California Superior Court, but not before attorneys for the City of Los Angeles secured a judicial order that his ballistics report – and the entire LAPD file on Bobby's assassination – should be kept secret; the ruling, on December 8, 1971, stated that "the public interest would be served by keeping it confidential".[338]

LA law – the alliance of the D.A.'s office and police department – appeared determined not to live up to the promise of disclosure made in 1969. In spring 1974, Baxter Ward – a former television investigative journalist who had been elected to the County Board of Supervisors – announced plans to hold public hearings which questioned the inconsistencies in the ballistic evidence.

"We presently have a situation in which it is claimed... that three bullets in the case do not match up," he explained. "They are a bullet from the body of Senator Kennedy, one from the

---

337 *Letter from Marshall Houts to Evelle J. Younger:* June 26, 1971. Robert F. Kennedy Assassination Archives, University of Massachusetts Dartmouth.

338 *DeWayne A. Wolfer vs. Barbara Warner Blehr:* Superior Court of The State of California, December 8, 1971. Robert F. Kennedy Assassination Archives, University of Massachusetts Dartmouth.

person of a spectator who was shot, and one from the test firing of the Sirhan weapon itself."[339]

Ward wanted Wolfer to testify before the hearings, but – backed by LAPD and L.A. District Attorney Joseph P. Busch – the criminalist refused to appear. Although the Supervisors heard evidence from nine witnesses, including three ballistics experts who supported William Harper's findings as well as from Coroner Noguchi, who re-stated his autopsy findings, without the co-operation of LA law enforcement Ward's enquiry stalled. It was, as he warned his fellow Board members, a position which undermined public confidence. "Until [the] authorities resolve these contradictions, there will be a perpetuation of the mystery, confusion and theories that have been allowed to develop and (in some cases) be sold for profit."[340]

The same thought had occurred to others. Allard K. Lowenstein, a former US Congressman who had helped Bobby write his "Ripple of Hope Speech" to South African students in 1966, was asked by Hollywood star Robert Vaughan to back a campaign for the re-opening of the assassination case. Lowenstein was reluctant, believing that claims Sirhan had not murdered Bobby were "absurd" and he planned to persuade Vaughan "to avoid further involvement in such foolishness." He discovered instead that such evidence as had been disclosed all pointed towards Sirhan's innocence of the assassination.

"The police report agreed with the coroner about the range (point blank) and the direction (from behind) of the bullets that hit Senator Kennedy," he wrote later. "So I proceeded through

---

339 Baxter T. Ward, County Supervisor: press release, April 4, 1974. Robert F. Kennedy Assassination Archives, University of Massachusetts Dartmouth.

340 Baxter T. Ward, County Supervisor: *Memo to Board of Supervisors,* April 10, 1974. Robert F. Kennedy Assassination Archives, University of Massachusetts Dartmouth.

the Grand Jury and trial records, searching for testimony that placed Sirhan's gun to the rear and within inches of Kennedy. There was none."[341]

Lowenstein was even more troubled by the problems surrounding Wolfer's ballistics testimony and the apparent evidence of more bullets than Sirhan's eight-shot revolver could have fired. He made an appointment to meet the District Attorney in the hope that there would be a logical explanation for the inconsistencies. He was about to run into the strange reluctance of LA law enforcement to provide any answers.

"The official response to my questions was as peculiar as the contradictions in the evidence... every official I saw at the D.A.'s office was polite and talked about cooperation, but nobody did anything much... When a question was answered at all, the answer often turned out to be untrue – not marginally untrue but enthusiastically, aggressively and sometimes quite imaginatively untrue."[342]

A joint live appearance with District Attorney Busch on NBC's *Tomorrow* show in December 1974 highlighted this official willingness to lie. Challenged about the conflict between Noguchi's autopsy findings of point blank shots and eyewitness testimony which placed Sirhan several feet away, the D.A. flatly denied the problem existed.

"It was point blank, right in the ear of the Senator. The gun was right there... and we can show it." When Lowenstein fired back: "Who has said they saw it? Just name one witness that said they saw a gun, point blank, fired into Senator Kennedy's ear", Busch responded "Would you like Mr. Uecker, the man that grabbed his [Sirhan's] arm?"[343]

---

341 Allard K. Lowenstein: *The Murder of Robert Kennedy, Suppressed Evidence of More than One Assassin? Saturday Review,* February 17, 1977
342 *Ibid.*
343 *Tomorrow Show,* NBC TV, December 18, 1974

In the moments before the assassination Karl Uecker, the Ambassador Hotel's assistant *Maître D'*, was holding Bobby's hand and leading him through the pantry; as the closest witness, and the man who pinned Sirhan down on the steam table, he had been the prosecution's star witness at trial. In the intervening years he had returned to his native Germany; when Lowenstein tracked him down there, Uecker was adamant that Busch was lying. "I told the authorities that Sirhan never got close enough for a point-blank shot: never," he said.[344]

But, with all the original witness statements still locked away in LAPD's files, it was impossible to verify Uecker's claim, and Lowenstein's efforts received little coverage. They did, however, prompt further falsehoods from LA law enforcement. The morning after the *Tomorrow* show aired, Lyn D. Compton, the lead prosecutor at Sirhan's trial, wrote to the *Los Angeles Times* on the headed notepaper of his new employers – the California Court of Appeal.

Questioning Lowenstein's motives as "suspect", and denouncing his suggestion of a possible second gunman as "absurd" and "a disservice to the country", Compton pronounced that "not one single witness has ever testified to seeing anyone else firing a gun in that pantry."[345]

This, as Compton knew well, was simply untrue. Less than 25 minutes after the assassination, Don Schulman, the young film-runner for KNXT television, had been interviewed on tape by Continental News Service. He told reporter Jeff Brent that he saw a security guard draw his weapon and shoot back at the

---

344 Allard K. Lowenstein: *The Murder of Robert Kennedy, Suppressed Evidence of More than One Assassin? Saturday Review,* February 17, 1977

345 Lynn. D. Compton, Associate Justice, California Court of Appeal: *Letter to Los Angeles Times,* December 19, 1974 (published: December 30, 1975). Robert F. Kennedy Assassination Archives, University of Massachusetts Dartmouth.

suspected assassin. He had repeated this story to Ted Charach, in an interview for Charach's 1973 feature-length documentary *The Second Gun.*

"I was in the pantry-way following the Senator ... The Senator had just finished shaking hands with someone and ... the *Maître D'* ... took his hand. As we were slowly pushed forward, another man stepped out and he shot. Just then the guard, who was standing behind Kennedy, took out his gun and he fired also."[346]

Since Charach's film was then playing in movie theatres across the country, and had attracted reviews (both good and bad) in major newspapers, Compton's claim was as inexplicable as it was false. The former prosecutor must also have known that Schulman had been interviewed by Special Unit Senator: but his statements remained locked in the files which LAPD and D.A.'s office still refused to release.

Some indication of what was – or at least had been – in those files emerged in the wake of two law suits brought by Paul Schrade in the summer of 1975. As a surviving victim of the pantry shooting, Schrade had good reason to seek the truth, but he had initially been reluctant to join the growing calls for a new investigation. "It wasn't an easy decision for me," he recalled later. "I agonized over it, but after speaking with Allard Lowenstein and looking at the material Lillian Castellano and Floyd Nelson had developed, I agreed to get involved."[347]

On August 4, Lowenstein and Paul Schrade, supported by CBS TV, filed suit demanding a review of all the evidence. The case was unsuccessful, but a second attempt by Schrade, together with Baxter Ward and the Board of Supervisors, led the California Superior Court to order a re-inspection of the ballistic evidence. Seven independent firearms experts examined

---

346 *The Second Gun.* ©: Theodore Charach and Gérard Alcan, 1973.
347 Paul Schrade: interviews with Tim Tate, 1991–2016

the bullets recovered from the shooting victims: the consultants unanimously concluded that it was not possible to match them with Sirhan's Iver Johnson revolver – thus directly contradicting Wolfer's findings. Their report was careful, however, to stress that the panel's tests did not provide "substantive or demonstrable evidence to indicate that more than one gun was used to fire any of the bullets examined".[348]

LA law enforcement immediately put a misleading spin on this careful scientific statement, prompting newspaper reports that the panel of experts had conclusively ruled that "there was no second gun in the assassination of Senator Robert F. Kennedy".[349]

This misdirection infuriated one of the experts: veteran criminalist and forensic scientist Lowell W. Bradford issued a statement denouncing the "improper" interpretation of the panel's report and stressing that "the firearms examination simply closes one episode of the evidence evaluation and should not constrain further efforts to resolve valid questions concerning the possibility of the firing of a second gun at the assassination scene".[350] LA's law enforcement bodies, however, seemed determined to prevent any such enquiries.

On August 21, LAPD announced that immediately after the shooting it had removed the pantry ceiling panels and door frames – including the centre dividers in the swinging doors which Bobby had passed through. Both the tiles and the woodwork bore apparent evidence of bullets or bullet holes – evidence

---

348 *Comprehensive Joint Report of the Firearms Examiners*, October 4, 1975. Robert F. Kennedy Assassination Archives, University of Massachusetts Dartmouth.

349 *Los Angeles Times,* October 8, 1975

350 *Statement of Lowell W. Bradford, Forensic Scientist,* October 7, 1975. . Robert F. Kennedy Assassination Archives, University of Massachusetts Dartmouth.

which had been photographed within hours of the shooting. Yet, according to LAPD's statement, it had destroyed all of these crucial materials, together with all records of what tests had been performed on them; it described the destruction as "routine".

On its own, the admission was shocking. But what followed showed that LAPD and the D.A.'s office were determined to obstruct further investigations into the issue.

In support of his law suits Schrade's attorney, Vincent Bugliosi, had tracked down the two LAPD officers shown, in the AP photograph taken on June 5, 1968, inspecting apparent bullet holes in the pantry woodwork. One, Sgt. Robert Rozzi, swore an affidavit for Bugliosi.

"Sometime during the evening [of June 4-5] when we were looking for evidence, someone discovered what appeared to be a bullet a foot and a half or so from the bottom of the floor in a door jamb behind the stage. I also personally observed what I believed to be a bullet in the place just mentioned. What I observed was a hole in the door jamb, and the base of what appeared to be a small calibre bullet was lodged on the hole ... I personally never removed the object from the hole, but I'm pretty sure someone else did."[351]

The importance of Rozzi's statement was that it was evidence of a ninth bullet – at least one more than Sirhan could have fired. But just as revealing was an affidavit by Bugliosi himself, describing his attempts to take a witness statement from the second officer shown in the photograph.

He interviewed Sgt. Charles Wright by phone on November 16. According to Bugliosi's sworn statement, Wright "unequivocally" confirmed Rozzi's account. "When I told him that Sgt. Rozzi had informed me that he was pretty sure that the bullet

---

351 *Affidavit of Sgt. Robert Rozzi,* November 15, 1975. Robert F. Kennedy Assassination Archives, University of Massachusetts Dartmouth.

was removed from the hole, Sgt. Wright replied 'There is no pretty sure about it. It was definitely removed from the hole, but I don't know who did it.'"[352]

Bugliosi arranged to meet Wright the following evening at LAPD's West L.A. Division house. But when he got there, Wright said "that he had just been instructed by Deputy City Attorney Larry Nagen not to give me a statement." [353]

After a series of phone calls to Nagen, Bugliosi finally secured permission to take the affidavit, but quickly discovered that Wright was now heavily qualifying his previously "definitive" recollections. The lawyer walked away, promising instead to subpoena Wright's testimony. But when he served the legal summons, LA's new District Attorney, John Van de Kamp[354] and Evelle Younger went to court and overturned it: Sgt. Wright was not permitted to provide an affidavit.

Bugliosi, a former prosecutor with a formidable reputation – he had won 105 of his 106 jury trials and had successfully brought Charles Manson and his murderous 'family' to justice – was undeterred. He quickly traced further witnesses who had seen evidence of bullets or bullet holes in the pantry woodwork.

Angelo Di Pierro was the Ambassador Hotel's senior *Maître D'* in June 1968. He gave Bugliosi a statement in which he said that after the shooting he had observed "a small calibre bullet lodged about a quarter of an inch into the wood on the center divider of the two swinging doors". He also made clear that he was well-qualified to know a bullet when he saw one: "I am quite familiar with guns and bullets, having been in the Infantry for

---

352 *Affidavit of Vincent P. Bugliosi,* November 17, 1975. Robert F. Kennedy Assassination Archives, University of Massachusetts Dartmouth.

353 *Ibid.*

354 Joseph Busch had died, unexpectedly, during the summer.

three and a half years. There is no question in my mind that this was a bullet and not a nail or any other object."[355]

Martin Patrusky was one of the hotel's waiters and, as an eyewitness to the shooting, had testified for the prosecution at Sirhan's trial. He had also been present when Wolfer and the crime scene specialists arrived at the Ambassador and watched the police team examine the woodwork.

His statement was as unequivocal as DiPierro's. "One of the officers pointed to two circled holes on the center divider of the swinging doors and told us that they had dug two bullets out of the center divider ... I am absolutely sure that the police told us two bullets were dug out of these holes ... and I would be willing to testify to this under oath and under penalty of perjury."[356]

Together, the statements of Sgt. Rozzi, DiPierro and Patrusky were strong *prime facie* evidence that there were more bullets and bullet holes than Sirhan could have fired. Coupled with the photographic evidence, they should have led to a re-investigation of the assassination. LAPD and the D.A's office chose to ignore them: instead, they embarked on a truly bizarre public relations exercise.

On December 18, Van de Kamp obtained a court order to mount a full search and examination of the Ambassador Hotel pantry with a view to locating any bullets or bullet holes in its various doorframes. Since he already knew that LAPD had removed all this woodwork immediately after the shooting – and indeed subsequently destroyed it – the search would plainly be futile. To cap the absurdity, Van de Kamp provided the court with statements taken two days earlier from hotel carpenters Dale Poore

---

355 *Statement of Angelo DiPierro*, December 1, 1975. Robert F. Kennedy Assassination Archives, University of Massachusetts Dartmouth.
356 *Statement of Martin Patrusky*, December 12, 1975. Robert F. Kennedy Assassination Archives, University of Massachusetts Dartmouth.

and Wesley Harrington in which they described removing the doorframes at the request of LAPD in June 1968.

Despite this, the D.A. and LAPD played out a cynical charade. For six hours, police officers and lawyers painstakingly examined the crime scene, recording at least half of the search on videotape. The recording showed them solemnly inspecting and then removing the crime scene woodwork, knowing all the while that what they were so carefully peering at had been installed after the assassination; they then pronounced themselves duly satisfied that all visible holes had been caused by carpentry nails. Thereafter, and with remarkable chutzpah, LA law enforcement insisted that this bogus exercise proved that the much-photographed bullet holes in the actual woodwork were nothing more sinister than nail holes.

According to a federal investigator who had been in the pantry in the hours following the shooting that claim was "completely false and erroneous".[357] From 1966 to 1971 William A. Bailey was an FBI Special agent based in Los Angeles: on the night of the assassination he was dispatched to the Ambassador Hotel to interview eyewitnesses and examine the crime scene. According to an affidavit Bailey swore for Bugliosi in November 1976: "At one point during these observations I (and several other agents) noted at least two small calibre bullet holes in the center post of the two doors ... there was no question in any of our minds as to the fact that they were bullet holes."[358]

Bailey was a solid and professional witness. After he left the Bureau, he was appointed assistant professor of police science at Gloucester County College, New Jersey; several weeks after

357 William A. Bailey: interviews with Tim Tate, 1992
358 *Declaration of William A. Bailey,* November14, 1976. Robert F. Kennedy Assassination Archives, University of Massachusetts Dartmouth.

he signed the affidavit, investigators working for the District Attorney questioned him there.

"I told them," he later recalled, "exactly what I saw. There were two bullet holes in that center divider. And you could actually see the base of a bullet in each hole. Anyone who says anything else does not know what they are talking about. And the importance of them is that they indicate the presence of two more bullets than Sirhan's gun was capable of firing. LAPD said it had accounted for all eight bullets in Sirhan's gun – and in that account, those two bullets in the center divider do not figure. What that meant was pretty simple: there was another gun in the pantry and it was fired. Sirhan's gun and the bullets fired from it are responsible for wounding five other people, but it did not fire the bullets that killed Bobby."[359]

Despite this, and although Bailey never wavered from his statement, the D.A. made no further enquiries. It simply buried his interview amongst all the evidence it still refused to release publicly.[360] In private, however, the District Attorney's office was working on an attempt to dismiss, once and for all, the claims that there had been a second gunman in the pantry.

In August 1975 the DA and the County of Supervisors had commissioned a "Special Counsel" to examine the evidence and produce a report for public consumption. Thomas Kranz, a local attorney, had been a volunteer on Bobby's 1968 campaign and had been in the Ambassador Hotel on the night of June 4. For two years he was given access to official files, LAPD and the FBI; in March 1977 he published his findings which, he hoped, would

---

359 William A. Bailey: interviews with Tim Tate, 1992
360 *Request to the Los Angeles County Grand Jury,* p. 26; March 30, 1992. Robert F. Kennedy Assassination Archives, University of Massachusetts Dartmouth.

"help to shed light on one of the most tragic occurrences in Los Angeles' history".[361]

Unfortunately they did not. Kranz's conclusions were little more than a lengthy re-statement of the official version of events. Although he criticized Wolfer, saying that "it is impossible to positively match the specific bullet which killed Robert Kennedy ... to the Sirhan revolver", given recent entries on the criminalist's file he could hardly have done otherwise: in November 1974 Wolfer was reprimanded by the City of Los Angeles for improper conduct[362] and a year later the California Appeals Court ruled that he had given false testimony in another case "with a reckless disregard for the truth" which "borders on perjury"[363] [364]

Kranz also allowed that "there is always the remote possibility that Sirhan acted within a conspiracy, either overt or covert"; nonetheless, the Special Counsel blithely – and inaccurately – dismissed the publicly-known inconsistencies in LAPD's evidence.

"Eyewitness testimony, ballistic and scientific evidence, and over six thousand separate interviews conducted by numerous police and intelligence agencies over the past eight years, all substantiate the fact that Sirhan acted alone."

Far from being, as the D.A. intended, a thorough and conclusive response to those clamouring for the case to be re-opened, Kranz' report was littered with 75 basic factual errors [365] and

---

361 *The Report of Thomas F. Kranz on the Assassination of Senator Robert F. Kennedy*, March 1977. California State Archives
362 *Los Angeles Times*: November 12, 1974
363 *Los Angeles Times*: December 3, 1975
364 In 1980 Wolfer was also suspended for 30 days for mishandling, misstoring and improperly analyzing ballistics evidence in another murder case. *LAPD Suspends Forensic Chemist, Los Angeles Times,* May 31, 1980
365 *Request to the Los Angeles County Grand Jury*, p.9; March 30, 1992. Robert F. Kennedy Assassination Archives, University of Massachusetts Dartmouth.

was, in the words of criminalist William Harper, an "amateurish piece of whitewash"[366].

More problematic still was that the evidence on which the Special Counsel based his conclusions remained strictly secret. It would take another 10 years – and a succession of fiercely resisted public interest law suits – for LAPD and the District Attorney to honour their promise of "full disclosure".

When those case files were finally opened to public scrutiny, they revealed thousands of original documents and dozens of tape recordings which undermined every aspect of the official story. But they also disclosed clear evidence of numerous conspiracies – and an official determination to cover them up.

---

366 William W. Harper: *Letter to Los Angeles County Board of Supervisors,* April 28, 1977. Robert F. Kennedy Assassination Archives, University of Massachusetts Dartmouth.

CHAPTER TEN:
DISCLOSURE

O n July 30, 1985 the Los Angeles Police Commission announced – grudgingly – that it would order the release of LAPD's 10 volume, 1,453-page summary report into Bobby's assassination.

The decision overrode objections from police chief Daryl Gates, who argued that "there are still people around who would be harmed" by disclosure[367], and it was qualified by the Commission's insistence on censoring the report prior to publication: the District Attorney's office was instructed to redact information "with due respect to issues of privacy and national security." But, seventeen years after the shooting in the pantry, it was the first crack in the previously impenetrable walls of official secrecy.

That secrecy stood in stark contrast to America's openness about other *causes célèbres*. The Warren Commission Report into the assassination of President John Kennedy had been published in September 1964 – three days after it was delivered to the White House – and by 1966 almost all of its 26 volumes of evidence and working papers were released to the National Archives. Senator Frank Church's post-Watergate Senate Select

---

367 *Opening the files on RFK: Philadelphia Enquirer,* August 4, 1985

Committee investigating the CIA, NSA and FBI had held open hearings, and published its highly-critical report within months of wrapping up in the spring of 1976.

The House of Representatives' Select Committee enquiring into the assassinations of President Kennedy and Dr. Martin Luther King issued its final report in 1979, the year after the FBI had released many of its files on the murder of Dr. King.

Throughout all of this, LAPD and the Los Angeles District Attorney's office resolutely fought a succession of court battles to prevent release of any information about Bobby's murder.

A group of determined men and women were at the heart of the long campaign to open up the files. Paul Schrade had been joined by Dr. Philip Melanson, a political science professor at Southeastern Massachusetts University; Dan Moldea, an investigative journalist with a long track record of reporting on the Mafia; and Greg Stone, a former aide to Allard Lowenstein.[368] Together with Lillian Castellano and Floyd Nelson and Los Angeles attorney Marilyn Barrett, they formed the Assassination Truth Committee and harried the police commission to keep its promise. "There are unanswered questions about the case," Schrade told a hearing in February 1986. "You have been using every legal means to obstruct us getting them. I have grave concerns about the intent of the commission."[369]

Those concerns were justified when, on March 4, the LAPD Summary Report was released. Originally written in April 1969, it purported to be the definitive account of what the City Attorney's office described as "a very important event of historical

---

368 Lowenstein was himself murdered by a mentally-ill gunman in March 1980.

369 Paul Schrade: *Statement to Los Angeles Police Commission*, February 12, 1986. Robert F. Kennedy Assassination Archives, University of Massachusetts Dartmouth.

importance".[370] That ambition was rather defeated by the heaviness with which the censor had wielded his pen: 72% of witness names – and a host of entire pages – had been blacked out.

The Assassination Truth Committee began another exhausting round in the seemingly-endless battle with LA law enforcement, arguing that "approximately 95% of the police file currently remains withheld"[371]. It was backed by a coalition of voices from politics – Bobby's confidantes Arthur M. Schlesinger and Frank Mankiewicz – and Hollywood: actors Robert Vaughan, Paul Le Mat and Martin Sheen all demanded honest disclosure of the files. Sheen wrote to the Police Commission: "As someone who has played the role of Robert Kennedy on television, and who feels very deeply the loss to our country when leaders of his stature and greatness are struck down by violence ... I believe it is extremely important that the _full_ police materials be released ... It is imperative that the American public gets the full and complete official record of this event at last."[372]

Eventually the pressure told. In December 1986 Los Angeles Mayor Tom Bradley announced that all the files would be released and promised that researchers would have "quick access" to them[373]. The promise took months to fulfil: it was not until August 4, 1987 that LAPD finally turned over its SUS case materials to the California State Archives in Sacramento. Finally, eight months later on April 19, 1988, the state archives officially opened to the public its Robert F. Kennedy Assassination Investigation Records.

---

370 James H. Kahn, Los Angeles City Attorney; covering letter to Los Angeles Police Commission. California State Archives.

371 Press release: Greg Stone, June 3, 1986. Robert F. Kennedy Assassination Archives, University of Massachusetts Dartmouth.

372 Martin Sheen: letter to Los Angeles Police Commission, July 29, 1985. Robert F. Kennedy Assassination Archives, University of Massachusetts Dartmouth.

373 Statement of Mayor Tom Bradley, December 3, 1986. Robert F. Kennedy Assassination Archives, University of Massachusetts Dartmouth.

The sheer volume of material was staggering: 50,000 pages of police documents, including reports of many of the 3,470 interviews conducted, transcripts of eyewitness testimony, hundreds of audio and visual recordings as well as 990 photographs. In total the collection covered 36 cubic feet.

Cataloguing and indexing this archive – let alone sifting through the mountain of previously undisclosed data for revelatory information – would be a Herculean task. But it was what was missing from the files which was most immediately concerning. There was no trace of the tape recorded statements of 51 key witnesses, including 29 who had given accounts which "relate directly or indirectly to questions of conspiracy"[374]. More disturbingly still, there was evidence that LAPD had deliberately destroyed potentially vital evidence.

According to its logs, disclosed in the files, Special Unit Senator had amassed 3,400 photographs during its investigation; yet before Sirhan's trial had even begun it had destroyed 2,410 of them. A file note recorded that on August 21, 1968 SUS had "deposited these photos in the [County General] Hospital incinerator and witnessed their destruction."[375] There was no record of who had shot these photographs nor of what they showed.

What made this more remarkable was that the incineration took place one day after the head of S.U.S. formally instituted a policy for the retention of photographs: a memo from Captain Hugh Brown ordered that "all photographs received from outside sources shall be dated and initialled by the person accepting ... Pictures of no value at this time shall be filed alphabetically by contributor and shall be indexed in the master card file."[376]

---

374 John Burns, California State Archivist: Press conference, April 19, 1988.
375 *Employee Report: Burning of S.U.S. Photographs, 8-21-68.* Special Unit Senator files, Volume 27; p.199. California State Archives.
376 Memo from Capt. Hugh Brown to Chief Robert A. Houghton, August 20, 1968. Special Unit Senator files, Volume 24; p.121. California State Archives.

Nor was this the only unexplained destruction of evidence. In addition to disposing of the ceiling tiles and pantry door frames, in July 1968 S.U.S. had sent two of its "student workers", Richard Groller and Thurston Best, to the General Hospital to "burn important papers". There was no explanation of what these documents were: only the fact that the pair had a traffic accident, and had to write up an explanation of the damage to their police cruiser, preserved any record of the decision to destroy "important" S.U.S. papers.[377]

According to former FBI Special Agent (and assistant professor of law enforcement) William Bailey, LAPD's burning of photographs, documents and physical pieces of the crime scene evidence ran contrary to the fundamental tenets of policing. "There's no good reason to have destroyed, at such an early stage, all that evidence. I cannot come up with a reason – not a logical reason – for why they would have done that."[378]

But the most surprising act of destruction concerned the Iver Johnson revolver with serial number H 18602 – the weapon which, according to LAPD criminalist DeWayne Wolfe's notes, had been used to fire test bullets for comparison with those recovered from the victims. Throughout his various court appearances in the 1970s, Wolfer had never been able to resolve the question of whether he had used this gun for the tests or whether he had actually fired Sirhan's revolver, serial number H 53725, and simply made a clerical error in recording the serial number. LAPD's decision to destroy H18602 in either July 1968 or 1969 – the files disclosed two contradictory dates for this – prevented new tests to establish once and for all which revolver Wolfer had used for bullet comparison.

---

377 Traffic Accident reports by Thurston Best and Richard Groller, July 18, 1968. Special Unit Senator files, Volume 31; p.79-80. California State Archives.

378 William A. Bailey. Interviews with Tim Tate, 1992

The files also included the criminalist's analysis of the shots fired in the pantry – including photographs and a diagram – which purported to explain the trajectory and flight path of all eight bullets from Sirhan's gun. None of this had been addressed in the murder trial, since the defence team had chosen not to examine, much less challenge, any of the crime scene evidence. The 1987 release of the S.U.S. papers would reveal Wolfer's thesis to be physically impossible.

His account of what he termed the "#2 bullet" stated that it "passed through the right shoulder pad of Senator Kennedy's suit coat (never entered his body) and travelled upward striking victim Schrade in the center of his forehead".[379] He had supported this with a diagrammatic sketch and, most tellingly, photographs of a re-enactment taken at the crime scene on June 5, 1968. These showed Wolfer wearing Bobby's jacket with long metal rods passing through the bullet holes to demonstrate their flight path. The rod simulating the trajectory of bullet #2 was almost vertical: for it to have hit Paul Schrade would have required Schrade to be performing a bizarre contortion.

"I would have to be around nine feet tall – and to have somehow put my head down on Bob's shoulder – for that to be possible," Schrade said. "It was completely absurd."[380] It was also contradicted by LAPD's own evidence elsewhere in the files. The detectives had drawn up a schematic diagram – based on all the eyewitness testimony – which showed the position of each of the shooting victims in the pantry: it placed Schrade several feet behind Bobby.

"Wolfer's claims about this bullet did not make any sense," Schrade recalled, "and that makes me question whether the

379 DeWayne A. Wolfer: Bullet trajectory study, June 5, 1968. Special Unit Senator files, Volume 33; p.166 California State Archives.
380 Paul Schrade. Interviews with Tim Tate, 1991–2016

whole trajectory analysis was invented to fit with the preconception that only Sirhan fired his gun. What's certain is that the bullet which passed through Bob's jacket could not have been the one which hit me. And that makes me believe there was more than one gun fired."[381]

Nor was this the only problem with the trajectory analysis. According to Wolfer, "bullet #8 struck the plaster ceiling and then struck victim [Elizabeth] Evans in the head. This bullet was recovered from the victim's head and booked as evidence."[382] Once again, LAPD's own documents in the S.U.S. files contradicted Wolfer's claim that the slug was on a downward path: its report detailing Evans' injuries stated that "the bullet entered the scalp of the forehead, just below the hair line, off center to the right and travelled upward."[383] Since both versions could not simultaneously be accurate, LAPD had concealed, for 20 years, its own knowledge that Wolfer's trajectory report was – at best – questionable.

What made it even more dubious was the diagrammatic sketch the criminalist had produced to support his thesis[384]. This showed "bullet #8" being fired from a point well to the rear of all the other shots, before passing through a ceiling tile and ricocheting downwards to hit Ms. Evans. There was no evidential basis for this alleged firing position – indeed all the eyewitness testimony about Sirhan's position directly contradicted it. Instead, the drawing appeared to have been an attempt to account for the maths of the pantry. Its dimensions, and the height of the ceiling meant that had he placed the gunman accurately it would have been impossible to line up "bullet #8" with Ms Evans; only

---

381 *Ibid.*

382 DeWayne A. Wolfer: Bullet trajectory study, June 5, 1968. Special Unit Senator files, Volume 33; p.166 California State Archives.

383 LAPD crime report – Elizabeth Evans, June 6, 1968. Special Unit Senator files, Volume 77; p.97 California State Archives.

384 Special Unit Senator files, Volume 46; p.13 California State Archives.

by artificially putting Sirhan further back – for this shot alone – could Wolfer make the angles work.

The files also revealed that LAPD had suppressed eyewitness evidence which conflicted with the autopsy findings. S.U.S. officers had identified 71 people (in addition to the six victims) in the pantry at the time when Sirhan opened fire[385]: not one placed him in a position to fire the shots which Coroner Noguchi identified as coming from behind at a distance of no more than one to three inches. Instead, all those who saw the shooting placed Sirhan between one and a half and six feet from Bobby – and always in front of him.

In particular, of the five eyewitnesses designated as "best" by the District Attorney's Office because they were physically closest to Bobby, four gave accounts which could not be reconciled with the fatal wounds (the fifth was never asked about Sirhan's position when he opened fire). Karl Uecker, who had been leading Bobby through the pantry was interviewed, on tape, at Rampart station on June 5, 1968. He repeatedly told the detectives that Sirhan was "right in front of me ... right in front"[386]. This indicated that Uecker was physically between Bobby and Sirhan's gun – which would have made it impossible for Sirhan to have fired the fatal shots. The officers didn't question Uecker about the distance between Sirhan and Bobby, but at the Grand Jury hearing, held behind closed doors two days later Deputy D.A. Morio Fukuto specifically asked him: "How far was the suspect from Senator Kennedy and yourself at the time that the first shot took place?". Uecker replied: "How far? As far as my left hand can reach ..."[387]

---

385 *Victims and Witnesses in Kitchen*: Special Unit Senator files, Volume 85; p.149 California State Archives.

386 Transcript of recorded interview with Karl Uecker, June 5, 1968. Special Unit Senator files, Volume 102; p.232-243 California State Archives.

387 Karl Uecker, transcript of Grand Jury testimony, June 7, 1968. Special Unit Senator files, Volume 97; p.106-107 California State Archives.

Hotel bus boy Juan Romero was possibly the last person to shake Bobby's hand before the shooting and, according to LAPD's log of his interview in the early hours of June 5, had been close enough to receive facial powder burns when the gunman opened fire.[388]

Two days later he was interviewed by the FBI and told the Agents that he "noticed that the gun was approximately one yard from Senator Kennedy's head".[389] LAPD's card index recorded that S.U.S. received a copy of this interview.[390] On the same day that Romero gave his account, the FBI also took a statement from Vincent DiPierro. He was just behind Bobby at the time of the shooting and said that "the revolver was about three to five feet from Senator Kennedy's head."[391]

Attorney Frank Burns, a senior campaign official who was standing behind Bobby when the shooting began, gave a written statement to LAPD in the form of a letter, dated June 12, 1968. In it he described seeing an "extended arm holding a gun" in front of him and that he estimated "the gun would be about even with the front edge of the serving table."[392] Burns later told Dan Rather, in an interview for CBS TV, that Sirhan's gun was "never closer than a foot and a half to two feet" to Bobby; when Rather questioned whether the muzzle of the gun could have been closer, Burns insisted "No way".[393]

LAPD attempted to square this circle of conflicting evidence by claiming, in its Summary Report, that Sirhan had "lunged

---

388 Special Unit Senator files, Volume 51; p.153 California State Archives.
389 Interview with Juan Romero, June 7, 1968. FBI files, X-1 – Vol.2. p.72-76. California State Archives.
390 Special Unit Senator files, Volume RI-SA; p.188 California State Archives.
391 Statement of Vincent Thomas Di Pierro, June 7, 1968. X-1 – Vol.2. p.67-71. California State Archives.
392 Statement of Frank J. Burns, June 12, 1968. Special Unit Senator files, Volume 102; p.338-343 California State Archives
393 Frank J. Burns interview with Dan Rather, CBS TV, January 5, 1976

towards the Senator with his right arm fully extended" and that this – somehow – enabled him to fire his gun at "point blank range" from behind Bobby's right ear.[394] But the full files showed that it had manipulated and distorted the fragmentary evidence on which it based this suggestion.

Lisa Urso, the 18-year-old San Diego college student and campaign volunteer, was one of LAPD's ostensible key witnesses. She had been several feet in front of – and facing towards – Bobby when the shooting began and, according to an internal police memo, "saw Sirhan reach to his waist area with his right hand. He removed a gun and lunged towards the Senator with his right arm fully extended."[395]

Unfortunately for LAPD the report of Urso's interview with S.U.S., on June 27, 1968, revealed that she had made no mention whatsoever of any "lunge" by Sirhan, and although she had used the phrase "point blank range" this was so heavily qualified to raise severe doubts that the teenager understood its meaning. "She was not sure of the distance," the reporting officer noted, "but from what she observed she thought the shot was fired from point blank range"[396]. LAPD chose to omit this cautious caveat from its public statements; instead it spun Urso's testimony as definitive proof that Sirhan had been close enough to fire the fatal bullets. It would not be the last time that LA law enforcement suppressed her problematic testimony.

Between 1968 and 1977, LAPD and the D.A.'s office staged three reconstructions of the shooting: each was filmed by LAPD.

---

394 Summary report of the Los Angeles Police Department Investigation of the Senator Robert Kennedy Assassination, p.149. California State Archives.

395 Internal LAPD memo, May 10, 1974: Special Unit Senator files, Volume 122, p.138. California State Archives.

396 Lisa Urso interview, June 27, 1968. Special Unit Senator files, Volume 61; p.185-186 California State Archives

The first, on November 12, 1968, featured Juan Romero, Karl Uecker, Vincent DiPierro and his father Angelo, waiter Martin Patrusky and Lisa Urso, standing in the positions they had occupied in the pantry when the shots were fired.

The following day a second re-enactment was staged with Frank Burns, Jesse Unruh, Rafer Johnson and three other bystanders depicting how they reacted after the shooting began. Both recordings showed quite clearly that these eyewitnesses placed Sirhan several feet in front of Bobby – a position from which he physically could not have fired the fatal shots.

But it was the third reconstruction, filmed by the D.A. in 1977, which was most telling. It once again featured Lisa Urso, and it was filmed against the backdrop of the Schrade and Bugliosi attempts to have the assassination re-investigated. Urso was shown facing an unidentified man representing Bobby while the camera microphone recorded her clear recollection of what had happened. "Somebody brushed my side and looked as if they were going to shake hands with the Senator and … the person who had the gun in their hand was about three or four feet from the Senator"[397].

All of these videotaped re-stagings contradicted the official account of the assassination, and all had been suppressed by LA law enforcement for twenty years – kept under lock and key at Parker Center and in the D.A.'s office, along with the 50,000 pages of S.U.S. files.

Those files also contained the key to uncovering evidence about the number of bullets and bullet holes found at the crime scene. Wolfer claimed to have accounted for all eight shots Sirhan had fired – which meant that if any additional slugs had been found in the woodwork or walls of the crime scene, there must have been a second gunman.

---

397 Videotape reconstruction by Los Angeles District Attorney's Office; 1977. California State Archives.

Between 1988 and 1990 journalist Dan Moldea, working with the Assassination Truth Committee, used LAPD's internal memos and reports to track down police officers and Los Angeles County Sheriff's deputies who had examined the pantry and surrounding corridors in the hours after the shooting. Some refused to speak, while others could not remember anything in detail; but seven lawmen gave tape-recorded interviews in which they unequivocally said they had seen clear evidence of more than one gun being fired.

Thomas A. Beringer was a sheriff's deputy. On the night of the assassination he and his colleague arrived at the Ambassador Hotel shortly within minutes of the shooting and found themselves confronted with a crowd of up to 100 people in or around the crime scene. Beringer saw one man, dressed in a tuxedo, using a knife to dig in the middle of the centre divider at about eye-level.

"I remember one person trying to take a bullet out of the wall with a knife, a silver knife, for a souvenir ... as I recall it was a silverware knife. It wasn't doing any good."

Beringer stepped in, stopped the man from doing any further damage and reported the incident to LAPD's "crime scene people ... and then later on that's where the bullet was, I think." When Moldea challenged him about whether he was sure it was a bullet Beringer replied: "It wasn't a nail. It was a definite bullet hole."[398]

Raymond M. Rolon, then an LAPD sergeant, assigned to the crime scene area told Moldea that a plain clothes detective had pointed out a bullet hole to him. "I'm standing there, looking around there, and he says, 'Oh, we've got a bullet over there in

---

398 Transcript of interview with Thomas A. Beringer by Dan Moldea, December 19, 1989. Robert F. Kennedy Assassination Archives, University of Massachusetts Dartmouth.

the door jamb …"[399]. Charles Wright, the LAPD officer who was shown in the AP photograph kneeling by a doorframe and pointing at a bullet said "My opinion then was that it was a bullet. And I stand by it."[400] Since the D.A.'s office and LAPD had prevented Wright from giving an affidavit to Vincent Bugliosi in 1975, his unequivocal statement to Moldea carried the strong implication that he knew something LA law enforcement wanted to conceal.

The recollections of the officers who spoke to Moldea suggested that LAPD had found numerous additional bullet holes and even bullet fragments at the crime scene. Ken Vogl was Wilson's partner at Rampart Division: he arrived at the Ambassador Hotel shortly after the shooting and remained on duty from the early hours of June 5 through to the evening. At the time of his interview in 1989 he was still a serving police officer, having risen to the rank of detective in LAPD's Central Division.

"We were looking for bullet fragments and stuff in the kitchen where the shooting occurred," he said. "There was more than one bullet found: there was one on the floor by the wall: it was either a bullet hole or a piece of bullet by the floor. And there was at least one bullet hole in the ceiling – high." [401]

Charles Collier was LAPD's civilian photographer. In 1968 he was 51 and a veteran of the US Army's 101st Airborne Division during World War Two: he had been with LAPD since 1952 and had risen to supervisor in the photo lab at Parker Center. In the

---

399 Transcript of interview with Robert M. Rolon by Dan Moldea, March 18, 1990. Robert F. Kennedy Assassination Archives, University of Massachusetts Dartmouth.

400 Transcript of interview with Charles A. Wright by Dan Moldea, January 19, 1990. Robert F. Kennedy Assassination Archives, University of Massachusetts Dartmouth.

401 Transcript of interviews with Kenneth E. Vogl by Dan Moldea, December 28-29, 1989. Robert F. Kennedy Assassination Archives, University of Massachusetts Dartmouth.

early hours of June 5 he arrived at the crime scene with DeWayne Wolfer and was assigned to take "orientation photos". "They told me…'we want all of the bullet holes and all of the blood and everything'". Collier saw, and photographed, "six or seven" bullet holes "in the walls in the pantry of the kitchen", and was certain of what he had observed through his camera lens. "I remember taking lots of pictures of bullet holes…and a bullet hole looks like a bullet hole if you've photographed enough of them."[402]

Wolfer and his men, according to another LAPD officer, recovered slugs from the centre divider which held the pair of swinging doors though which Bobby had entered the pantry. Robert F. Rock was an inspector in the Patrol Bureau and, in the aftermath of the shooting, was put in charge of press liaison at the Ambassador Hotel.

He told Moldea that he didn't see bullets himself but said that he knew the criminalist had recovered one from the wood-work. "In fact, they took a whole door frame to preserve it." [403]

Ken Vogl watched DeWayne Wolfer's crime scene team reconstruct the bullet flight paths by stretching lines of string from Sirhan's shooting position to the points in the walls, wood-work and ceiling where the slugs – or their fragments – had embedded themselves. "There were strings all over the place because I think there were more bullets in the ceiling. More than one, anyway…there was more than one string going up there." When Moldea asked him, on a scale of one to ten, how certain he was about these recollections, Vogl replied: "Oh, it was a ten. There's no doubt. I saw fragments…I can't say that it was over

402 Transcript of interview with Charles Collier by Dan Moldea, December 16, 1989. Robert F. Kennedy Assassination Archives, University of Massachusetts Dartmouth.
403 Transcript of interviews with Robert F. Rock by Dan Moldea, February 10, 1990. Robert F. Kennedy Assassination Archives, University of Massachusetts Dartmouth.

half the bullet or whatever. But I'm sure there were bullet fragments ... I saw them on the floor."[404]

Wolfer's deputy on the night was Scientific Investigation Division officer Sgt. David Butler. He had joined the department a week before the shooting and considered Wolfer a "mentor and close personal friend". At the time of his 1990 interview with Moldea, Butler was still employed as a firearms examiner in the unit. He said that he arrived at the Ambassador Hotel two hours after the shooting, and was present for much of Wolfer's examination of the crime scene.

At one point, he said, the criminalist "took the two bullets out of the wall"; he then clarified that it was the centre divider, rather than a wall, explaining that the SID team "tore" the divider out because "we had to disassemble it to find the bullets". When Moldea asked him whether they had found bullets, Butler answered "yes". "Basically we knew the bullets were in the walls or in the mouldings. We knew we were going to have to come back and get them ..." For good measure Butler also confirmed that he had been present when the bullets were dug out of the divider.[405]

Butler also recalled finding bullet fragments beside the steam table in the pantry. He explained that these were the result of ricochets – "When bullets hit concrete they shatter", [406] he told Moldea. But, since none of Sirhan's bullets (not even the Evans bullet) struck the hard pantry ceiling nor even hit the ceiling's softer drop tiles, the only concrete his bullets could hit would

404 Transcript of interviews with Kenneth E. Vogl by Dan Moldea, December 28-29, 1989. Robert F. Kennedy Assassination Archives, University of Massachusetts Dartmouth.

405 Transcript of interviews with David Butler by Dan Moldea, January 3, 1990. Robert F. Kennedy Assassination Archives, University of Massachusetts Dartmouth.

406 *Ibid.*

have been many feet from the steam table and further down the pantry.[407] The logical conclusion was that the fragments Butler found came from a second gun firing *towards* the steam table and from *behind* Bobby.

In total the files revealed substantial and fundamental problems with the official version of the assassination: the information within them suggested clearly that LAPD knew it was physically impossible for Sirhan to have killed Bobby.

Wolfer's trajectory analysis was simply impossible; the number of bullets, bullet fragments or bullet holes exceeded the number of shots Sirhan could have fired from his eight-chamber revolver; and the testimony of every eyewitness was incompatible with Thomas Noguchi's autopsy findings. All of this evidence had been suppressed by LA law enforcement for two decades.

"It appears they concluded within about an hour of the shooting that Sirhan acted alone," said Marilyn Barrett, the lawyer working with the Assassination Truth Committee. "They decided that would be their conclusion and they then tailored all of the evidence to fit it. They destroyed, altered or falsified anything which contradicted their presumption – and then they covered it up for twenty years."[408]

Schrade, Melanson and Stone, whose years of persistence had forced the files' disclosure issued a public statement castigating the "numerous errors and self-contradictions of the key police forensic science officer" and calling for the entire case to be re-opened.

"The release of official police and FBI records[409] which was expected to answer the major questions about the RFK

407

408 Marilyn Barrett: interviews with Tim Tate, 1991–2016

409 Prompted by Freedom of Information Act requests by Schrade and Melanson, the FBI released its files on the assassination between 1986 and 1988.

assassination, has instead thrown many of them into greater doubt," they argued. "What is unmistakable is that impartial efforts are now essential in order to clarify the facts of this case."[410]

But the key to uncovering the truth of what really happened in the Ambassador Hotel pantry on the night of June 4-5, 1968, was a single audio tape, turned over along with other materials to the California State Archives by LAPD and filed away in the mass of storage boxes in Sacramento. What was recorded on it was scientific proof of a second gun being fired: yet despite the official opening of the police investigation files in April 1988, the audio recording's monumental importance would go unnoticed for another sixteen years.

---

410 *Statement of Professor Philip Melanson, Paul Schrade and Gregory Stone,* May 15, 1990. Robert F. Kennedy Assassination Archives, University of Massachusetts Dartmouth.

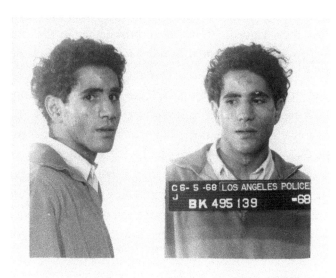

Los Angeles Police Department's mugshot of Sirhan Sirhan, taken within hours of the shooting.

The Iver Johnson .22 calibre revolver, serial number H53725, wrestled from Sirhan in the pantry. The serial number would come back to haunt Los Angeles Police Department.

Bystanders and Kennedy aides restraining Sirhan in the pantry, seconds after he began shooting. Hotel assistant Maître D Karl Uecker (in bow tie) looks on.

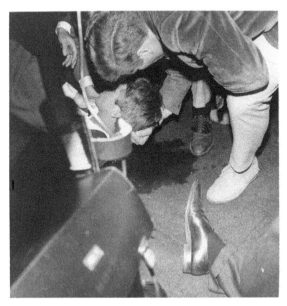

Robert Kennedy lies, mortally wounded, on the pantry floor.

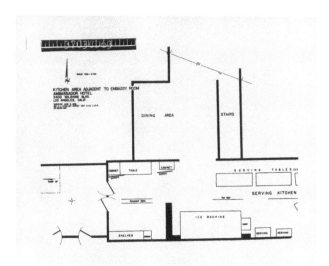

Los Angeles Police Department's diagram of the pantry layout and surrounding areas.

Sandy Serrano on the external staircase where she encountered the polka dot dress girl and her companions.

Robert Kennedy gives his victory speech at the Ambassador Hotel; less than a minute later he was shot and mortally wounded.

Surrounded by photographers and with his wife, Ethel at his side, Robert Kennedy gives his victory speech at the Ambassador Hotel.

"Now it's on to Chicago – and let's win there." Robert Kennedy speaks to his supporters at the Ambassador Hotel. Less than a minute later he would be shot in the hotel pantry.

V for Victory: winning the California Democratic primary put Robert Kennedy on course to challenge for the White House.

LAPD criminalist DeWayne Wolfer pointing to apparent bullet holes in the centre divider at the back of the pantry. The existence of additional bullet holes disproved the case against Sirhan, and this photograph was suppressed for two decades.

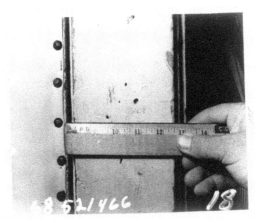

A scene of crimes officer measures an additional bullet hole, which has previously been identified by an LA Sheriff's Department officer. His badge number – 723 – is inscribed underneath the hole.

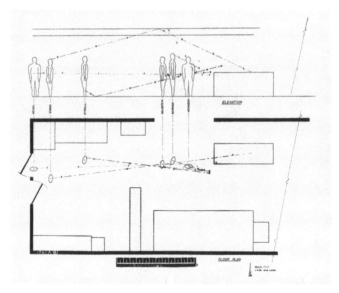

LAPD's diagrammatic explanation of the shooting. It was contradicted by the sworn testimony of every witness.

Wolfer, Coroner Thomas Noguchi and a scene of crimes officer use metal rods to recreate the angle of the shots which hit Robert Kennedy. Like most of the forensic evidence this contradicted LAPD's subsequent version of events.

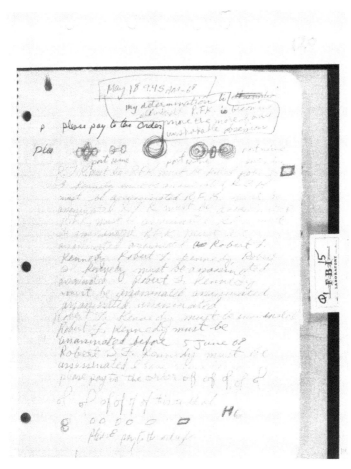

"RFK Must die". One of the pages from Sirhan's notebook, apparently showing that he planned to assassinate Robert Kennedy. Sirhan has no memory of writing this.

CHAPTER ELEVEN:
THE PRUSZYNSKI RECORDING

It arrived at the California State Archives in Sacramento in the huge volume of material turned over by the Los Angeles Police Department on August 4, 1987; but it was not catalogued and made available to the public – as Tape #CSA-K123 – until May 31, 1990. Even then, the Archives' description of the audio recording was bland and gave little clue to the true importance of its contents:

"CSA-K123 Pruszynski, Stus I-4837 June 4-5, 1968

At Ambassador Hotel on June 4; tape is his recording of events at the hotel. Includes end of RFK's speech, possible shots being fired, post-shooting hysteria in kitchen, and interviews with a man who claims Sirhan was not alone. Pruszynski narrates what he is seeing."[411]

Perhaps because of this unexciting label, or due to the delay in processing it, the release of the single audio recording would pass completely unnoticed for many years. And yet Tape #CSA-K123 is the single most important piece of evidence in the assassination. It is the only recording to have captured the sounds of the shooting in the Ambassador Hotel kitchen pantry: and it would, in time, provide scientific proof of more than one gunman.

---

411 Tape # CSA-K12. California State Archives.

***

In the spring of 1968 Stanislaw Pruszynski – "Stash" to his friends and colleagues[412] – was a 32-year-old Cold War-era Polish immigrant to Canada. He was also a reporter at the *Montreal Gazette*. In May he took an unpaid leave of absence and, armed with a cheap cassette tape recorder, set out to follow Bobby as an international news correspondent on the campaign trail.

"Things were moving in the United States and there was a lot of action ... and here I was in Montreal ... doing, you know, nothing very exciting," he recalled in 2007. "And then Eugene McCarthy decided to run for president ... Robert Kennedy came in and ... I decided this is where I have to be."[413]

At the time, Pruszynski was planning to write a book – "an outsider's view of the whole American political circus"[414] – and was surprised how quickly and easily he had been given a press pass and a place on the candidate's jet and train. "Security around Robert Kennedy was non-existent," he recalled later. "I arrived from Montreal, landed in Indiana. I met him first time at the airport in Indianapolis, and I presented him my business card, which was no longer really valid because I was on leave of absence from the Gazette ... And on the basis of that they accepted me with open arms."[415]

---

412 *"Stus"* was a mistyping by the RCMP which found its way into the archived records.

413 Documents held at the John F. Kennedy Presidential Library and Museum, Boston, Massachusetts, show that Pruszynski contacted Bobby's presidential campaign in late March 1968, just days after he announced his White House bid, and that by May Pruszynski was a member of the traveling Kennedy press corps.

414 Stanislaw Pruszynski, interview with Creative Differences, Warsaw, Poland, 2007

415 *Ibid.*

For the next month he travelled with Bobby's campaign through Nebraska, Oregon and, finally, California. "I always carried a tape recorder just in case so I wouldn't miss anything, and it was easier in many ways. It was hanging on my neck. It was easier than taking out a piece of paper and making notes."[416]

On the night of June 4, Pruszynski was in the Ambassador Hotel Embassy Room ballroom. He climbed on to the podium and placed his microphone and cassette recorder on the lectern to record the candidate's victory speech. When Bobby walked away after his victory speech, the young reporter set off behind him.

"I went over to the podium and I detached my tape recorder…and then as I walked with the crowd following Bob Kennedy, I suddenly heard a cry, lots of people shouting."[417]

Pruszynski had turned off his machine with a flip of his microphone switch. But in his haste to follow Bobby, he had unknowingly flipped it back on; as a result, his cheap cassette recorder captured the gunfire in the pantry, from a range of approximately 40 feet. But it was only later that he realised what he had recorded. "When I was there I didn't hear it. I mean I heard them [the shots], but of course it didn't register. But once I played the tape, the shots were very clear."[418]

Stash Pruszynski returned to Montreal a few days later and abandoned his dreams of writing a book about the campaign. He put away the cassette and forgot about it, until the Royal Canadian Mounted Police knocked on his door and asked, on behalf of the FBI, to borrow the tape. RCMP then dubbed a major portion of Pruszynski's cassette to a reel-to-reel tape and sent the open reel to the Bureau, which forwarded it on to its specialist laboratory in Washington D.C. for analysis.

---

416 *Ibid.*
417 *Ibid*
418 *Ibid.*

In June 1969, the laboratory reported that the RCMP's reel-to-reel dub had "been recorded at a non-standard speed on ½-track recorder and contained an interfering hum." The FBI lab overcame these problems by "adjusting the speed for a natural sound and equalizing the frequency response to enhance intelligibility". It then made two enhanced copies of the RCMP's open reel dub.[419]

The FBI evidently failed to realise the significance of the Pruszynski recording. It sent a copy of its version of the tape to LAPD, but noted that "after a review of the recording was made at Los Angeles ... it does not appear that anything pertinent to this investigation is contained in the recording."[420] It would be almost 35 years before anyone realised the fundamental importance of what Stash Pruszynski had, unwittingly, captured.

Brad Johnson had been interested in the controversies surrounding the assassination since the 1970s. From the late 1990s, while working as a writer for CNN in Atlanta, he began seeking out material held at the California State Archives in Sacramento, Dr. Philip Melanson's Robert F. Kennedy Assassination Archives at the University of Massachusetts Dartmouth, as well as from other sources, including America's three original broadcast television networks, CBS, NBC and ABC.

He painstakingly sought out audio recordings, film footage and video, eventually acquiring the videotaped live feeds from the TV cameras covering primary election night at the Ambassador Hotel. In time these enabled him to put together a unique synchronised timeline of the June 4-5, accurate to fractions of a second, and to identity the exact moment that the shooting was under way in the hotel's kitchen pantry. The

---

419 *Copy of tape recording made by Stus Pruszynski:* FBI files X-8, Vol.21, p.102. California State Archives
420 File note [undated]: FBI files X-8, Vol.21, p.6. California State Archives

materials were essential because only the immediate aftermath of the shooting – not the assassination itself – had been captured on camera and, three decades later, there was still no confirmed audio recording of the gunshot sounds.

In spring 2004 Brad requested copies of several audio tapes from the archives in Sacramento; one was Tape # CSA-K123. From its online description, indicating some "possible" shot sounds recorded, he didn't expect it to contain anything particularly significant; but when, on May 31, he listened to it on high-quality headphones, he immediately realized its importance. Not only had the Pruszynski recording captured *some* of the gunshots, there was a strong possibility it had picked up all of them. Moreover, the shot sounds matched exactly the earliest point in his timeline when, from the reactions from people in the ballroom, the shooting was evidently in progress: 12:16:05am.

By studying the recording and the videotaped live feeds together, Brad was now able to add to his timeline by pinpointing the moment the shooting began – 12:15:59am – and the time it concluded just over five seconds later as an unidentified woman gave a long high-pitched scream from somewhere inside, or just outside, the pantry.

The discovery – made 14 years to the day after the CSA had released the Pruszynski recording to the public – was a major break-through. For decades researchers and investigators had believed that there had been no recording of the assassination; but none had, according to their books or published papers, ever listened to the Pruszynski recording. Brad began making arrangements to have his CSA dub of the recording professionally examined.

He also went in search of Stanislaw Pruszynski. In the years following the assassination, "Stash" had emigrated; Brad eventually tracked him down to Poland where Pruszynski was a popular café owner in Warsaw. Although he no longer possessed either the original audiocassette or the recorder it had been made on, he was able to describe the machine, and to recall exactly his movements both before and during the shooting – including the path he had taken from the stage in pursuit of Bobby and his entourage. With this, and a description of the distinctive yellow shirt "Stash" had been wearing on the night, Brad was able to identify him on the video and film footage. This would prove vital in determining the position and movements of the reporter and his microphone as the shots were being fired backstage and out of camera range.

In late July Brad took the CSA copy of the Pruszynski recording to a top sound technician at Paramount Studios in Hollywood: his informal opinion was that more than eight shots could be detected in the recording. Next, Brad asked P. Spencer Whitehead, an audio expert at Georgia Institute of Technology to undertake a more thorough analysis; after several months Whitehead determined that there were between nine and eleven shots captured on the tape.[421]

The implication of these two assessments was enormous: any more than eight shots meant that a second gun had been fired. If the experts were right, the Pruszynski recording was scientific proof of someone other than Sirhan shooting in the pantry. With the stakes so high, Brad knew he needed additional opinions as well as a formal and unimpeachable forensic analysis of the recording.

Audio engineer Philip Van Praag had worked in the field of magnetic recording for more than 40 years. He held a master's degree in electrical engineering, had taught at the Ampex Corporation – one of the world's biggest tape technology innovators – and had quite literally written the book on the development and history of the audio recorder.[422] In the late spring of 2005, Brad

---

421 CNN: *Back Story*, June 5, 2009
422 *Evolution of the Audio Recorder*, Philip M. Van Praag, Ec Designs Inc., April 1997.

asked him to conduct a rigorous examination of the Pruszynski recording.

The tape Van Praag received from the California State Archives was an analogue dub of the reel-to-reel tape it had received from LAPD. Unimpressed with its consumer-grade quality, he asked the archivists for permission to make his own copies – both analogue and digital – from the open reel master; he took these back to his laboratory in Tuscon, Arizona, in September and began a highly detailed sequence of tests.

After a general examination of the entire recording (which included material recorded before, during, and up to half an hour after the assassination) Van Praag started work on the crucial period: from the moment Pruszynski inadvertently flipped his microphone back into recording mode while removing it from the ballroom's stage lectern to the noisy and chaotic aftermath of the shooting backstage in the kitchen pantry. He found that this section of the recording was "contiguous" – in other words, that it contained no additional stop-and-starts, had not been edited and that it had captured the event exactly as it had happened. Then, using sensitive filtering equipment, he screened out background hum to create a cleaner 'picture' of the sounds Pruszynski had recorded.

But the young reporter had been on the move while his machine was running and Van Praag knew that this would have had an important determining effect on the sound patterns captured on the tape. Scanning the multiple camera feeds from the Embassy Room which Brad had assembled, the engineer was able to pinpoint the moment Pruszynski's recorder was inadvertently flipped back on as he lifted it from the lectern; this enabled Van Praag to synchronise the audio recording with the footage, and, using maps of the hotel, to recreate precisely, the microphone's direction of travel and its distance from the shooting.

"With Pruszynski's movements known," Van Praag recorded in a subsequent affidavit, "together with dimensional data, information concerning the locations of Sirhan and Senator Kennedy at the time of the shooting, and an accurate approximation of Pruszynski's equipment, I was then able to begin examining the shot sounds."[423] Using analogue test equipment and digital computer-based software Van Praag attempted to identify the number of shots that had been recorded.

"Given the recording equipment limitations, together with the general noisy crowd environment, and Pruszynski's distance from the area from which the shots emerged, it was not possible to definitively determine the exact total number of shots fired. However, thirteen shot sounds were identified ... [and] it is possible that the total number exceeds thirteen, in view of the fact that loud screams emerged within seconds from the people closest to the shooting scene as they became aware of what had just occurred. These emerging screams and loud shooting may have obscured the capture of discernible additional shot sounds."[424]

Van Praag realised the significance of what his tests revealed. Sirhan's one and only gun held just eights bullets and he had no opportunity to reload. Thirteen shots meant that a second gun held by someone other than Sirhan had also opened fired in the pantry. But that was only the first discovery.

"With multiple guns fired over a short period of time (slightly more than five seconds), and by more than one individual, it occurred to me that this would result in a random timing distribution among the occurrence of those shots during that brief

---

423 Declaration of Philip Van Praag, Sirhan Bishara Sirhan vs. George Galaza, Warden, et al. [Filed] November 20, 2011, US District Court, Central District of California.

424 *Ibid.*

interval. And, that the spacing of some of those shots could, by chance, be quite narrow."[425]

To investigate this, the audio engineer studied the visual images of each shot sound on a computer program which displayed their wave forms on a timeline, calibrated in tiny fractions of a second. Two separate groupings – shots 3, 4 and shots 7 and 8 – revealed clear evidence of "double shots": two bullets fired so closely together that to the human ear they would sound like one, but which Van Praag's computer program was able to identify as separate events. The margin between them could only be measured in thousandths of a second: shots three and four were separated by 149 milliseconds, and the gap between shots seven and eight was just 122 milliseconds. This firing rate – averaging out at almost eight shots per second – made Van Praag doubt whether one person could have fired all of them.

"According to firearms experts, two or three shots per second is considered rather fast," he wrote in his 2008 self-published book about the case, "and the world's record is reported to be about 140 milliseconds (using an optimized competition-grade weapon).

"The Iver Johnson Cadet 55SA used by Sirhan was a 1950s design low-priced revolver, known for its heavy trigger pull... It would have been literally impossible for Sirhan to have fired any two shots that rapidly."[426] Intrigued, Van Praag began a deeper and even more detailed analysis.

Gunshots create what forensic specialists term "impulse sounds". Particularly in noisy environments, the human ear can mistake these for fireworks, car backfires and even balloons popping. But transforming the raw sound into a visual display of its waveform – its shape, in layman's terms – enables audio

---

425 *Ibid.*

426 Philip Van Praag and Robert Joling: *An Open and Shut Case*, p. 15. J V & Co. LLC, 2008

engineers to distinguish the sound of a genuine shot from a more innocent "impulse sound". Gunfire has a "unique trailing edge acoustic audio pattern" – essentially a sound signature – which Van Praag plotted on his array of spectrographic and oscillographic equipment.[427]

But he knew also that the impulse sounds captured by Pruszynski's microphone had been affected by three fundamental issues. The first was the amateur nature of the 1960s equipment itself: by studying the video feeds Brad had obtained from TV networks, as well as CSA documents LAPD had received along with the FBI's open reel dub, it was possible to determine the likely make, model and specifications of the reporter's consumer cassette recorder and microphone. Van Praag needed this information because, he wanted to conduct a test which would re-create Pruszynski's recording of the assassination.

He played a digitally recorded .22 calibre revolver gunshot through his laboratory speakers, capturing it on "a cassette recorder and microphone closely approximating to Pruszynski's equipment … and using cassette tape generally available in that year".[428] He was careful to note a very precise, and limited rationale for this experiment.

"The optimized recording conditions utilized for this test did not attempt to 'reconstruct' the actual room conditions under which the Pruszynski recording was made … Rather, the purpose of the test was to determine the <u>minimum</u> degree of degradation to be expected from recording a gunshot onto this consumer-grade cassette recording."[429] In other words, it set a

---

427 *Declaration of Philip Van Praag, Sirhan Bishara Sirhan vs. George Galaza, Warden, et al.* [Filed] November 20, 2011, US District Court, Central District of California.
428 *Ibid.*
429 Philip Van Praag and Robert Joling: *An Open and Shut Case*, p. 17. J V & Co. LLC, 2008

base-level parameter for understanding the impulse sounds on the 1968 recording.

But the primitive technology of Pruszynski's equipment was only the first limitation. The reporter's cassette tape had been duplicated – first by the Royal Canadian Mounted Police, then by FBI and finally by Van Praag himself at the California State Archives: all of the 1969 dubs were made on analogue equipment, and each resulting tape was a generation further away in quality from the one which Pruszynski had handed over to RCMP. Because understanding this generational loss played an important role in producing a scientifically accurate analysis, Van Praag painstakingly unearthed the makes and models of the machines which had been used to make these dubbed versions – as well as the type of recording tape available at the time – and replicated each stage in the process to create a multi-generation test tape which could be compared with the Pruszynski original.

There was one additional control element to factor into the analysis. Sound signatures are affected by the distance of the microphone from what it records and whether the recording is stationary or made on the move.

By matching and syncing the Pruszynski recording to the multiple television live feeds Brad had unearthed, and studying maps of the ballroom, backstage hallway and the pantry, Van Praag was able to determine the distance between the reporter's microphone and the gunfire – 40 feet – and to plot its movement towards the shooter.

To replicate this, he conducted a further experiment using two .22 calibre revolvers – one an Iver Johnson Cadet 55SA, identical to Sirhan's weapon, the second a very similar Harrington & Richardson 922. Van Praag chose this second weapon because, from evidence contained in the LAPD files, one of the security guards in the pantry had owned exactly this weapon at the date of the assassination.

"The outdoor field test was set up with microphones located 40 feet from the guns, to mimic the average distance between Pruszynski's microphone and the guns. One microphone was positioned in front and slightly to the side of the guns, the other positioned behind and slightly to the side."[430] To ensure that climactic conditions did not produce distortions in the result, the experiment was performed twice, with two weeks between elapsing between each test.

With all the data loaded on to computer, and after feeding in all the information yielded by his duplication studies, Van Praag began analysing the results: they were startling. As well as confirming the initial diagnosis of at least 13 separate shot sounds, and the incidence of definite double-shots (careful analysis proved that these could not have been merely echoes, ricochets or non-gunshot sounds) Van Praag made two remarkable discoveries.

The first – indicated by tell-tale trailing edge wave-form patterns – was that the Pruszynski tape captured two different weapons being fired in the pantry. One was that of Sirhan's .22 calibre Iver Johnson revolver, the second – present in five of the thirteen shot sounds – matched the characteristics of the H&R 922.

But the second finding was, if anything, even more significant. The data showed that the gunshots on the tape came from two opposing directions. "From a preponderance of witness accounts," Van Praag recorded in his sworn declaration, "Sirhan was firing in a westward direction. Pruszynski, and the microphone he was holding, was moving in an eastward direction, toward the kitchen pantry and therefore toward the source of the shots.

---

430 *Declaration of Philip Van Praag, Sirhan Bishara Sirhan vs. George Galaza, Warden, et al.* [Filed] November 20, 2011, US District Court, Central District of California.

"That put Pruszynski's microphone in front of Sirhan's gun, essentially facing the barrel of Sirhan's gun. As my field test results placed the second gun firing in a direction facing away from the microphone, therefore that second gun was firing in an eastward direction, opposite that of Sirhan's direction of fire."[431]

This distinction – Sirhan's gun pointing and firing westward, the second gun pointing and firing eastward – solved the mystery of the conflict between Coroner Thomas Noguchi's autopsy findings and the eyewitness testimony showing that Sirhan never got behind Bobby. It provided an explanation for the wounds suffered by the five surviving victims – Paul Schrade, Elizabeth Evans, Ira Goldstein, Irwin Stroll and William Weisel – who had all been hit by bullets travelling westward – and for the eastward direction of the shots which mortally wounded Bobby.

Van Praag summarised the results of his tests in unequivocal terms: "That 13 shots, or more, were fired in the pantry during that brief five second period of time; that five of those shots were fired from a ... direction opposite to the direction that witness accounts report as the direction in which Sirhan was firing ... and that in two instances within those five seconds there were virtually simultaneous, or 'double' shots ... In my opinion the conclusion is inescapable that there was a second gun fired by a second shooter during the shooting that resulted in the death of Senator Robert F. Kennedy."[432]

This detailed and sophisticated succession of tests was the first scientific proof that someone other than Sirhan had assassinated Bobby. Because of its fundamental importance, Brad arranged for it to be evaluated independently by two other audio experts. As part of a documentary for the Discovery Times

---

431 *Declaration of Philip Van Praag, Sirhan Bishara Sirhan vs. George Galaza, Warden, et al.* [Filed] November 20, 2011, US District Court, Central District of California.

432 *Ibid.*

television channel[433], two engineers from Audio Engineering Associates in Pasadena, were brought in to assess Van Praag's findings. Separately, Eddy B. Brixen, a renowned Danish authority on acoustics, double-checked AEA's assessments.

The two Pasadena-based engineers, Wes Dooley and Paul Pegas, were well-credentialed and had a solid reputation in the audio industry. Dooley had trained in recording studios and radio stations in the late 1960s and gone on to become a world-renowned expert on microphone technology. Pegas was a graduate of the Peabody Conservatory of Music, the University of Maryland and the Edgar Stanton Audio Recording Institute.

Together they loaded copies of Van Praag's analogue and digital masters of the Pruszynski cassette into their equipment and Pegas created a spectrograph of the recording: this displayed the audio frequencies of all the sounds on the tape, and was accurate to 1000th of a second. He also applied a computer program which allowed him to slow the playback without changing the pitch of the sounds.

Over a period of two days, Dooley and Pegas subjected the material to their own rigorous testing. At the end of their two allotted days, Dooley reached the conclusion that Van Praag was right, and Eddy Brixen reviewed and confirmed Dooley and Pegas' analysis in his Copenhagen studios. "So he felt there's ten different places where it looked like there were shots," Dooley told the programme-makers. "So we're getting very similar results." [434]

Nor did the experts rule out the possibility of more than ten shots in the pantry: once AEA's analysis showed the presence of more bullets than Sirhan could have fired, the producers, operating to a strict budget, ceased funding new work for the documentary.

---

433 *Conspiracy Test: The RFK Assassination*. Discovery Times: June 6, 2007
434 *Ibid*

The network did, however, pay for additional field tests to investigate the double-shot evidence Van Praag had uncovered. The producers located an authority from the gun-industry and commissioned him to examine how quickly an expert could fire an Iver Johnson Cadet 55SA. Phil Spangenburger, had worked with firearms for more than 35 years; he was a Hollywood gun coach and firearms editor for *True West* magazine. Using an industry-standard electronic timer, Spangenburger was filmed firing the gun as quickly as he could.

After several attempts his fastest time to empty the eight shot cylinder was 2.93 seconds – an average of 366 milliseconds between shots – significantly longer than the 120-149 milliseconds Van Praag reported in his analysis. As an additional test measure Spangenburger then fired just two shots as quickly as possible.

The result, recorded on the calibrated timer, was .55 seconds: a total 550 milliseconds for the two, or an average 275 milliseconds per shot. If an expert gun handler could not match the extremely rapid fire captured on the Pruszynski recording, neither was Sirhan – an untrained amateur with limited experience – likely to have been able to achieve such speeds.

"When I hear 120 milliseconds between shots, that sounds incredibly fast," Spangenburger told the film crew. "I think anybody with any experience would realise that had to be more than one firearm."[435]

Given the implications of the various scientific tests carried out on the Pruszynski recording it was, perhaps, inevitable that there would be attempts to undermine their findings. Mel Ayton, a British author, had previously published books "dispelling the myths" (as he termed them) surrounding the killings of President John Kennedy and Dr. Martin Luther King. At the time of the Pruszynski audio analysis, he had been working on

---

435 *Ibid.*

a new book which, in his view, proved that Sirhan was a lone assassin, motivated by "fanatical Palestinian nationalism and his hatred for RFK" [436] In May 2006 Ayton obtained a copy of Van Praag's digitized dub of the recording.

For one of his conspiracy-debunking books on the John Kennedy assassination Ayton had worked with Steve Barber, a rock musician-turned self-proclaimed audio expert. In the summer of 2006 he sent the Pruszynski recording to Barber asking for his opinion: Barber, together with two other veterans of the JFK controversy, Dr. Chad Zimmerman and Michael O'Dell, subsequently reported that the tape captured between six and eight shots. Barber told Ayton that "I have counted nothing more than seven shots"; O'Dell said he was "willing to identify six for certain", while Zimmerman – who had conducted "a thorough examination of the tape using computer software" – discerned "eight or fewer shots".[437]

Ayton reported their findings in his book without disclosing either the nature of the tests Barber, O'Dell and Zimmerman had carried out, or the equipment on which they had done so. He did, however, commission a rather more expert opinion from a highly-regarded British firm which specialised in analysing audio recordings for court hearings.

Dr. Philip Harrison had a raft of degrees in acoustical engineering, phonetics and phonology and linguistics. As a forensic consultant employed by J.P. French Associates, he had worked on more than 100 cases "in the areas of authentication, enhancement, transcription and speaker comparison", notching up appearances before the English Court of Appeal and the International War Crimes Tribunal.[438]

---

436 Mel Ayton: *The Forgotten Terrorist*, Potomac Books, 2007.
437 Mel Ayton: *The Forgotten Terrorist*, p. 133-134. Potomac Books, 2007.
438 Dr. Phillip Harrison: *Summary Curriculum Vitae*. J.P. French Associates: http://www.jpfrench.com/staff/philip-harrison/

Harrison's credentials were serious, and his analysis of the Pruszynski recording as presented in Ayton's book (it has not been lodged anywhere else) demonstrated a more rigorous examination than those disclosed by Barber, O'Dell and Zimmerman. "I have listened to and analysed the CD copy of the Pruszynski recording within specialised audio analysis software," he wrote to Ayton. "In doing so I have discussed my findings and conclusions with a colleague, Professor Peter French, who is in agreement with my interpretations."[439]

Harrison concluded that he could discern "seven impulse sounds" on the tape, and "taking into account the events of the early hours of June 5, 1968 and considering the entirety of the recording and the characteristics of the seven sounds, it is fair to conclude that these are the sounds of Sirhan's gun being fired."[440]

There were, however, substantial flaws in Harrison's analysis. The first was a classic example of confirmation bias: having discerned the sound of shots, Harrison made the assumption that these emanated from Sirhan's gun and no other. But the second problem was even more fundamental.

Harrison found, according to his report, a large number of impulse sounds. He separated these into three categories: the first was a cluster of seven, the second a group of three, and the third was a collection of additional sounds, whose total number he did not appear to have counted. He designated the first group as the sound of shots being fired, but – without explanation – chose to consider the second group of three impulse sounds as candidates for an eighth shot, rather than the more logical possibility that they were Shots 8, 9, and 10. As for the final group of unnumbered impulse sounds, Harrison simply noted that he could not identify their source.

---

439 Mel Ayton: *The Forgotten Terrorist*, p. 280. Potomac Books, 2007.
440 *Ibid.*

"There are," his report to Ayton advised, "several other impulse sounds surrounding the shots and many others across the thirty-five minutes of recording. Determining the actual source of these sounds is not viable as the quality of the recording is not adequate and there are no reference sounds with which to compare them."[441]

In summary, Harrison's results suggested that he could not rule out hearing ten shots – and possibly more. Despite this, Ayton's response was to pronounce unequivocally that Harrison and French had "found no more than eight shots were present on the recording" and to attack those who claimed otherwise.

"Van Praag's and Wes Dooley's findings will be rejected by the scientific community on the basis they have not provided a written report for consideration by their peers, they have unwittingly (or consciously) provided scientifically unsupported results to conspiracists who have their own agenda in promoting an unproven conspiracy to murder Robert F. Kennedy."[442] For good measure he denounced the Discovery Times documentary (in which he appeared), claiming it had "duped the American public".[443]

There were, however, a number of problems with Ayton's argument. The first was his charge that Van Praag and Dooley should be disregarded since they had not provided a report for peer assessment; since none of those on whose opinions Ayton relied had done this either (nor, unlike Van Praag, have they ever sworn "under penalty of perjury" an affidavit detailing their findings), the complaint exhibited a remarkable degree of *chutzpah*.

---

441 Mel Ayton: *The Forgotten Terrorist*, p. 281-282. Potomac Books, 2007.
442 *Ibid.* pp. 279-290
443 Mel Ayton: *How The Discovery Channel Duped the American public About the RFK Assassination Acoustics Debate.* November 29, History News Network. http://historynewsnetwork.org/article/44466

More fundamental, as Van Praag noted in his subsequent court declaration, was the glaring absence of much in the way of forensic science in the opinions Ayton had apparently garnered. Barber "largely relied upon listening to a copy of one of my masters for his conclusions ... the question begs to be asked as to exactly what scientific process(es) did he use to categorically rule out the possibility that there could have been more than eight shots fired?" [444] Harrison's analysis, meanwhile, "was conducted without the examiner knowing where Mr. Pruszynski was standing and, most significantly, what was the location of his microphone, and how was it moving towards the pantry as the shots were fired ... These deficiencies, contrasted with the mandatory standards ... that I employed, bring into question the credibility of Harrison's opinion." [445]

But the biggest hole in Ayton's assertions – which California's Attorney General would subsequent cited as solid evidence [446] – lay in what Dr. Phillip Harrison actually told him. For a start he was unable to explain the 'double shot' phenomenon which Van Praag had identified, determining only that these were unlikely to be mere echoes of the bullets exploding from the muzzle of Sirhan's gun. And far from unequivocally stating that Stash Pruszynki had captured "no more than eight shots", the British analyst had, in fact, carefully hedged his bets by reporting the existence of other unexplained "impulse sounds".

Moreover, since Harrison's report did not suggest that he had deployed any of the "mandatory standard" tests which Philip

---

444 Declaration of Philip Van Praag, Sirhan Bishara Sirhan vs. George Galaza, Warden, et al. [Filed] November 20, 2011, US District Court, Central District of California.

445 *Ibid.*

446 *Kamala Harris, Attorney General of California: Sirhan Bishara Sirhan vs. George Galaza, Warden, et al.* Reply Brief on Actual Innocence, [filed] 1 February 2012, US District Court, Central District of California

Van Praag had used (much less the sophisticated and careful test gunfire recordings and comparisons) to identify those additional "impulse sounds" as gunfire, it was hardly surprising that he was unable to say with certainty what they were. What he did not, however, conclude was that they were definitely *not* gunshots.

In September 2012, 43 years after its laboratory belatedly examined the copy dubbed and sent to Washington by the RCMP, the FBI returned to the question of what exactly was captured on the Pruszynski recording. It did so after Robert F. Kennedy Jnr. wrote to US Attorney General Eric Holder asking him to order a new examination of what was now accepted as the only audio recording of the shooting.

According to documents Brad prised from the FBI under the Freedom of Information Act, between October 2012 and February 2013 the Bureau carried out tests on the original Pruszynski open reel dub stored in the FBI's archives, and on a consumer-grade cassette copy provided by the California State Archives. (Curiously, the Bureau did not examine either the CSA's higher-quality open reel copy of the recording, or Phil Van Praag's carefully-enhanced versions; nor did it bother to speak with Van Praag himself, or trouble itself to establish the position and movement of Pruszynski's microphone).

The results of these somewhat half-hearted examinations resulted only in an assessment that the recording was "of insufficient quality to definitively classify the impulse events as gunshots, confirm the number of gunshots or determine the identification of specific weapon(s)".[447] Since every other audio analyst – regardless of whether they supported or dismissed evidence of a second gunman – had clearly identified impulse sounds as gunshots, the FBI's inability to do so was inexplicable.

---

447 FBI Digital Evidence Laboratory: Report of Examination, May 13, 2013.
    Copy in authors' possession

Ultimately, and in the absence of any genuine and verifiable data to the contrary, Van Praag's thorough investigations must stand. And since they provide scientific proof that a second gunman, firing a different weapon, from a different direction to Sirhan's weapon, took part in the shooting, they pose a simple, logical question: who was the second shooter – and why did he open fire?

CHAPTER TWELVE:
SUSPECTS

There was – or at least had been – no shortage of other suspects.

Major murder investigations frequently attract an initial flurry of calls from members of the public, offering tips and potential leads. In a case as politically charged as the assassination of a major candidate for the White House – particularly one who was the brother of a murdered President – it was inevitable that Los Angeles Police and the FBI would be deluged with alleged sightings of the chief suspect and other suspicious characters, as well as allegations of wide-ranging conspiracies.

"The implications and allegations that the crime was an international or subversive plot were obvious and numerous," LAPD's Summary Report noted.[448] The first such reports reached the police within hours of the shooting in the pantry, even as Bobby still clung to life in the Good Samaritan Hospital. Over the following days and weeks LAPD was contacted by dozens of individuals claiming to have knowledge that Sirhan had been involved with communists, Arab nationalists or anti-Castro

---

448 *Summary Report of the Los Angeles Police Department Investigation of the Senator Robert Kennedy Assassination*, p.(vi). California State Archives.

Cuban activists, or that he had been overheard discussing the assassination of Bobby Kennedy in the days leading up to California's primary election night. Many of these were untrue or inaccurate, though most were probably well-intentioned. Nevertheless, Special Unit Senator devoted hundreds of detective man-hours to investigating (by its own count) 20 separate alleged conspiracies.

But by the time Chief of Detectives Robert Houghton wrote the Summary report in June 1969, his team had discounted each one as nothing more than the imaginings of "publicity seekers, political adventurers, opportunists and the honestly mistaken"[449], some of whom were "either using the assassination to further their own private cause or to enhance their position among their associates".[450]

The full S.U.S. files, however, told a different story. Whilst some of the tips were, inevitably, misguided, the investigations into substantive leads on other suspects were shown to have been abruptly curtailed, abandoned without resolution or – in some cases – simply never followed up. Since the alleged conspiracies identified in these reports involved some of Bobby's historic enemies – notably organised crime and the CIA – the failure to pursue them was, at best, strange.

One of the first – and ultimately most time-consuming – investigations began on the afternoon of June 5, 1968, when Oliver Brindley "Jerry" Owen walked into LAPD's University station house. Owen, a burly 55-year-old ex-prize fighter, sometime horse dealer and itinerant evangelist – he billed himself as "The Walking Bible" due to his self-claimed recall of every verse of the scriptures – had a colourful history of brushes with the law, but had never been convicted of a crime in California, at

---

449 *Ibid.*
450 *Ibid.* p.61

least[451]. In a lengthy taped interview, beginning at 5pm, Owen related a complicated and outlandish story.

He claimed that two days earlier he had been driving through downtown Los Angeles; when he stopped at a traffic light two young men and a woman asked him for a ride. One, he told the detectives, looked like the photo he had seen in the newspaper of the man arrested with a smoking gun in the pantry at the Ambassador Hotel.

"He appeared to be in his early 20s, I thought he was Mexican, dark bushy headed kid, looked like a Mexican, but spoke very good English," the transcript of his taped interview stated. "As we went out [on] Wilshire he asked me if I could stop for a little while at the big hotel and stated that he had a friend that worked there, that he'd only be a few minutes."[452]

The "big hotel" turned out to be the Ambassador, and the friend who the young man went to visit worked in the kitchen there. Owen said he waited outside the entrance for ten minutes, at which point his hitch-hiker re-appeared, got back in the truck and struck up a conversation about horses. "He wanted to know if I had horses and what kind of horses … he stated that he was an exercise boy at the race track." The young man also quizzed Owen about his religious heritage: "He wanted to know if I was Jewish … and he said [he had] no use for Jews. He said that as a boy he lived in Jordan … that he was raised in Jordan and left there when he was 13 or 14 years old."[453]

Owen then said that he told Sirhan he had a palomino pony, and agreed to sell it to him for $250 dollars; they arranged to

---

451   FBI files show him to have been arrested for, but not convicted of, robbery, arson, and fraud in a docket dating back to 1930 and stretching across the country.

452   Transcript of interview with Jerry Owen, June 5, 1968. Special Unit Senator files, Volume 40, p.168-172. California State Archives.

453   *Ibid.*

reconvene later that evening to complete the transaction. When they met, at 11pm in the Hollywood area, Sirhan said he didn't have the money.

The preacher gave the detectives a good description of Sirhan, and of his two companions. The woman was a Caucasian, in her early 20s with "straight dirty blonde hair" and who "needed a bath"; the man was in his 30s, had long, dark brown hair and wore a gold turtleneck sweater with a medallion round his neck. Those descriptions would, in time, become vital information in the search for additional suspects.

According to its account in the Summary report, LAPD spent several months trying "to conclusively establish the truth regarding Owen's allegation. On the surface his statements were not self-incriminating, and Owen presented himself as a volunteer witness who was interested in assisting the police. Essentially investigators needed only to establish the falsity of Owen's statements to refute his allegations or to verify the truth of his statements and use Owen as a material witness."[454]

However, this bland statement of routine police practice was at considerable variance from the true facts revealed by the full S.U.S. files. Whilst Owen was unquestionably a slippery character, and some parts of his account did not check out, LAPD spent much of its time seeking to discredit him and – most particularly – two journalists who inserted themselves into the story.

Jonn Christian was a garrulous freelance with a severe drink problem, given to a belief in elaborate conspiracy theories and with a penchant for wild and self-aggrandizing schemes to make money[455]. His colleague, William Turner, was a former

---

454 Summary report of the Los Angeles Police Department Investigation of the Senator Robert Kennedy Assassination, p.81-82. California State Archives.

455 Jonn Christian: interviews and correspondence with Tim Tate, 1991 – 1994.

FBI Special Agent who had been fired by the Bureau in 1961 for making "various untrue or unjustified statements" and for lacking "the truthfulness, accuracy and responsibility required of an FBI agent".[456] After a succession of failed appeals against his dismissal, he ran – unsuccessfully – in the 1968 Democratic Party's congressional primary race.

In the interim, he had written a series of articles, attacking the FBI and Director J. Edgar Hoover, and had worked with the New Orleans DA Jim Garrison's investigations into an alleged conspiracy behind the assassination of President John Kennedy. Throughout the summer of 1968, Christian and Turner doggedly pursued private investigations into Owen's story, claiming to have found witnesses who remembered seeing the preacher with Sirhan at various times and places in the months before the shooting in the pantry, as well as evidence indicating a conspiracy to kill Bobby "because he would stop the Vietnam War"[457]. Some, if not all, of this was good, solid journalism: but their habit of summoning detectives to listen to Christian's long and rambling monologues, coupled with their unashamed attempts to drum up support from city and state politicians, as well as Turner's involvement with Jim Garrison, led to LAPD disregarding almost everything the pair unearthed: one internal file note denounced Christian for "established phoniness".[458]

The journalists came to believe the police were harassing and threatening them, and claimed that LA law officers were involved in an attempt by Owen to have Christian arrested for alleged

456 Re; William Turner, undated LAPD report. Special Unit Senator files, Volume 68, p.243. California State Archives.
457 The Assassination of Robert F. Kennedy: Christian & Turner, Random House, 1978.
458 Capt. Hugh Brown, Daily Summaries of Activity, October 11-16, 1968. Special Unit Senator files, Volume 25, p.308. California State Archives.

libel[459]. Christian went into hiding and, for the rest of his life claimed to be in fear for his life. By the early 1990s he was suffering from severe alcoholism, and was living, near-destitute, in a remote shack in the Mojave Desert.[460]

Despite the genuine and troubling evidence that Owen had known Sirhan – and had probably met him and a male and female companion sometime before the night of the assassination – after a polygraph test administered by Lt. Hank Hernandez indicated "he was being untruthful... [and] cannot honestly say that he picked up, talked to or saw Sirhan Sirhan on June 3, 1968"[461], LAPD eventually abandoned the investigation into his association with Sirhan.

On its own – and given both the holes in his account and the unreliability of Christian and Turner as witnesses – the failure to get to the bottom of Owen's potential involvement in the assassination might be excusable. But the S.U.S. files contain internal reports showing that the police ignored other, much stronger, evidence of a conspiracy underpinning the assassination. All of this involved organisations with known grudges against Bobby.

On July 17, 1968 detectives interviewed Richard Lubic, a 31-year-old television producer who had been standing next to the pantry's ice machine a few feet to the right of Bobby, and who was designated as "a pertinent witness in that he actually witnessed the shooting".[462] However, the focus of the tape-recorded session was not his recollection of the event but rather his involvement with a team of researchers, sent to Los Angeles

---

459 Chapter 15 of Christian and Turner's book, *The Assassination of Robert F. Kennedy* contains a lengthy account of this bizarre sequence of events.

460 Jonn Christian: interviews with Tim Tate, 1991 – 1994.

461 Report of Polygraph Examination of Jerry Owen. Special Unit Senator files, Volume 34, p.162-164. California State Archives.

462 Notes from an inter-agency meeting, 9am, December 3, 1968. Special Unit Senator files, Volume 26, p.34. California State Archives.

by New Orleans D.A. Jim Garrison, to investigate alleged links between Bobby's murder and the assassination of President John Kennedy.

The full S.U.S. files show that LAPD was keenly aware of Garrison's interest and in the summer of 1968 seriously considered an offer from Ted Charach to "get inside the Garrison organisation" and covertly feed back information on its activities.[463] The detectives' interview with Richard Lubic provided them with details of what the New Orleans D.A. believed he had uncovered.

Garrison's investigator had been in contact with the television producer since Bobby's victory in the Indiana primary election in May. He told Lubic that the New Orleans team had evidence of an overarching conspiracy linking the assassinations of John Kennedy, Dr. Martin Luther King and Bobby. "Garrison ... has a document on which are the initials of three people to be eliminated, JFK, MLK and RFK," LAPD's report of the Lubic interview noted. "This paper was obtained from a raid of the National States Rights Party headquarters."[464]

The National States Rights Party was a far right white supremacist organisation, founded in 1958 by a Tennessee chiropractor called Edward Reed Fields, and was vehemently opposed to the advance of civil rights for African-Americans. One month after John Kennedy's assassination, the FBI had warned the U.S. Secret Service that he posed a threat to those under its protection.[465]

---

463 Memo from Sgt. D.D. Varney to Lt. Higbie, LAPD, August 1, 1968. Special Unit Senator files, Volume 48, p.76. California State Archives.

464 LAPD report of interview with Richard Lubic, July 17, 1968. Special Unit Senator files, Volume 48, p. 310-314 California State Archives.

465 National States Rights Party. FBI Archives: https://vault.fbi.gov/ National%20States%20Rights%20Party/National%20States%20 Rights%20Party%20Part%201%20of%201%20

Lubic told S.U.S. that he had been shown the evidence implicating NSRP in the conspiracy. " 'There was a document which I saw … that said we must eliminate three people, and they were all initialled, J.F.K., M.L.K, and R.F.K. just on a piece of paper which was taken by a certain police department in the South that raided the headquarters and took all this hate stuff, and these documents."[466]

Garrison's investigator also told Lubic that the Party had formed links with "rich oil people [who] wanted JFK killed. JFK was going to do away with the oil depletion allowances which would cost these people possibly billions of dollars." And he gave what he claimed were details of the way the plot had worked. "The key conspirators are called the committee. The group was in three levels: the committee, the bookkeepers, and the actual shooters. The committee agreed to put up approximately ten million dollars. The money would be distributed as needed by the bookkeepers. The actual shooting would be done by Cubans or Latins who hated Kennedy for the Bay of Pigs fiasco."[467]

But according to the account of Lubic's interview recorded by LAPD, he had also warned that the conspirators were well connected. "These groups had certain contacts in government agencies [such] as the CIA, FBI and even the Dallas police and sheriff's depts …"[468]

Throughout his interview Lubic was careful to stress that he had no direct personal knowledge of any such conspiracy, merely that he was passing on to LAPD what Garrison's team had, allegedly, uncovered. In addition to sending his investigator to Los Angeles, the New Orleans D.A. had also taken the trouble

---

466 Transcript of Interview with Richard Lubic, July 17, 1968. file Special Unit Senator files, Volume 96, p.290-291 California State Archives.
467 LAPD report of interview with Richard Lubic, July 17, 1968. Special Unit Senator files, Volume 48, p. 310-314 California State Archives.
468 *Ibid.*

to meet Lubic personally in the days following Bobby's assassination; in the passenger lounge at Salt Lake City airport, Utah, he had passed on his belief that "Sirhan Sirhan was probably a conspiracy man: meaning that Sirhan could have been working with the committee [and that] if Sirhan had missed [then] other people would have killed RFK."[469]

Lubic also suggested that LAPD meet Garrison and hear for itself what he had uncovered. This evidently met with a frosty reception. At the end of the interview the detectives gave Lubic a copy of Judge Alarcon's gagging order and told him "not to discuss the case with anyone".[470] Since the order applied only to state and local officials, precluding them from disclosing information received in the course of their duties, handing it to Lubic might be interpreted as a crude attempt at intimidation.

What is certain is that within a week Chief of Detectives Robert Houghton complained about Lubic at an inter-agency case review meeting with representatives of the FBI, the Los Angeles District Attorney and the federal US Attorney General's office, for "attempting to stir up conspiracy angles."[471] Six months later, Houghton denounced him in rather more forthright terms.

"Lubic is a self-styled entrepreneur, former TV producer, and political adventurer," the detective told a second inter-agency meeting. "[He] alleges associations with Garrison, William Turner, Jan [sic] Christian, and all the other sinister figures in the assassination"[472]. In the interim Garrison and his investigators returned to Los Angeles to pursue their enquiries; LAPD files

---

469 *Ibid.*
470 *Ibid.*
471 Inter Agency meeting between LAPD, FBI, DA and US Attorney General's Office, July 22, 1969. Special Unit Senator files, Volume 47 p.69
472 Inter Agency meeting between LAPD, FBI, LA Sheriff's Office , LA DA, and US Attorney General's Office, July 22, 1969. Special Unit Senator files, Volume 26, p. 34. California State Archives

show that the New Orleans team specifically "requested SUS to make a special report."[473] There is no trace of any response from LAPD, nor of any "special report".

Garrison was (and remains) a divisive figure in the myriad controversies surrounding the assassination of President Kennedy – though it is fair to note that in 2013 the CIA itself admitted to have perpetrated a "benign cover-up" by deliberately withholding from the Warren Commission the Agency's involvement with the Mafia in its determined attempts to assassinate Castro.[474]

But regardless of the merits, or otherwise, of Garrison's claims, LAPD's disinterest in examining them is striking. And it matched a pattern: in sharp contrast to the way it handled even the most minor supposed sightings of Sirhan – tape recorded interviews, multiple and lengthy questioning and polygraph tests were the order of the day – allegations of conspiracies involving Bobby's known enemies were quickly dismissed, and then suppressed for two decades.

Roy Donald Murray was a "prosperous cotton rancher" who owned 900 acres of land around the small northern California town of Earlimart. The community lay in Tulare County and was just 10 miles from Delano – the seat of Cesar Chavez' struggle of behalf of migrant farm labourers where Bobby had challenged the local sheriff over his unlawful policy of locking up striking workers. In May 1968 – just after the assassination of Dr. Martin Luther King, and approximately five weeks before the shooting in the pantry, Murray was drinking with friends

---

473 Daily log of Robert Houghton, Commander, Detective Bureau; entry for Aug 1 1968. Special Unit Senator files, Volume 36, p.28. California State Archives

474 *DCI John McCone and the Assassination of President John F. Kennedy*, David Robarge, CIA official historian; de-classified September 29, 2014. National Security Archive at George Washington University.

in the Earlimart Elks Club; their conversation was overheard by Lt. Ed Combs, from the Delano Police Department, who later reported it to the FBI.

"The general tenor of conversation had been for the King assassination and against the John F. Kennedy assassination," Combs told the FBI's Special Agent. "Someone in the group had mentioned that they had shot the wrong Kennedy and it was too bad that it had not been Robert instead of John that had been kill[ed] ...

"[Murray][475] advised the group that he had received a long distance telephone call from friends in the Las Vegas area requesting a contribution from him to help pay a one half to three quarter million dollar contract to assassinate Robert Kennedy. [He] stated that the assassination was to take place if it appeared Kennedy was to gain the Democratic Presidential nomination, and that California was considered as the conclusive proof point of that probable nomination."[476]

The rancher, who was noticeably intoxicated, also made clear that the phone call soliciting his help had come from "his Mafia friends" in Las Vegas.[477] He boasted that he had personally pledged $2,000 to the assassination fund, and "that he told the people from Las Vegas that he could probably drum up at least $50,000 to $100,000 in Delano, California alone."[478] The rationale for this, according to Lt. Combs, was that "the wealthy farmers in the area all hate Kennedy".[479]

---

475 His name is redacted in the FBI reports, but not in the copies held by LAPD

476 FBI report of interview with Lt. Ed Combs, Delano Police Department, June 12, 1968. FBI file Ser. 2726-2850, p.168-169. California State Archives.

477 Summary of Interviews that materially contributed to the investigation. Special Unit Senator files, Volume 77, p.244. California State Archives

478 FBI report of interview with Lt. Ed Combs, Delano Police Department, June 12, 1968. FBI file Ser. 2726-2850, p.168-169. California State Archives.

479 *Ibid.*

Combs had not been alone in hearing Murray's allegations of a murderous conspiracy. Delano Chief of Police James C. Aisles also told the FBI he had been present in the Elks Club. He and Combs had not questioned the rancher – much less arrested him – about his claims because "at the time, they merely discounted them as bragging on the part of Murray as he is a braggart and a 'loudmouth' when drinking."[480] But after the assassination both men realised that the plot appeared to match rather closely what had happened on the night of June 4 – 5.

Combs also gave the Bureau some relevant background information about Roy Murray: although he had no arrest record in Delano, the police officer knew him to be "a gambler with supposed connections in Las Vegas."[481]

Drunk or not, Murray's statements amounted to a solid claim of personal involvement in a conspiracy involving organised crime and wealthy farm owners – two groups who were known to be among Bobby's most powerful enemies. LAPD, for reasons it has never explained, took no action; instead, it left the FBI to conduct cursory enquiries. The Bureau interviewed Earlimart post-mistress Mrs. Loyette Osborne; she said that Murray had lived in the area for more than 40 years, was married with five children, and – as a member of the Lions and Elks Clubs, as well as the local Masonic Lodge – was "a well-known and respected member of the community".[482] Armed with this endorsement, the Agent went to question Murray himself. As recorded in the FBI files, it was very far from a rigorous interrogation.

"[Murray] was shown a statement of his rights which he read but declined to sign. He then furnished the following information. He recalled making a statement about six weeks ago to the effect

---

480 Undated memo Special Unit Senator files, Volume 74, p.80 California State Archives
481 *Ibid.*
482 *Ibid.*

that he had pledged two thousand dollars towards a total of 500 to 750 thousand dollars which was to be utilized to pay off a 'contract' to kill Senator Robert Kennedy in the event it appeared he could receive the Democratic nomination for the Presidency of the United States. He stated that he had no factual basis for this statement or for saying that La Cosa Nostra was behind this 'contract'.

"He added he was actually sorry he had uttered this. He described Senator Kennedy as a brilliant young man, and added although he disagreed with Senator Kennedy's policy in the Delano, California, area growers versus the Mexican faming laborers dispute and Senator Kennedy's repeated endorsement of Cesar Chavez, the head of the Mexican Farm Workers Association, he certainly had no desire to see Senator Kennedy harmed."[483]

And there the 'investigation' ended. Murray was not polygraphed, and there is no trace, in either the FBI or LAPD files, of any attempt to examine his bank or phone records, nor of any enquiries made by either agency to discover who his "Mafia friends in Las Vegas" might be. By the time the files were released to the California State Archives it was too late to ask Murray any further questions. Local records in Delano show that he died – cause undisclosed – in 1973: he was 52 years old.

Assassination conspiracies involving organised crime figured prominently in two other entirely separate reports given to LAPD in the summer of 1968. Both were given by eyewitnesses and contained enough detail to enable further investigation; but, like the Murray case, both were quickly dismissed on remarkably flimsy grounds.

In the hours immediately following the shooting, a 19-year-old woman walked into Los Angeles County Sheriff's office and asked to speak with a sergeant she knew in its intelligence division. Anita Stewart's husband, James, was then being held on remand in the

---

483 FBI File X-8, Vol. 21, p.84. California State Archives.

County jail, having been picked up six weeks earlier in a sting operation targeting petty criminals who fenced stolen jewellery.

She had met Sgt. Lee Stahl during the case; that morning Mrs. Stewart sought her out with information about Bobby's assassination. After hearing her story, Stahl handed her on to LAPD: on August 13, it sent Sgt. Jack Cochran, an S.U.S. officer, out to interview her.

Cochran's report shows that between July and September 1967 Mrs. Stewart had worked at an insurance broking firm on Wilshire Boulevard, Los Angeles, owned and operated by her father, Leonard Davis.

"Two weeks after beginning to work, her father was visited by a man named Tuffy... she was told that he was an ex-fighter. During this visit, Tuffy and her father discussed the setting up of [a] medical insurance center through the Teamsters Union... Two days after the above described meeting, Tuffy and two other men came into the office and met with Leonard Davis. These men were not introduced to Mrs. Stewart, but one of the men kept referring to Jimmy Hoffa as 'my dad'. She intimated [sic] from his conversation that he was Jimmy Hoffa's son. He is described as Male Cauc., in his early 20s, suntanned and good looking...

"The man whom she thinks was Jimmy Hoffa's son mentioned the fact that his dad was in jail [Hoffa was then serving an eight year sentence for the attempted bribery of a grand juror in Tennessee] and that Kennedy had exerted an unusual amount of harassment against him.

"There was a general discussion as to the possibility of Kennedy being elected president. The man she believes to be Jimmy Hoffa's son stated something to the effect that if Kennedy were elected President, that he would be rubbed out."[484]

---

484 Report of interview with Mrs. Anita Stewart, August 13, 1968. Special Unit Senator files, Volume 40, p.363-364 .California State Archives

Evidently Mrs. Stewart and her father did not have a good relationship. After she stopped working for him they had little contact until she called him on the morning of June 5, 1968 to remind him of the conversation she had overheard. According to Sgt. Cochran's report, the following day "at 4am, she received a phone call at home and a deep male voice stated 'Forget everything you heard in Lennie's office (her father) or you won't live to tell about it.'"

Then, in July, as she was driving on the freeway, "a grey Oldsmobile, 1964 Convertible with red and white out of state plates, containing two Cauc men started following her... They pulled up alongside her and forced her off the road. She states a traffic report was made and that she sustained injuries sufficient to hospitalize her for three weeks. She has been in fear of her life since this incident." Cochran listed the traffic report number for this incident, suggesting that – at least in part – there was some factual basis for this element of her story.[485]

Following the interview with Anita Stewart, he tracked down the people who had been in Leonard Davis' office. "Tuffy" turned out to be Theron Tyson, a Los Angeles-based official of James Hoffa Sr.'s Teamsters union (Local 389). He confirmed that he had visited Davis during the summer of 1967 and that Mrs. Stewart was present.

He also told the detective that "he did make mention of a threat on someone's life but, but he was alluding to the threat on James Hoffa Sr.'s life which had occurred in San Francisco in 1961. This comment was made offhanded and in a general conversation. There was no conversation relating to a threat on the life of Senator Robert Kennedy. Tyson knows James Hoffa Jr. personally, but states he was never present at Leonard Davis' office during any of their business meetings."[486]

---

485 *Ibid.*
486 *Ibid,* p.366

James Hoffa Jr. was then an attorney in private practice in Detroit. On August 14, Cochran phoned him to ask about Mrs. Stewart's allegation. It was not a long conversation. "He stated that he checked his attorney's calendar for the year 1967 and it indicates he was not in the Los Angeles area between June 1, 1967 and August 1, 1967. Additionally, he does not recall being in Los Angeles for several months prior to these dates. He stated he does know a Mr. Theron Tyson but is not acquainted with Leonard Davis or Anita Stewart, nor has he ever been in the insurance brokerage firm of Mr. Leonard Davis."[487] There is no indication anywhere in the LAPD files that S.U.S. made any attempt to verify Mr. Hoffa's assurance as to his travel schedule. Cochran simply seems to have accepted his word.

However, the detective also interviewed Mrs. Stewart's father. He confirmed that Tuffy Tyson had visited his office and that Anita had been working there when he turned up. He explained that the visit was "due to an insurance venture proposed to Davis by Tyson", which involved Davis obtaining a loan from an unnamed institution on behalf of the Teamsters; this finance was then to be underwritten by an insurance policy which David would draw up.

Tyson had gone to Davis because (so Davis believed) he "had been turned down by all the other lending institutions and this was the last ditch effort... Tyson told him that since the jailing of James Hoffa Sr. great difficulty in securing loans had arisen."

Apparently Davis thought the plan was doomed from the outset and, according to his account, Tyson did not visit the office again while Anita Stewart worked there. He also denied either knowing or ever meeting James Hoffa Jr.[488]

---

487 Ibid.
488 Interview with Leonard Davis, August 13, 1968. *Ibid*, p. 366

Whatever the truth about James Hoffa Jr. there were significant differences in the stories told by Leonard David and Tuffy Tyson. The union man recalled discussing a death threat – albeit one against Hoffa Sr. some years earlier; Davis didn't mention this unusual conversation. In a properly conducted police enquiry – particularly one dealing with claims of a conspiracy to assassinate a likely Presidential candidate by one of his sworn enemies – this would have been enough to justify further and more rigorous investigation. Instead, Cochran dismissed Anita Stewart's allegation on the basis that Davis said "his daughter is a pathological liar and has a vivid imagination. His daughter has had two abortions, once in Japan and once locally … Mr. Davis stated he knows his daughter Anita needs psychiatric care but has been unable to convince her to see a doctor".[489] Although there is no record of any factual verification for these claims in the S.U.S. files, the detective wrote a formal memorandum pronouncing the investigation over.

"It is apparent that it is a complete fabrication, probably due to an overactive imagination. I detected an undercurrent of melodrama in my interview with her and she seemed possessed by a desire to impress me with the sinister implications of her story. It is my opinion that further investigation of this matter is not warranted, and that her obvious hostility towards her father has manifested itself into her conjuring up these absurd allegations."[490]

Jimmy Hoffa's name – and claims that he was involved in an assassination conspiracy – would not, however, go away. On June 17, 1968 Edward Hugh Pole contacted the FBI to report a conversation he had overheard involving the Teamster's leader while in prison. According to the Bureau's report (copied in LAPD's files)

---

489 *Ibid*, p.364-365
490 *Observations and Conclusions of Investigating Officer* [undated]. Special Unit Senator files, Volume 52, p.43.California State Archives

Mr. Pole "stated that on or about Memorial Day 1967, he was in the dining hall at the Lewisburg Federal Penitentiary and at the table next to him was James Hoffa, who was talking to … two individuals [and said] that, 'I have a contract out on Kennedy and if he ever gets in the primaries or ever gets elected, the contract will be fulfilled within six months'."[491]

Pole said that two weeks later he asked Hoffa about this directly. "Recalling the prior conversation, he asked Hoffa what he thought about Kennedy. He stated Hoffa immediately began an emotional tirade over Kennedy's use of wiretapping and his (Hoffa's) conviction and incarceration at Lewisburg. He ended the conversation by stating, 'Right now Kennedy's in no danger; but if he ever gets into a primary or gets elected, I won't say how or when, but he'll get knocked off'." [492]

American law enforcement has a long – and often disreputable – tradition of using statements from 'jail house snitches' to charge and convict other inmates of serious crimes. Usually, the informant provides incriminating 'hearsay' testimony in exchange for a reduced sentence or parole, leading to accusations that the evidence is unreliable.

But Edward Pole did not, according to the FBI's reports, fall into this category. Although the document is heavily redacted, it appears to show that he was not in prison at the time he told his story to the Bureau's Agent; more telling was his insistence that "in view of Hoffa's power and influence in this country, he feared for his life and under no circumstances would he testify to the above information."[493] He therefore had nothing to gain from inventing his account of Hoffa's boast.

---

491 Interview with Edward Hugh Pole [name redacted in FBI files, but not in LAPD copy], June 17, 1968. FBI file Ser. 501-750, p. 304-306. California State Archives.
492 *Ibid.*
493 *Ibid.*

Against this background, the FBI's actions are inexplicable. Although he did not know their names, Pole gave the Bureau descriptions of the two men who had been sitting with Hoffa in the prison dining hall; these were sufficiently detailed for the Lewisburg records clerk to identify them as Samuel Desist and Anthony Provenzano. On July 23, a Special Agent travelled to the Penitentiary to interview both men.

Desist said that he "associates with Hoffa quite frequently but has never sat with him during any meal in the dining hall," the FBI report noted. "He stated he has never heard Hoffa make a statement even remotely similar to the one above concerning Senator Kennedy and has never heard him say anything which could indicate he or anyone else intended to harm Kennedy."[494] Provenzano, meanwhile, "advised he has closely associated with James R. Hoffa during his incarceration at the USP [United States Penitentiary], Lewisburg, Pa., and frequently has his meals at the same table with Hoffa in the dining hall." However, "he denied he had ever heard Hoffa make any statement indicating he or anyone else intended to harm Senator Kennedy in any way", adding that " 'if Hoffa ever made such a statement, my eight year old baby should have cancer in both eyes' ". [495]

The FBI knew that both Hoffa's dining companions were, even by the low standards of prison inmates, distinctly unreliable witnesses. Desist had been convicted in a four week trial of importing narcotics from France – a case which, according to the US Court of Appeals "involved what is alleged to be the largest single seizure of pure heroin in the United States, valued at sums as high as $100,000,000, and totalling some 209 pounds".[496] Provenzano –

---

494 Interview with Anthony Desist Lewisburg Federal Penitentiary, July 23, 1968. FBI files X-4, Vol. 15, p. 98. California State Archives

495 *Ibid*.p.99

496 The Court of Appeal affirmed Desist's conviction on Oct 13, 1967. US Court of Appeals for the Second Circuit – 384 F.2d 889 (2d Cir. 1967)

aka "Tony Pro" – was an even more serious criminal, and one with long-standing ties to Hoffa. A *caporegime* (captain) in the New York City Genovese Mafia, he had used his position as a Teamster's vice president to steal – with Hoffa's blessing – union funds for his personal use.[497] Inside Lewisburg Penitentiary, Tony Pro provided Hoffa with protection from the other inmates.

These antecedents should have led the FBI to treat both men's assertions of Hoffa's innocence with a degree of scepticism. There is no evidence that it did so. Instead, it sought an audience with the man himself. On July 23 the Special Agent read the prisoner his Miranda rights – which the pugnacious Hoffa refused to sign – and calmly asked him about Pole's story. But instead of flatly denying it, "Hoffa stated he would not answer such a 'stupid' allegation. He stated 'you know as well as I do how many nuts there are in this place who would say anything'. Hoffa said 'you have my statement' and refused to comment further regarding this allegation or the assassination of Senator Kennedy." [498]

And there the matter rested. Neither the Bureau nor LAPD – which was copied in on all the reports – ever sought to investigate further. There were no follow-up enquiries and no polygraph examinations of Pole, Desist, Provenzano or Hoffa. As with all other allegations of a conspiracy involving Bobby's known enemies, LAPD and the FBI simply buried the evidence in their locked files.

Nor was this the only suppression of significant evidence. Amid the thousands of pages of withheld investigative reports were documents detailing LA law enforcement's knowledge of a man who should have been a prime suspect for the role of the second gunman.

---

497 Provenzano was also a close friend of Richard Nixon: in his first public appearance after leaving the White House, the disgraced former President played golf with the organized crime boss.

498 *Ibid.* p.97

CHAPTER THIRTEEN:
THE SECURITY GUARD

L APD knew that at least two other guns were drawn in the pantry at the time of the assassination. They also knew that one eyewitness had reported seeing one of them being fired.

Don Schulman, the 28-year-old film runner for KNXT TV, gave two on the spot interviews outside the Ambassador Hotel, shortly after Sirhan was captured. In the second, he told one of his station's reporters, Ruth Ashton, that he was standing directly behind Bobby when the shooting began.

"I saw a man pull out a gun. It looked like he pulled it out from his pocket and shot three times. I saw all three shots hit the Senator.... I also saw the security men pull out their weapons. After then it was very, very fuzzy. Next thing I knew there were several shots fired..."[499]

Some minutes earlier Schulman had been interviewed by Jeff Brent, a reporter for the Continental News Service. "I was standing behind Kennedy as he was taking his assigned route into the kitchen. A Caucasian gentleman stepped out and fired three times... The security guards fired back..."[500]

---

499 Don Schulman: interview with Ruth Ashton Taylor, KNXT TV, Los Angeles. June 5, 1968
500 Don Schulman: interview with Jeff Brent, Continental News Service. June 5, 1968

Given the chaotic atmosphere Schulman's statements were understandably a little garbled. But in both accounts he was very clear about one thing: he saw a security guard – or guards – draw their weapons. Nor was he the only witness reporting additional guns.

Lisa Urso, the teenage campaign volunteer, claimed to have told the police that "the security guard had a gun and I think he went like this (drawing a gun) or he put it in a holster or something". Urso said the man had blond hair and was wearing a grey suit rather than a guard's uniform.[501] Community activist and journalist Booker Griffin also said he reported seeing a similar-looking man draw his gun; he was tall with dark, wavy hair and also wearing a suit.[502]

The accounts of Schulman, Urso and Griffin shared an additional characteristic: each appears to have been ignored by LA law enforcement. Neither of the somewhat cursory summary reports of Urso's interviews with LAPD and the FBI make any mention of the story[503], and she later told Dr. Philip Melanson that the police had "reacted with disinterest on one occasion, hostility on another."[504]

The report of Griffin's LAPD interview says that "he heard what he thought was 10 or 12 shots" and "recalled having the

501 Lisa Urso: interview with Dr. Philip Melanson, October 30, 1987. Request to the Los Angeles Grand Jury, 1992. Exhibit 60: evidence of Dr. Philip Melanson. Robert F. Kennedy Assassination Archives, University of Massachusetts Dartmouth.

502 Booker Griffin: interview with Dr. Philip Melanson, June 5, 1987. Request to the Los Angeles Grand Jury, 1992. Exhibit 60: evidence of Dr. Philip Melanson. Robert F. Kennedy Assassination Archives, University of Massachusetts Dartmouth.

503 LAPD interview with Lisa Urso, June 27, 1968. "Special Unit Senator" Vol. 61, p.185-186. California State Archives

504 FBI interview with Lisa Urso, July 19, 1968. FBI file X-4, Vol.13 p.103-104. California State Archives

feeling there was more than one person shooting",[505] while the FBI's account of its meeting with him makes no mention of any of this.[506]

But it was Schulman whose account apparently concerned LAPD the most. S.U.S. detectives didn't get around to speaking with him until August 9, 1968 when, according to the summary report of this interview – the only surviving record in the files – they did not ask him about seeing additional guns in the pantry[507]. But eight days earlier, an internal progress note flagged him (incorrectly) as "reportedly assisting the Garrison organization in collecting evidence".[508]

There was good reason for LA law enforcement to be concerned about Schulman's testimony: by identifying one or more uniformed security guards with drawn guns – and at least one of which had been fired – the young film-runner highlighted a major blunder by LAPD. It would also set in train one of the longest-lasting and most troublesome controversies surrounding the assassination.

There were seventeen guards on duty around the hotel on the night of June 4-5. Eleven were directly employed by the Ambassador, and with the exception of their two most senior men who sported suits, wore the hotel's own uniform; according to its policies they carried no weapons. The other six were private rent-a-cops, drafted in from Ace Security. They wore the

---

505 Interview with Booker Griffin, July25, 1968. Special Unit Senator Vol. 51, p.14. California State Archives
506 Interview with Booker Griffin, June 11, 1968, FBI files Interviews 2, p.50-51. California State Archives
507 Summary of interview with Don Schulman, August 9, 1968 1968, Special Unit Senator Vol. 57, p.102. California State Archives
508 Memo from Sgt. D.D. Varney (SUS) to Lt. Higbie re: Theodore Charach. August 1, 1968. Special Unit Senator Vol. 48, p.74. California State Archives

company's grey uniform and were required by their employer to be armed with .38 calibre revolvers.

When Bobby finished his victory speech, there were five guards in the vicinity of the Embassy Room, the kitchen pantry or the corridors nearby. Thomas Perez, an Ambassador security man, was in the anteroom behind the stage and to the east of the pantry; his plain-clothed superior, Fred. A Murphy, was outside the kitchen doors at its west end; and Ace supervisor Jack Merritt was guarding the main doors to the Embassy Room. As Bobby began moving towards, and then into, the pantry, Ambassador officer Stanley Kawalec and Thane Eugene Cesar, wearing Ace uniform, accompanied him – Kawalec in front, Cesar following just behind the candidate.

Merritt and Cesar were the only two of these five guards authorized to carry weapons. Merritt told S.U.S. investigators that when the shooting broke out "he drew his gun and ran into the pantry in time to see two men struggling with Sirhan."[509] The LAPD files contain only a brief and undated summary of his statement which makes no mention of the type of gun he carried, or what he did with it once he had drawn it. There is no evidence that the detectives seized or examined the gun.

The FBI's account of its interview with Merritt, conducted on June 13, 1968, is equally sparse. It contains no reference to him brandishing his gun and, like the Los Angeles Police, the Bureau seems to have evinced no interest in establishing its type, calibre or whether it had been fired.[510]

This might – perhaps – have been excusable, given Merritt's apparent arrival in the pantry after the shooting began. But there was no such justification for the disinterest shown by LA

---

509 Summary of interview with Jack J. Merritt August 9, 1968, Special Unit Senator Vol. 78, p.73. California State Archives
510 Report of interview with Jack J. Merritt, June 13, 1968. FBI files X-4, Vol.13, p.39. California State Archives.

law enforcement in the other armed guard: as a result, Thane Cesar would, in the minds of many researchers, become a prime suspect for the role of the second gunman. Ultimately, his story would exemplify the contradictions and controversies which remain unresolved fifty years after the assassination.

Cesar was 26, a full-time plumber employed by Lockheed Aircraft, and a part-time rent-a-cop who worked occasional shifts for Ace. He was interviewed by LAPD in the hours immediately after the shooting, telling detectives that he had hold of Bobby's right arm when he saw Sirhan point his gun towards them.

"I just happened to look up and ... all I could see was an arm and a gun ... and I reached for mine but it was too late. He had done fired five shots and when he did I ducked because I was as close as Kennedy was, and from what I can remember, from what I did, I grabbed for the Senator and fell back.

"When I ducked, I threw myself off balance and fell back and ... there's iceboxes right in this area ... and I fell against that and then the Senator fell down right in front of me and then I turned around; then [I] seen blood coming down this [right hand] side of his face ..."[511]

The police asked Cesar to identify the weapon he saw in the suspect's hand, showing him a .22 calibre revolver of the same make and specifications as that wrestled from Sirhan: he was unable to do so. But despite the fact that he described drawing his own gun, they made no attempt to establish its make, model and calibre, nor to examine it for evidence that it had been fired.

The FBI seemed equally lackadaisical. It questioned Cesar six days later and also failed to check – much less secure – the guard's weapon. And in the time between the two interviews Cesar's story had begun to shift: instead of falling over because

---

511 Transcript of recorded of interview with Thane Eugene Cesar, June 5, 1968. Special Unit Senator Vol. 94 p. 34-44. California State Archives

he ducked, he told the Agents he "was shoved by an unknown individual, and the next thing he remembered he was on the floor against the ice machine", and that he only drew his gun after he "scrambled to his feet".[512] He repeated this changed version of how he fell over in a second interview with LAPD on June 12.[513]

These were, to be sure, very small differences, but they would, over time, form part of a troubling pattern of inconsistencies which, had S.U.S. been doing its job, should have led the detectives to look a little more closely at Thane Cesar. Instead, despite the fact that he was one of the closest people to Bobby at the time of the shooting – he said that he was "about two feet from him"[514] – LA law enforcement seems to have had no further interest in his evidence. By his own subsequent account the D.A.'s office acceded to his request that he would "just prefer not to be involved"[515] in the trial of Sirhan, and for the next few years he disappeared from view.

But a less official investigator took a rather more robust interest. Ted Charach tracked Cesar down to his home in Simi Valley, California, and persuaded him to give an audio-taped interview for the reporter's self-declared "probe" into the assassination. The 27-minute recording, portions of which were included in Charach's 1973 feature-length documentary *The Second Gun*, established that Cesar confirmed to all three stereotypical characteristics of a murder suspect: opportunity, means and motive. He described walking immediately behind Bobby moments before the shooting began, and therefore clearly was in a position

---

512 Report of interview with Thane Cesar, June 11, 1968. FBI file: Interviews 2, p.15-17. California State Archives.
513 Handwritten statement of Thane Cesar, June 12, 1968. . Special Unit Senator Vol. 49, p. 91-94. California State Archives
514 *Ibid.*
515 Thane Eugene Cesar audio-taped interview with Ted Charach: [in] *The Second Gun,* ©: Theodore Charach and Gérard Alcan, 1973.

to fire the fatal shots. And he was surprisingly frank about both his right-wing political views and his dislike of the Kennedys.

"I definitely wouldn't have voted for Bobby Kennedy because he had the same ideas as John did, and I think John sold the country down the road. He gave it away to the commies...he literally gave it to the minority."[516]

That "minority", according to what Cesar told Charach, was the African-American community; he blamed both Kennedy brothers for their support for civil rights and de-segregation. "The black man now for the last four to eight years, has been cramming this integrated idea down our throat and so you've learned to hate him. And one of these days, at the rate they're going, there is going to be a civil war in this country. It's going to be white against the black, and the only thing I'd say is that the black will never win.

"I mean me, as an individual, I'm fed up...we have had it shoved down our throat enough. But one of these days it's going to be shoved too far and then we're going to fight back. First of all, I think the white man is going to try and do it with his voting power, and if they can't do it by getting the right person to straighten the thing out, then he's going to take it into his own hands. I can't see any other way to go."[517]

Nor was this an entirely passive political position. Cesar told Charach that he had worked for the Presidential campaign of George Wallace – the unashamedly racist former governor of Alabama who had publicly promised that he stood for "segregation now, segregation tomorrow, segregation forever".[518] Cesar said he "passed out handbills" and donated $3 to support Wallace's 1968 bid for the White House.

---

516 *Ibid.*
517 *Ibid.*
518 George Wallace, Inaugural Governor's Address, Montgomery, Alabama, January 14, 1963.

Since the case against Sirhan had cited his dislike of both Bobby and his pro-Israeli position, Cesar's statements seemed to give him an equally powerful political motive for murder. But it was the question of Cesar's gun – the means to kill – which would prove the most problematic.

Neither LAPD nor the FBI had asked about the gun he was carrying in the pantry; but in his interview with Charach Cesar said he was carrying a .38 calibre revolver – a substantially more powerful weapon which used much larger bullets than the .22 calibre slugs recovered from the shooting victims, and whose characteristics ensured it could not have been fired accidentally.

"The only way it could have come off [sic] is if I had pulled the trigger, because the hammer wasn't cocked. It would have taken more pressure… I would have had to want to fire the gun… It wouldn't have been something where I could have slipped on the trigger. It wouldn't have been that easy. You'd have had to put pressure against the trigger and pull it."[519]

Since LAPD had not checked Cesar's gun during its first interview with him just after the shooting there was no way to confirm the truth of his story. But Charach also established that the .38 was not Cesar's only weapon; Cesar told Charach he had owned a .22 calibre Harrington & Richardson 9-shot revolver which, as he freely admitted, was "just like the one that was used on Bobby… it's exactly the same kind of .22… same length barrel, same size".[520]

He claimed, however, that he had got rid of the gun a few months before the assassination, selling it to a friend and former work colleague who had since moved to another state. Charach diligently tracked down the man, Jim Yoder, to the tiny Blue

519 *Ibid.*
520 *Ibid.*

Mountain hamlet in Arkansas. Yoder gave a significantly different version of events: he had indeed bought the H&R from Thane Cesar, but the date of the purchase was September 6, 1968 – three months *after* the assassination. He could be certain about this because he retained the receipt, which specified the gun's serial number and description, the sale price ($15) and date; it also bore Cesar's signature as the vendor.[521]

None of this should have come as a surprise to LA law enforcement. On July 14, 1971, Cesar had been called in to the District Attorney's Office and for a new interview. Questioned by representatives of the DA and LAPD, he confirmed that he had owned the .22, but claimed – as he had done in Charach's as yet un-broadcast film – that he had sold it to Yoder in February 1968.

But during the same tape-recorded session Cesar also claimed that he had offered to show the gun to an S.U.S. investigator during a meeting at his home on June 24, 1968. "I don't remember if I showed it to him, but I did mention I had a gun similar to the one that was used that [assassination] night".[522]

There was an obvious flaw in this statement: Deputy DA Sidney Trapp asked how, if he had sold the gun in February, "did you show it to the sergeant the night he came out?" Cesar's attempts at backtracking only made the position worse, first saying "I didn't ... I just told him about it and I wanted, you know, I was telling him what it was," then immediately, "I wanted to show it to him, you know what kind of gun it was."[523]

521 Sales receipt for Harrington & Richardson .22 calibre pistol, serial no: Y-13332; September 6, 1968. Robert F. Kennedy Assassination Archives, University of Massachusetts Dartmouth.

522 Transcript of Recorded interview with Thane Eugene Cesar, District Attorney's Office, North Spring Street, LA, July 14, 1971. Robert F. Kennedy Assassination Archives, University of Massachusetts Dartmouth.

523 *Ibid.*

Despite this distinctly unsatisfactory and contradictory explanation, the officials didn't explore the issue further: instead, after asking Cesar to confirm that was carrying his .38 on the night of the assassination, they spent much of the remaining 20 minutes probing his involvement with Ted Charach.

Towards the end of the meeting the DA's detective, De Witt Lightner, made Cesar repeat his account of drawing his gun after he got up from the pantry floor – "maybe for five seconds and then [I] put it back"- before asking directly "did you ever fire a shot?". Cesar said he did not. Shortly afterwards, the transcript records a decision by the assembled law enforcement officials to take a break so that a polygraph operator could be brought in to administer a lie detector test.

However, when the recording resumed, Trapp announced that the examination had been cancelled or postponed. "We may perhaps ask you, perhaps not," he told Cesar, without giving – on tape at least – any explanation for the change of heart.[524] For the next few years, Thane Eugene Cesar would disappear from public view.

But the question of whether he – or any other security guard – had fired his weapon in the pantry would not go away. On July 6, 1971 – eight days before Cesar's interview in the DA's office – KHJ News Channel 9 broadcast a new interview with Don Schulman. "I saw the security guards draw their weapons out and I assumed that they were security guards because – well, as I said it was an assumption, they would be the ones with weapons," he told the station's Baxter Ward.

"I was interviewed by LAPD ... and I told them my story and what I had seen, and at that time they disagreed with me on seeing other weapons. And I told them I was positive

---

524 *Ibid.*

I had seen other weapons and then they filled out the report, thanking me very much and said they had enough witnesses and I probably would not be called [to give evidence at Sirhan's trial].[525] He gave a similar account in Ted Charach's film, *The Second Gun*, which opened in movie theatres two years later. "I told the story to several different people including several police departments ... I didn't see everything that night ... but the things I did see, I'm sure about. And that is Kennedy was shot three times [and] the guard definitely pulled out his gun and fired".[526]

Both Schulman's claims and Cesar's ever-changing and contradictory statements featured heavily in the repeated requests made by former US Congressman Allard Lowenstein to LA law enforcement in the early 1970s, although, as he later complained, he never received substantive answers. But tucked away in the S.U.S. files was a confidential internal LAPD report, written in 1974 for the force's then-Assistant Chief, Daryl Gates, though never publicly released.

Titled "Reply to questions submitted by Allard K. Lowenstein" it set out a series of "Troublesome and misleading statements by officials" which could cause problems if they were revealed. Cesar's ownership of the .22 H&R, and his false claims to have sold it before the assassination featured prominently. And it also raised the question of his cancelled 1971 polygraph.

"Mr. Cesar voluntarily appeared and answered all questions put to him in a thorough, straightforward and honest manner. He volunteered to take a polygraph examination to verify his statements. Since all questions were satisfactorily answered and the evidence given by Mr. Cesar coincided with other evidence

---

525 Don Schulman interview, KHJ News Channel 9, Los Angeles. July 6, 1971
526 Thane Eugene Cesar audio-taped interview with Ted Charach: [in] *The Second Gun*, ©: Theodore Charach and Gérard Alcan, 1973.

received by investigators, it was decided that a polygraph examination would not add to the investigation"[527].

This was blatantly misleading: Cesar's answers were the polar opposite of "straightforward and honest". Nor was it the document's only falsehood: "In addition," the writer, Lt. F.J. Patchett, reported, "no-one in the pantry was given a polygraph examination."[528] LAPD knew its own records showed that at least one of the pantry witnesses, Vincent Di Pierro, had been polygraphed because his original testimony exposed another flaw in the S.U.S. investigation.

Perhaps as a result of the fundamental problems Lt. Patchett's report identified, LAPD made a belated attempt to investigate at least one of the weapons Cesar had owned. It tracked down Jim Yoder in Blue Mountain, Arkansas, and asked about the .22 he had bought. Unfortunately, by the time it did so – December 1974 – the gun was gone, stolen in an apparent burglary on Yoder's home.[529] There was, therefore, no prospect of testing it for comparison with the bullets recovered from the pantry shooting. It would be another year before the District Attorney's Special Prosecutor, Thomas Kranz, picked up the issue and questioned Cesar again.

Kranz' report showed that when he met Cesar, in his lawyer's office in November 1975, the now ex-guard insisted that he

---

527 *Reply to Questions Submitted by Allard K. Lowenstein*: confidential report for LAPD Asst, Chief Daryl F. Gates, December 20, 1974. Special Unit Senator Vol. 123, p.135. California State Archives.

528 *Ibid.*

529 Although Yoder insisted he had reported the theft, when LAPD officers spoke to the local sheriff's department they discovered the office holder had changed, and that prior to leaving the outgoing sheriff had destroyed all the department's records. "There was nothing in the office but paint," one of the new sheriff's officers told LAPD on Christmas Eve, 1974. *Report of interview with Deputy Penn Smith, Logan County Sheriff's Department, Arkansas.* December 24, 1974. Special Unit Senator Vol. 123, p.130 California State Archives

"did not fire his gun [and] was never questioned regarding this action by either LAPD or FBI officials in the weeks following the shooting of Senator Kennedy."[530] When the Special Counsel asked "'Why didn't you fire your gun? You were here to protect Kennedy', Cesar replied "simply and quickly, 'I was a coward'".[531]

This apparently self-deprecating explanation was yet another variation in his account: nor was it the only one. Evidently conscious of LAPD's glaring failure to secure the gun Cesar admitted having drawn in the pantry, he and the police now offered an entirely uncorroborated claim that they had done so within hours of the shooting.

"Cesar states, and the LAPD orally verifies, but have no documents to substantiate, the fact that the .38 caliber weapon Cesar had on his person that night as part of his Ace Guard Service assignment, was examined by an unnamed LAPD officer, but was not seized or subsequently test-fired". Even Kranz – whose report was denounced for its inaccuracies and credulity – wasn't buying that.

"In hindsight," he noted, "it seems obvious that the LAPD should have seized the .38 weapon that Cesar was carrying ... the very fact that he had been inside the pantry, and had held a weapon in his hand during some of the confusion, and the fact that at least five victims in addition to Senator Kennedy were involved in the mass shooting, should have given notice to the LAPD to seize the weapon, if only for precaution's sake.

"Additionally, it was proved by the very determined and thorough investigative research conducted by Ted Charach that Cesar owned a .22 caliber revolver at the time of the shooting. Cesar was somewhat vague as to when he had sold the weapon...

---

530 *The Report of Special Counsel Thomas F. Kranz on the Assassination of Robert F. Kennedy,* March 1977. SUS file 124, p.299

531 *Ibid.,* p.300

"Such inconsistencies in the statements of the security guard, and the fact that he had been carrying a weapon in the pantry, suggested that good judgment required the LAPD to at least inspect and test the weapon beyond a cursory search at the Rampart Division ... It can be expected that continued accusations will be made by conspiracy buffs, and the misinformed, concerning Thane Eugene Cesar and his .38 caliber revolver."[532]

Journalist Dan Moldea conformed to the first of those characteristics. As a celebrated organized crime reporter – the evidence detailed in his 1974 book on Jimmy Hoffa[533] helped persuade the U.S. House Select Committee on Assassinations that the Teamsters' leader and Mafia bosses Carlos Marcello and Santos Trafficante played a role in the John Kennedy assassination – Moldea cheerfully acknowledges that he dealt, by definition, with crimes of conspiracy.[534]

In March 1987 Moldea, then working simultaneously for Paul Schrade and Philip Melanson's Inquiry and Accountability Foundation and on a forthcoming magazine feature, tracked down Cesar in California and persuaded him to agree to an interview. The transcript of their three-hour meeting, stored in Melanson's Robert F. Kennedy Assassinations Archive at the University of Massachusetts, Dartmouth, began with the reporter putting his interviewee at ease, saying that he believed Ted Charach had "set him up pretty good". Cesar replied that he had "learned to live with" news stories implying he had killed Bobby: "basically, I ignore people like you," he explained, because LAPD had told him he had nothing to worry about.

---

532 *Ibid.*, p.301-302
533 *The Hoffa Wars: Teamsters, Rebels, Politicians and the Mob.* Paddington Press, 1978.
534 Dan E. Moldea. Interview with Tim Tate, Washington DC, July 3, 2016.

"The police department...told me: 'There's no way we're going to prosecute you. We know you didn't do it. We've got the man that did it. We're happy with it.' ...In fact, they told me that they had to spend a lot of time and money to prove that I didn't. That's what they were doing and that's what they did. They felt they proved conclusively that I had nothing to do with it."[535]

He went on to re-iterate his right-wing political views and dislike of the Kennedys. "I wasn't ashamed of what I said [to Charach]...I mean there's nothing wrong that I liked Wallace. I still like Wallace. I'd still vote for Wallace...Wallace had a lot of good ideas...I've never cared for Democrats since John F. Kennedy....I had no use for the Kennedy family, you know (laughing); none of them...I mean I've read a lot of history on the Kennedy family. I think they're the biggest bunch of crooks that ever walked this earth. And I'm not ashamed to say it today..."

However, he went on to qualify this, adding: "I felt bad about the fact that he [Bobby] got shot. I wouldn't want anyone to get shot...I didn't like him as a politician. But, as a human being, he was fine...Just because I don't like Democrats don't mean I go around shooting them."[536]

But what disturbed Moldea most were the repeated inconsistencies in Cesar's story about when he sold his Harrington & Richardson .22. During the interview, he reverted to his claim that he had shown the H&R to LAPD during his June 24, 1968 interview at his home. "That guy, when he came out, I even showed him my .22 pistol that I owned. Because we were talking in depth about how easy it is to conceal a weapon like that and how Sirhan did it...And so I brought this .22 out, and I says, 'His

---

535 Thane Eugene Cesar: transcript of interview with Dan Moldea, March 27, 1987. Robert F. Kennedy Assassination Archives, University of Massachusetts Dartmouth.

536 *Ibid.*

is just like mine, except for it was a different brand.' ... So they knew about this gun, this .22 pistol."[537]

Towards the end of the meeting, Moldea asked, point–blank, whether he had shot Bobby "intentionally or accidentally": Cesar said he had not, and agreed to take a polygraph test if the reporter arranged one.[538]

Moldea's resulting feature was published in *Regardie's* – a Washington-DC based monthly business magazine – in July 1987. It set out a detailed case, based on the evidence then available, that there had been a second gunman in the Ambassador Hotel pantry, and concluded that "the evidence to support Cesar's possible role in the shooting is extensive and clearly demonstrates means, opportunity and motive"; but, struck by the ex-guard's apparent openness, the reporter also sounded a note of caution. "Gene Cesar may be the classic example of a man caught at the wrong time in the wrong place with a gun in his hands and powder burns on his face – an innocent bystander caught in the crossfire of history."[539]

In 1992, Moldea secured a commission to write a book about the assassination. "My proposal was a complete pro-conspiracy proposal," he later recalled. "They attached my proposal to the contract, for which I received $75,000. And I said 'two guns in the room, probably Cesar who did it – intentionally or accidentally'."[540] The publishing deal enabled the reporter to revive his ambition to set up a lie detector test. Cesar was willing, and Moldea had a very clear idea of its purpose. "The reason for the polygraph on Cesar was not to determine definitively whether he was innocent or guilty. I've seen the polygraph used enough to

537 *Ibid.*
538 *Ibid.*
539 Dan E. Moldea. *Who Really Killed Bobby? Regardie's,* June 1987.
540 Dan E. Moldea. Interview with Tim Tate, Washington DC, July 3, 2016.

see that it should get a person off the hook but it shouldn't necessarily get a person on the hook.

"I was spending an enormous amount of time and money on Cesar and I couldn't figure out whether he was innocent or guilty. I had asked him every question I could think of asking him – repeatedly – and he was contradicting himself, he was giving me conflicting answers on things…

"I needed some test or measurement… If he had failed the polygraph I would have spent every moment of my time and every cent that I had going after him. But I decided that if he passed, I would ease up."[541]

On the advice of his extensive contacts in law enforcement, Moldea hired Edward Gelb, a past-President of the American Polygraph Association – "the world's leading association dedicated to the use of evidence-based scientific methods for credibility assessment"[542] – who had achieved wider public recognition from his appearances on a nationally-syndicated television program called *Lie Detector.*[543] Since Gelb was also a former LAPD officer, the selection was controversial, but to the reporter it was simply a question of securing the best man for the job. "I had a choice," he said in 2016. "I could spend very little money and have one of Gelb's associates do the polygraph, or I could have Gelb do it himself for the top dollar. And I chose Gelb to do it himself: he's the best, and I want the best to do it."[544]

After a lengthy pre-test interview in Gelb's Los Angeles office, Cesar was strapped into a Stoelting Ultrascribe polygraph machine; Gelb asked him a series of test interrogatories to calibrate a base-level response before moving on to the four key questions: " 'Did you fire a weapon on the night Robert Kennedy

---

541 *Ibid.*
542 *American polygraph Association*: http://www.polygraph.org/
543 *Lie Detector*: Columbia Pictures Television, 1983.
544 Dan E. Moldea. Interview with Tim Tate, Washington DC, July 3, 2016.

was shot? Did you fire any of the shots that hit him in June 1968? Could you have fired at Kennedy if you wanted to? Were you involved in a plan to shoot Robert Kennedy?'"[545]

According to the account in Moldea's subsequent book, Gelb's formal report exonerated Cesar completely. "Based on the polygraph examination and its numerical scoring, Thane Eugene Cesar was telling the truth when he answered 'No' to the above questions." In other words, according to Moldea, "Cesar did not fire a weapon the night Robert Kennedy was killed, nor was he involved in a conspiracy to kill Kennedy."[546]

Ordinarily, that should have ended the speculation about Cesar and his role – or lack of it – in Bobby's murder. But, in twists that encapsulate all that blights genuine understanding of the assassination, Moldea's subsequent actions failed to put out the fires. The polygraph test led him to a radical change in direction: convinced that Cesar was "to all intents and purposes innocent"[547], he turned his attention to Sirhan. Over the course of three interviews, conducted in California's Corcoran State Prison, Moldea reached the conclusion that the original trial decision had been correct: Sirhan, he told his incredulous publisher, had been a lone gunman.

"If a look could kill I would have been melted," he recalled. "I thought he was going to cancel [but] he said 'you better make this work'".[548]

The resulting book showed Moldea executing a dramatic *volte-face*. After setting out the substantial evidence of a second gunman – eyewitness testimony, extra bullets and LAPD's malfeasance, he pronounced that Sirhan, and only Sirhan, had

---

545 Dan E. Moldea: *The Killing of Robert F. Kennedy – An Examination of Motive, Means and Opportunity*: p.287 W.W. Norton, 1995
546 *Ibid.* p.289
547 Dan E. Moldea. Interview with Tim Tate, Washington DC, July 3, 2016.
548 *Ibid.*

assassinated Bobby. It was greeted with anger and dismay by his former colleagues, Paul Schrade and Philip Melanson – the latter denounced it for "speculative conclusions that have little or no foundation" and which "simply misreport or mischaracterize the record".[549]

But it was the reporter's personal involvement with Cesar which most undermined him. In the years following the polygraph, Moldea accepted an invitation to become godfather to Cesar's son,[550] and he went on to act, essentially, as Cesar's agent – handling requests for interviews from journalists and documentary makers, and offering to broker deals at up to $50,000 a time.

Moldea rejects any suggestion of a conflict of interest or impropriety. "Since 1995, I have received many calls and letters about the RFK case. Most of those who contact me are people I have never heard of," he wrote on his own website. "And I have learned from a series of harsh experiences that if they haven't been referred by someone I know, then I don't trust them or their motives.

"To be sure, almost all of them want to talk with Cesar, who is simply tired of this nonsense and has told me that if anyone wants to waste his time, it will cost $50,000."[551]

Was Thane Eugene Cesar the second gunman in the pantry? Certainly, Phil Van Praag's audio analysis, revealing the sound signature of a nine-shot .22 H&R – the very model of gun which Cesar owned and then lied about – raises questions which need to be answered. Or, as Moldea suggested, was Cesar merely "the

549 *The Fatal Flaws in 'The Killing of Robert Kennedy*: Philip H. Melanson, Professor of Political Science and Chair of the Robert F. Kennedy Assassination Archive, 1995. Robert F. Kennedy Assassination Archives, University of Massachusetts Dartmouth.

550 Dan E. Moldea. Interview with Tim Tate, Washington DC, July 3, 2016.

551 Dan Moldea: http://www.moldea.com/Response-SOS.html. Posted: July 3, 2008

classic example of a man caught at the wrong time in the wrong place with a gun in his hands and powder burns on his face – an innocent bystander caught in the crossfire of history"[552]? The Gelb polygraph test would appear to suggest the latter. But that report has never been formally published: although Moldea has promised to open it to public scrutiny[553], a quarter of a century after it was conducted he decided against doing so. "With regard to the Cesar-polygraph paperwork, I have no plan to release it," he wrote in May 2017. "It has some value, and I can use it for bargaining power when and if the occasion arises."[554]

Without this – and in the absence of an honest and thorough inquiry by LA law enforcement – the troubling flaws in LAPD's original investigation remain unresolved. One issue in particular – its handling of eyewitness evidence describing the escape of self-declared assassins – seems to point to the existence of a carefully-planned conspiracy.

---

552 *Regardie's* – op.cit.
553 Dan E. Moldea. Interview with Tim Tate, Washington DC, July 3, 2016.
554 Dan E. Moldea: e-mail to Tim Tate, May 11, 2017.

CHAPTER FOURTEEN:
THE GIRL IN THE POLKA DOT DRESS

Within hours of arresting Sirhan, Los Angeles Police issued an all-points bulletin for two suspected accomplices who had been seen with him on the evening of June 4-5, and who had, according to eyewitnesses, fled from the scene of the crime. One was a young Hispanic-looking man; the other, a young white woman wearing a black and white polka dot dress. For the next sixteen days Special Unit Senator would ostensibly put enormous time and resources into identifying the mystery woman: as a result, 'The Girl in the Polka Dot Dress' would become, in LAPD's own words "the most publicized of the conspiracy allegations"[555].

The hunt for the polka dot dress girl involved questioning hundreds of people who had been at the Ambassador Hotel on the night of the shooting, as well as handling phone calls from members of the public who claimed to have seen her in the days before or after the assassination. Dozens of detectives – often aided by Special Agents from the FBI's Los Angeles Field Office

---

555 Special Unit Senator: Final Report, p. 62. April 4, 1969. California State Archives

and lawyers from the District Attorney's staff – dutifully logged every alleged sighting before LAPD abandoned the investigation and announced that the search for Sirhan's female accomplice had been a wild goose chase: nothing more than the invention of an "overwrought" 20-year-old campaign worker. But there was far more to the story than the police or the District Attorney's office was prepared to admit.

By the start of Sirhan's trial, the DA knew that his last conscious memory, minutes before the shooting, was of encountering an attractive girl wearing a polka dot dress. On January 26, 1969, prosecution psychiatrist Dr. Seymour Pollack and defence psychiatrist Dr. Bernard Diamond, accompanied by defence chief investigator Robert Blair Kaiser, had tape-recorded a lengthy interview with Sirhan in his cell at the county jail. According to Diamond's trial testimony, Sirhan described meeting the girl and drinking a coffee with her.

"He described this girl and he did not know who she was, Sirhan did not know her name and she never told him her name … he was really planning whether or not he could persuade the girl to leave the hotel with him … all he was thinking of was the girl and coffee."[556]

After drinking the coffee, Sirhan's next conscious recollection was of being "choked" on the steam table in the kitchen pantry immediately after the shooting. Then, in a bid to unblock memories locked in his unconscious, Diamond put Sirhan into a hypnotic trance: when the psychiatrist asked "Who was with you when you shot Kennedy?" Sirhan mumbled "Girl the girl the girl…"[557]

556 *People vs. Sirhan Bishara Sirhan,* Certified trial transcript Vol. 24, p.148. California State Archives…

557 Recording of interview under hypnosis by Dr. Seymour Polack, January 25, 1969. California State Archives.

Though Sirhan could not have known it, his fragmented story of the girl with whom he shared a coffee bore several similarities to the police statements of twenty-five eyewitnesses. Each described a girl wearing a striking polka dot dress, and thirteen of them reported seeing her with a man matching Sirhan's description.

Those statements – which suggested Sirhan had not acted alone on the night of the assassination – would be suppressed for almost 20 years. Not until the S.U.S. case files were opened to public scrutiny at the California State Archives in 1988 would the extent of this testimony emerge: and within those files was disturbing evidence that LAPD had ignored potentially vital exhibits, bullied witnesses into recanting their stories or, when that failed, grossly distorted their accounts.

* * *

Sandy Serrano needed air. The 20-year-old Latina co-chair of Youth For Kennedy in Pasadena-Altadena had arrived at the Ambassador Hotel around 9.15pm with campaign colleagues and her roommate Irene Chavez. After more than two hours the California primary election result had still not been announced and the overcrowded room where she'd spent most of the evening was hot and stuffy, so Serrano stepped out on to an external stairway to cool off. It was sometime after 11.30pm.

Five minutes later, two men and one woman walked up the stairway towards the door which led up into the Embassy Room. As they passed her, the woman said 'Excuse me'. Serrano noticed that one of the men had on "rather messed up clothes and he had a lot of hair: looked like he needed a haircut. And to me he looked like what we call a "*borracho*"[558], somebody who just

---

558 *Borracho* is a slang word for someone who is drunk and unkempt.

never looks right"[559]. The second man was Mexican-American, approximately 23 years old, wearing a white shirt with a gold-coloured sweater.

The woman was Caucasian, five foot six inches tall with dark brown hair; her dress was white with black polka dots.[560] At the time, Serrano later recalled, she "didn't think anything of it. I was just sitting there, feeling really tired and thinking how good it felt to be away from the crowd and to be cool again. I didn't know who these people were, but the three of them definitely seemed to be together."[561]

Then, a little over half an hour later the girl and the man in the gold sweater burst out of the door from the Embassy Room and ran back down the stairway; as they passed Serrano, the girl uttered a phrase which would come to haunt the investigation into Bobby Kennedy's murder.

"She practically stepped on me," Serrano told LAPD detectives. "And she said 'we've shot him. We've shot him'. Then I said, 'who did you shoot?' And she said 'we shot Senator Kennedy'. And I says, 'oh sure'. And she came running down the stairs and the boy in the gold sweater came running down after her..."[562]

Serrano was startled and upset. She ran down the stairway and back into the ground floor Ambassador Room, asking everyone she met if it was true that Kennedy had been shot. News of the shooting had yet to filter downstairs, and at first she was met with blank incomprehension. Five minutes later she found Irene Chavez in a hallway outside the Ambassador Room.

According to an undated note of an LAPD interview with Chavez, Serrano was crying and told her roommate about

559 LAPD – 1st interview with Sandy Serrano; 2.25am, June 4, 1968. SUS files, Volume 95; pp 83-96. California State Archives.
560 Ibid.
561 Sandy Serrano-Sewell: interviews with Tim Tate, 1991 – 2016
562 Ibid.

"seeing a man and a woman run down the stairway where she had been sitting. The woman said something about they had shot Kennedy"[563]. After this, Serrano found a payphone and called her parents in Ohio. They, too, would later tell LAPD that she was crying.

Sgt. Paul Sharaga was the first LAPD officer to arrive at the Ambassador Hotel site. He had been out in his patrol car when he heard a radio alert: he pulled into the parking lot at 12.20am. Within a few minutes he was approached by an elderly couple[564] who told a very similar story to Sandy Serrano. Sharaga had no doubt they were sincere and honestly relating to him exactly what they had just witnessed. "They were quite hysterical and spontaneous," he remembered later.[565]

As Sharaga subsequently told S.U.S. investigators, "She and her husband were on the balcony outside the Embassy Room of the Ambassador Hotel when a young couple, early twenties, came running from the direction of the Embassy Room shouting 'We shot him, we shot him', when asked who, the young couple replied, 'Kennedy, we shot him.'"[566] The story, as related by Sharaga, suggests that the older couple not only saw the young male and female running down the outer stairway but may have witnessed their encounter with Serrano.

In a filmed interview some years later Sharaga recalled: "I immediately put out a broadcast with the description of the suspects: a male and a female Caucasian, the female Caucasian wearing a polka dot dress." [567] The sole substantive difference between

563 Summary of interview with Irene Chavez, Special Unit Senator Final Report, p. 907. April 4, 1969. California State Archives.
564 Sharaga could not, with any certainty, recall their name. He thought that it might have been "Bernstein".
565 Paul Sharaga: interviews with Tim Tate, 1991 – 1992.
566 Interview with Sgt. Paul Sharaga, September 26, 1968. Special Unit Senator Files; Volume 72, p 3. California State Archives.
567 Paul Sharaga: interviews with Tim Tate, 1991 – 1992.

the elderly couple's description and that given by Serrano was that they described polka dot dress girl's male companion as Caucasian, not Hispanic – though that could have been due to limited visibility under the moonlight.

LAPD's official log shows that Sharaga's call to the Communications Division (responsible for issuing APBs) was timed at 12.29am. But strangely, it recorded only one fleeing suspect. "2L30[568], description of a suspect in the shooting at 3400 Wilshire Boulevard, male Caucasian, 20-22, 6' to 6'2", very thin build, blond curly hair, wearing brown pants and a light brown shirt – it's a light tan shirt – direction taken unknown at this time".[569]

When he subsequently saw the log, Sharaga could not understand why his description of the female suspect in the polka dot dress had been omitted. "I definitely called in both the descriptions I had been given by the old couple. I also wrote down what they told me in my notebook and sent it back, by courier, to Inspector John Powers, who was in charge at Rampart Detectives Division. I can't think of any reason why only the male suspect's description was issued."[570]

Around 12.30am, Sandy Serrano was at the main guest entrance to the Ambassador Hotel and still trying to find someone to whom she could tell her story. Without knowing who he was, she approached Los Angeles County Deputy District Attorney John Ambrose. He described the encounter in a statement to LAPD.

"At that time a short, heavy, Mexican-American girl came up to me, obviously excited, and said that she had to tell someone what she had seen. She related that she was standing in a

---

568 Sgt. Sharaga's call sign
569 LAPD Telephone and Radio Transmissions, June 4-5, 1968. Special Unit Senator, Vol.39; p.26. California State Archives.
570 Paul Sharaga: interviews with Tim Tate, 1991 – 1992.

corridor of the Ambassador Hotel before she had heard any announcement of the shooting when a Mexican-American male, about 23-years old, wearing a gold sweater, and a Caucasian girl, between 22 and 26 years of age, approximately 5-5, wearing a white dress with black polka dots and heels, with a good figure and a bib collar on the dress, which also had long sleeves, walked by her and said 'we just shot him'.

"To which statement the girl asked the two, 'who shot who?' to which the girl in the polka dot dress answered 'we just shot Senator Kennedy'. The girl in the polka dot dress and the Mexican-American then departed. I secured the name address and telephone number of the girl who identified herself as Sandra Serrano ... I then took her toward the main halls of the Ambassador where the main body of police and press men were. I identified myself as a Deputy District Attorney and indicated that the girl with me was a witness whose statement the police would be wanting ... one police officer led Sandra and myself to a room in the Ambassador where the detectives were."[571]

By now television networks broadcasting news of the shooting. At 1.30am, in a live on-air interview, Serrano repeated to NBC correspondent Sander Vanocur the gist of what she had told Ambrose about the fleeing polka dot dress girl and her male companion.

"This girl came running down the stairs in the back, came running down the stairs and said 'We've shot him, we've shot him'. 'Who did you shoot?' And she said, 'We've shot Senator Kennedy!' ... She was Caucasian. She had on a white dress with polka dots, she was light skinned, dark hair, she had black shoes

---

571 Statement of John Ambrose, Deputy District Attorney. Special Unit Senator; Vol. 70, pp.339-340. California State Archives.

on and she had a funny nose. It was, it was, I thought it was really funny – all my friends tell me I'm so observant'.[572]

Serrano's interview was short and did not dwell on details. She didn't describe the first encounter with the polka dot dress girl, as she and her two companions climbed up the stairway; nor did she give a description of what the girl's companion was wearing. Nonetheless, John Ambrose was surprised that the police had allowed Vanocur access to a witness with what seemed potentially crucial information.

"At that time I indicated to one of the officers whether he thought it was a good idea to have Sandra interviewed by the press before the police had gotten the story, to which the reply was 'I guess there is nothing we can do about that now'... Sandra Serrano impressed me as a very sincere girl who had been a dedicated Kennedy fan, not interested in publicity in any way."[573]

At 1.43am – minutes after Vanocur had wrapped up his live interview with Serrano – Sgt. Paul Sharaga was called on his police radio by Inspector Powers at Rampart Station. "He asked me if I was responsible for putting out the APB with description of the two suspects. When I confirmed this he told me that he was going to cancel it. He said: 'We've got the suspect in custody. We don't want to make a federal case out of this.'"[574].

LAPD logs confirm that Powers cancelled Sharaga's APB about the male suspect at 1.44am, lending some credibility to his overall account, including his encounter with the elderly couple and their report of fleeing suspects. The story itself would later

572 Sander Vanocur live interview with Sandy Serrano; NBC, June 5, 1968, 1.30am.
573 Statement of John Ambrose, Deputy District Attorney. Special Unit Senator; Vol. 70, pp.339-340. California State Archives.
574 Paul Sharaga: interviews with Tim Tate, 1991 – 1992.

peter out in a miasma of unresolved loose-ends when the elderly couple's contact details disappeared from police files.[575]

After her television interview Sandy Serrano was taken to Rampart Division – LAPD's station closest to the Ambassador. At 2.35am, Sgts. Chiquet and Henderson from LAPD's homicide unit, began interviewing her about what she had seen. Serrano's account, recorded on tape, was consistent with what she had told Ambrose and Vanocur: she recounted both encounters with the polka dot dress girl: the first on the girl's way up the stairway with two men, the second on the way down with only one. Her description of the first, '*borracho*', man matched that of Sirhan who – though she did not know it – was already in custody; she said the second man wore a gold-coloured sweater.

Serrano also told Chiquet and Henderson that the girl was wearing a knee-length white dress with black polka dots and a bib collar; and that she a had a "funny nose … turned up like, you know, like … a pixie."[576] At 2.55am, Chiquet ended the interview, turned off the tape recorder and sent Serrano back to a holding room to wait for further instructions. At some point during the hour that followed she sat with a witness to the shooting in the pantry, 19-year-old student Vincent DiPierro. The two – who had never met or spoken before – spent less than an hour together, and Serrano denies that they discussed the assassination in any detail.

"We were just looking at each other and saying 'what are you here for?'" Serrano recalled in 2016. "He said he worked in the kitchen. I told him why I was there and he told me what he had seen. He didn't really say much – I mean he was as scared as I was: we were afraid. But I said 'oh – maybe we shouldn't be talking to each other'."[577]

---

575 Ibid.

576 LAPD – 1st interview with Sandy Serrano; 2.25am, June 4, 1968. SUS files, Vol. 95; pp 83-96. California State Archives

577 Sandy Serrano-Sewell: interviews with Tim Tate, 1991 – 2016

Despite this, the mere fact that they had met would later be used to question the stories each separately told LAPD's detectives.

By 4am Serrano had been taken the two miles from Rampart Station to LAPD's Parker Centre headquarters. In Room 318, two new detectives – Sgts. Patchett and Melendrez – accompanied by Deputy District Attorney John Howard, made her repeat her account of the meetings on the stairway: once again her story matched the ones she had given to Ambrose and Vanocur, Chiquet and Henderson. But she was able to add a few more details to the descriptions of the three suspects.

The girl had "an attractive build" and her dress was of white voile with black polka dots, each around one eight of an inch in diameter; it had long or three-quarter-length sleeves. The man who ran down the stairway with her had dark olive skin and dark black hair – "[It] was like straight and it came out in peaks like and it was awfully greasy" – and his sweater was "autumn gold" in colour with buttons down the front. The other man - – the *borracho* male – was around 5' 5" with dark hair, and looked "like somebody that had had a few, maybe. He didn't look drunk but sort of messy... seedy." [578]

In the middle of this account, Serrano also mentioned that just before her second encounter with the girl and her olive-skinned companion she had heard a car backfire. "I was sitting there for a while and then I thought it was a backfire of a car, and so I thought, to me, I thought I heard six shots; six backfires... and I just looked around, looked for a car you know, I just looked for a car..."[579]. It was a casual remark, intended to be helpful; but it would later be distorted and used to discredit all of Serrano's testimony.

---

578 LAPD – 2nd interview with Sandy Serrano; 4am, June 4, 1968. SUS files, Volume 91; pp 314 – 339. California State Archives
579 Ibid.

At 4.25am, Patchett, Melendrez and Howard called student Vincent DiPierro into Room 318. DiPierro's father, Angelo, was head *Maître D* at the Ambassador and got his son casual shifts as a waiter. DiPierro Jnr. had arrived at the Ambassador at 11.15pm on June 4 and, after spending some time in the Ambassador Room, walked up to the first floor pantry behind the Embassy Room. At a quarter past midnight, as Bobby left the Embassy Room stage and walked towards the pantry, Vincent was waiting just outside the doors.

"I stuck my hand out and he shook my hand," the young student told the detectives. "I tapped him on the back and said 'Congratulations Mr. Kennedy'. And I walked with him as far as I could ... I was just so happy that he was winning."[580]

As they entered the pantry, DiPierro noticed a couple of people standing beside a tray stand next to the ice machine. One of them, a young man, seemed to have climbed on to the tray stacker itself. He "looked like an ordinary Latin ... he was in a kind of funny position, because he was kind of down – like if he were trying to protect himself from something ... and ... I thought he was going to go and shake his [Bobby's] hand 'cause he had his hand down ... like if he had a sore hand or something, and then he kind of swung around and he went up on his – like his tiptoes – and he stuck over with his gun and he shot".[581]

The detectives realized that DiPierro was a key eyewitness: he had been so close to Bobby when the shooting started that he was splattered in blood – either from the Senator or from Paul Schrade, who had been hit in the forehead by a bullet, and literally fell into the young man's arms. His testimony would

---

580 Interview with Vincent DiPierro; 4.25am, June 4, 1968. SUS files, Vol. 94; p 47 – 73. California State Archives

581 Interview with Vincent DiPierro; 4.25am, June 4, 1968. SUS files, Vol. 94; p 47 – 73. California State Archives

therefore potentially form a vital part of the case against the suspected shooter. Sgt. Patchett then questioned DiPierro closely about the gunman and why he had noticed him in the seconds before the shooting. The transcript of the interview shows that DiPierro clearly described the gunman as "together" with an attractive girl.

"DIPIERRO: When I saw him first there was a girl behind him too. I don't know if you need that. There were two people that I saw … The only reason he was noticeable was because there was this good looking girl in the crowd there.

PATCHETT: All right, was the girl with him?

DIPIERRO: It looked as though, yes … she was up next to him – behind, and she was holding on to the other end of the tray table an she – like – it looked like as if she was almost holding him … I glanced over once in a while. She was good looking so I looked at her.

PATCHETT: What is it in your mind that makes you think they were together, the fact that they were standing together?

DIPIERRO: No, no, he turned when he was on the tray stand once and he had the same kind of stupid smile on, you know, and then he kind of turned and said something. I don't know what he said."

Deputy District Attorney John Howard then took over the questioning:

"HOWARD: You did see him speak to her?

DIPIERRO: He turned as though he did say something, whether he said anything –

HOWARD: Did she move her mouth like she was speaking to him?

DIPIERRO: No, she just smiled …

HOWARD: And would it seem to you that she smiled at something that had been said … Or that she was smiling because the Senator was walking towards her?

DIPIERRO: No, when she first entered she looked like she was sick also."[582]

DiPierro gave the detectives a solid description of the girl: white Caucasian, between 21 and 24, "very shapely", with dark brown hair just above the shoulders, one side "puffed up a little". She wore "a white dress with either black or violet polka dots" and a collar round the top. This matched exactly the dress described by Sandy Serrano: nor was it the only such account.

Booker Griffin, co-chair of the African-American *New Images* community organization, was also in the pantry when the shooting started. Within 24 hours he published an article in the *Los Angeles Sentinel* newspaper.

"The man that did the shooting was in the corridor-way as I left in advance of the senator. He was there with a tall Caucasian male and a Caucasian female in a white dress. I noticed the man because I had seen him several times before during the evening. I had seen him first downstairs in the Ambassador Room around 10.15pm. I remember distinctly because we had stared each other down. I vaguely remember the girl also with him.

"Between 11pm and the actual shooting I travelled between the Embassy Room and the press room ... maybe six or eight times. The last three or four times I noticed the gunman, the girl and the other guy. When I left the stage and went to the press room the last time before the shooting there were a few kitchen employees and the gunman and his two friends. I distinctly remember this because the gunman had sneered at me as I went past ... When the shooting occurred I ... had a full view of the whole room ... I distinctly saw the other man and the girl flee through a side corridor heading out of the hotel as I raced to the feet of the fallen Senator.

"There is no doubt in my mind that on several trips past the trio that they were together. I tried to get through to pursue them

---

582 *Ibid.*

TIM TATE & BRAD JOHNSON

down that corridor but couldn't get through. I was pushed and shoved by newsmen and Kennedy staff. I kept yelling 'they're getting away'."[583]

On the day Griffin's article appeared, Kennedy field worker Darnell Johnson was interviewed in Rampart Station by LAPD, the FBI and an official of Los Angeles County Human Relations Commission. According to an S.U.S. report: "He stated that as Kennedy finished talking and started towards kitchen area, he entered kitchen area by another entrance and as Kennedy and party were approaching him down the kitchen aisle he observed a group of five people between he and the Kennedy party.

"The group was standing close enough that there was physical contact between the five people and they all appeared to be talking with the exception of the suspect that was taken into custody. The suspect did not appear to be engaging in the conversation..."[584]

Johnson was shown the police mug shot of Sirhan and identified him as 'the suspect'; he also gave the detectives a description of his apparent companions. The next day he was re-interviewed at his office and gave a more detailed account of one of them: "A white female wearing a white dress, with 25¢ size black polka dots; the dress was fitted, was not miniskirt but was above the knees; was not a loose shift but was fashionable for the time. She was 23-25 years of age, tall, 5'8", medium build, well built, 145 pounds, long light brown hair, carrying an all-white sweater or jacket, pretty full face, stubby heel shoes in the fashion of the time."[585]

583 *Fatalism, Destiny: Fear Now Real*: Booker Griffin, Los Angeles Sentinel, June 6, 1968.
584 Interview with Darnell Johnson; June 6, 1968. SUS files, Vol. 40; p 297 – 298. California State Archives.
585 Interview with Darnell Johnson, June 7, 1968. FBI Los Angeles Field Office file X-1 – Vol.2; pp.101-102. California State Archives.

The FBI also interviewed another polka dot dress girl witness on June 7. George Green was Booker Griffin's *New Images* co-chair, and was on his way into the pantry when Kennedy was shot. Its report recorded that: "Green stated that once inside the kitchen door he noticed a woman in her 20s with long blond free-flowing hair in a polka dot dress and a light colored sweater, and a man 5'11", thin build, black hair and in his 20s.

"Green stated that this man and woman were running with their backs towards him and they were attempting to get out of the kitchen area. Green stated that the reason he noticed them was that they were the only ones who seemed to be trying to get out of the kitchen area while everyone else seemed to be trying to get into the kitchen area."[586]

Green's description of the polka dot dress girl differed slightly from the other sightings: he reported her hair as blond, not brown, but like Johnson he said she was wearing a light coloured sweater. And it substantially matched the account given by one of the security guards on duty on the night of June 4/5. On June 13, the FBI interviewed Jack Merritt at his home in Sepulveda: he told the Agent what he observed when he ran into the pantry just after the shooting began.

"In the confusion he noticed, among others, two men and a woman leaving the kitchen through a back exit. He could not see the woman's face but believed she was approximately 5'5" tall, with light colored hair and wearing a polka dot dress. One of the men was about 6'2" tall with dark hair and wearing a dark suit. The other man was approximately 5'5" or 5'6" tall and also wearing a suit."[587]

586 Interview with George Green, June 7, 1968. FBI Los Angeles Field Office file X-1 – Vol.2; p.96 California State Archives.
587 Interview with Jack Merritt, June 13, 1968. FBI Los Angeles Field Office file X-4 – Vol.13; p.39. California State Archives.

Throughout the sixteen days following the shooting, twenty-five eyewitnesses gave statements to LAPD in which they described seeing the girl in the polka dot dress with at least one male companion throughout the afternoon or evening of June 4 – 5. In many of the accounts, the woman had behaved strangely, as if she was deliberately trying to attract attention.

Nineteen-year-old Suzanne Orrick was sitting in the hotel coffee shop at 1.30pm on Election Day: at a nearby table she noticed an attractive young girl in a blue and white polka dot dress with a "full red blooded American type" man. The couple caught Miss Orrick's attention because the woman was wearing a Eugene McCarthy supporter's hat in the Kennedy campaign's election HQ[588].

Conrad Seim was a 50-year-old press photographer covering the Kennedy campaign. At 9.30pm he was standing in the south west corner of the Embassy Room, beside a bank of TV cameras when a woman "approached him and asked him if she could borrow his press pass. He wouldn't let her have it; approx. 15 minutes later [she] asked him again."[589]. LAPD's report of Seim's interview on June 7 shows that he described the woman as around 25 years old, slender with olive skin and short dark hair. She was wearing a white dress with dark blue polka dots, and Seim "noticed she had a funny nose – poss. broken at one time."[590] [591]

Kennedy campaign worker Susan Locke subsequently saw an identically-dressed woman in the Embassy Room, before Bobby spoke there. She told FBI that the woman attracted her

---

588 Interview with Suzanne Minett Orrick; June 10, 1968. SUS files, Vol. 51; p.308. California State Archives.
589 Interview with Conrad Seim; SUS files, Vol. 40; p.319. California State Archives.
590 Ibid.
591 For unexplained reasons, LAPD re-interviewed Mr. Seim three weeks later, on July 1, 1968. He repeated the same account of events as detailed in his previous statement. SUS files, Vol. 40; p.317. California State Archives.

attention for two reasons. "She observed that the girl was not wearing a yellow press badge and thought this to be very unusual since it was necessary to have such a badge to gain entry into the Embassy Room ... The girl was expressionless and seemed somewhat out of place where she was standing. She was a Caucasian in her early twenties, well proportioned, with long brown hair pulled back and tied behind her head. Her hair appeared to be dried out similar in appearance to hair of a girl who does a lot of swimming".[592]

Around 10.30pm Nina Ballantyne and Eve Hansen were at the crowded 'Casino level' bar on the ground floor. LAPD's interviews with the two women recorded that they were approached by a white woman in her mid-twenties wearing either a white or light blue dress with black or navy polka dots. She told Mrs. Hansen, "You'll never get served at this end of the bar. I've been waiting up the other end, I know". She then gave Mrs. Hansen the money for drinks and when they arrived made a toast, "To our next President". The woman then left the bar, telling Ms. Ballantyne that she was going upstairs "to where the Senator was going to be".[593]

A group of six young women from Panorama City 'Students For Kennedy' campaign was upstairs in the area between the lower Ambassador Ballroom and the upper Embassy Room where the Senator was due to speak. Three – Irene Gizzi, Elizabeth Miller and Janet Parker – were adults in their twenties; the other three were each fourteen years old. Five of the group gave statements to LAPD in which they reported seeing a woman in a polka dot dress in the foyer leading to the Embassy Room: each said the woman was with either two or three scruffy-looking men, and gave the impression of being out of place amid

592 Interview with Susan Locke, June 7, 1968. FBI Field Office files, Ser. 3002-3095; p.254-255. California State Archives.
593 Interviews with Eve Hansen and Nina Ballantyne. SUS files, Vol. 52; p.189 & Volume 48; p.248. California State Archives.

the exuberant crowd. Gizzi, the 29-year-old chair of Youth for Kennedy recalled that the "female Caucasian" was in her mid-twenties, with dark hair combed up in "love locks" and she wore a white dress with dark polka dots[594]. Schoolgirls Katie Keir and Jeanette Prudhomme independently gave identical descriptions in their police statements.[595]

But whilst accounts of the polka dot dress girl attracted most attention, the details of her male companions, given by the young Kennedy supporters, were even more significant. Janet Parker and Jeanette Prudhomme both identified one of the "grubby-looking" men with her as Sirhan[596].

Prudhomme, Gizzi and Keir also gave very similar descriptions of the third man in the suspicious group: they all – independently – told LAPD he was wearing a gold-coloured sweater. This matched the description Sandy Serrano had given detectives in her police interviews. But, crucially, she had not mentioned this in her live interview with Sander Vanocur, nor had it been publicized elsewhere, which made it highly unlikely that the 'Youth For Kennedy' girls could simply have been repeating something they had seen on television or in the newspapers.

There is no indication in LAPD's files that any of its officers realized the importance of this. What makes this more remarkable is that the gold-coloured sweater had also featured in a formal statement previously given to detectives by another volunteer witness – and one who had not been in the Ambassador Hotel on election night. On the afternoon of June 5, Jerry Owen, the

---

594 Interview with Irene Gizzi, August 6, 1968. SUS files, Vol. 40; p.101. California State Archives.

595 Interviews with Katherine Keir and Jeanette Prudhomme, August 7 & 8, 1968. SUS files, Vol. 40; p.124-125 & Volume 40; p.135. California State Archives.

596 Interviews with Jeanette Prudhomme (Op. cit.) & Janet Parker, June 8, 1968; SUS files, Vol. 46; p.219. California State Archives.

self-styled 'Walking Bible', recounted his convoluted story about picking up Sirhan and a male and female companion two days earlier. According to the transcript of his interview, he described the unidentified man with Sirhan and the girl as "[the] biggest of the whole bunch, gold turtleneck, fair suit, long... dark brown hair..."[597]

As with Sandy Serrano's police statements, Jerry Owen's account had not been made public. Nor is there any evidence that he ever knew, or communicated with, Serrano, Prudhomme, Gizzi or Keir. And yet somehow they all described seeing Sirhan in the company of a girl and a man wearing a gold-coloured sweater. Moreover, one of the 'Youth For Kennedy' girls remembered an additional detail about this man: Janet Parker told LAPD that he wore "a large medallion" over his shirt[598]. Jerry Owen's statement also described the man in the gold sweater as having "a medallion around his neck". [599]

There were simply too many near-identical sightings of Sirhan with the polka dot dress girl, and her gold sweater-wearing male companion, to be dismissed as mere coincidence. In an honestly-run and thorough police investigation, the confluence of so many contemporaneous accounts should have strongly suggested that Sirhan was not alone on the night of June 4 -5. But the full S.U.S. files contain a number of LAPD internal documents, spread in seemingly randomly fashion throughout its 50,000 pages, which indicate that despite its high public profile, the polka dot dress girl investigation was neither honest nor thorough.

Between June 6 and June 10 1968, LAPD was ostensibly still rigorously investigating the evidence given by Sandy Serrano and Vincent DiPierro. On June 7, the District Attorney had

---

597 Statement of Jerry Owen, June 5, 1968. SUS files Volume 40; pp. 168-178. California State Archives.

598 Statement of Janet Parker. Op. Cit.

599 Statement of Jerry Owen. Op. Cit.

presented DiPierro to the Grand Jury as an eyewitness to the shooting. Under oath, the young man repeated his account of seeing Sirhan with the girl in the polka dot dress. The same day, LAPD and the FBI took Serrano back to the Ambassador Hotel and made her re-enact the incident on the stairway.

On June 10, she and DiPierro separately took part in official videotaped sessions during which they were shown an assortment of eight polka dot dresses and asked to pick out the one which most closely resembled the one they had seen on the mysterious girl. Serrano later recalled that she found the experience intimidating.

"At first they were really nice, just asking me what I saw. But the second officer who came in was mean and told me to describe the dress. About two hours later he brought in polka dot dresses and hung them all around the room and told me to pick the dress that most looked like what I'd seen. He went on at me – he was relentless – about what size the polka dots were: like, the size of a dime? Or a nickel? And I was so scared I remember just pointing to a dress – any dress – just to get it over with."[600]

LAPD's actions were stranger than even Serrano realized. Amid the thousands of pages of the full S.U.S. files was a report showing that the day before it mounted the costume line up, it had taken custody of a polka dot dress which, despite its particular colour pattern, should – at the very least – have been considered as a potential candidate for the one worn by the mysterious woman.

At 3pm on June 6, a Mrs. Edith Goldstein discovered a green paper sack lying in an alley behind South Crescent Heights Boulevard in west Los Angeles – a little over five miles from the Ambassador Hotel. Inside it she found a pair of black patent shoes, a black slip, a padded size 34B brassiere, panties, a girdle,

---

cosmetics – and a "polka dot dress, white dots with dark gray background ... size estimated as 9-11 ... The above items of were in new or almost new condition and contained no indication of ownership."[601]

According to the FBI report, Mrs. Goldstein – who had no connection with the campaign and not been at the Ambassador on the night of the assassination – "was aware of the publicity being given the unknown lady in the polka dot dress": after trying to speak to LAPD – she received "no response" – she contacted the District Attorney's Office. Three hours later detectives "working out of the office of the Chief of Police" came to her home and collected the sack of clothing and make-up.[602]

There is no record in the S.U.S files of any interview with Mrs. Goldstein, but the following day LAPD's Latent Prints Section examined the contents of the sack. According to the Summary Report "numerous fingerprints were found and photographed. These fingerprints were only adequate for elimination purposes."[603] There is no trace of any photographs or laboratory reports to support this statement.

If LAPD had been serious about identifying – or eliminating – the polka dot dress, it would have been good practice to include Mrs. Goldstein's discovery in the collection of garments shown to Sandy Serrano. It did not do so. According to the Summary Report S.U.S. did, however, send the Goldstein dress over to De Wayne Wolfer's Scientific Investigation Division for additional tests. There were good reasons for this: the clothes were stained, the panties were inside the girdle and the bra straps

---

601 Memo from Special Agent [redacted] to Special Agent in Charge, Los Angeles, June 6, 1968. FBI file Ser.1-250, p.237. California State Archives.

602 Ibid.

603 Special Unit Senator: Final Report, p.417. California State Archives.

were undone[604] – all of which suggested that the clothes had been worn at least once. Despite this, S.I.D. found no human hair or blood and "concluded that the clothing was new and ... that the stains were probably caused by the clothing coming in contact with the lipstick and liquid make up."[605] Perhaps inevitably, given Wolfer's known laxity over record-keeping, the full files contain no lab tests reports and no evidence to support the Summary's contention. Nor does it appear that any further attention was paid to the mysteriously-discarded polka dot dress and sack of garments.

One explanation for LAPD's antics can be found in hand-written notes of its reports of interviews with some of the other witnesses. They suggest that as even as these events took place, the man leading the conspiracy investigations team of Special Unit Senator had already decided the entire polka dot dress story was untrue. Conrad Seim's interview report has a cover sheet, signed and apparently written by Lt. Manny Pena, which states: "Polka Dot story a phoney and Girl in Kitchen ID settled. Lt. Pena. Witt. can offer nothing of further value". It is timed and dated 3.15pm on June 7, 1968. It also bears the scrawled instruction, 'Don't Type'.[606]

The Suzanne Orrick report has a similar handwritten note: "No further investigation. Polka dot story of Serrano – false". It, too, is signed by Lt. Pena and is dated June 10.[607]. Another file note – not clearly dated[608] – shows that the young women from 'Youth For Kennedy' were to be pressured to retract their

---

604 S.U.S. Card index file – Edith Goldstein, June 18, 1968. Vol. GA-GW, p.144. California State Archives.
605 Special Unit Senator: Final Report, p.418. California State Archives.
606 SUS file Volume 104; p.107. California State Archives.
607 SUS file Volume 51; p.307
608 SUS file Volume 40; p.103. The date on the memo is June 6, 1968 – several days before the women were originally interviewed.

statements about seeing the polka dot dress girl and her companions with Sirhan. "Re-interview all persons named in this interview. Inform that Serrano story (false). Offer tactful opportunity to correct statements. Re-interview 8/5/68"[609]

These notes may also explain the treatment meted out by LAPD to other prominent polka dot dress girl witnesses. Darnell Johnson was dismissed as "extremely unreliable" because he had "made statements which contradict fact" about the respective positions of Ethel Kennedy and Rafer Johnson in the pantry.[610]

Meanwhile, Booker Griffin was alleged to have retracted his story of seeing the polka dot dress girl and her companion fleeing the scene of the crime. An internal Progress Report – again signed by Lt. Manny Pena – stated: "Booker Griffin … was re-interviewed … As a result it was determined that the statements made by him were a projection of incidents and people seen at other times, rather than fact. This he acknowledged in a transcribed statement on 7-25-68".[611]

The "transcribed statement" referred to by Lt. Pena does not bear out this assertion. Instead, it shows that although LAPD's interviewers repeatedly told Griffin that he had not seen the polka dot dress girl and her companion with Sirhan – or witnessed her subsequent escape from the pantry – he said only that while he could not be absolutely definite, he was sure that the incident happened as he had described it[612]. "They really tried very hard

---

609   A subsequent internal LAPD note indicates that Katherine Keir "and other girls who also thought they saw Sirhan B. Sirhan in the hotel" retracted some or all of their statements "in the presence of their parents". There are no documents containing any such retractions in the SUS files. SUS files Volume 47; p.240. California State Archives.

610   SUS files Volume 40; pp.295-296. California State Archives.

611   *Progress Report – Case Preparation For Trial*; July 20, 1968. SUS files Volume 103; p44. California State Archives.

612   Interview with Booker Griffin, July 25, 1968. SUS files Volume 51; pp. 17-35. California State Archives.

to break me down and lead me rather than listen to what I was telling them," he said later. "They were trying to embarrass me and question my sanity and question my intent".[613]

The evidence given by Griffin, Green and the Youth For Kennedy girls' was not made public. By contrast, the stories Vincent DiPierro and Sandy Serrano told received widespread press and television coverage. S.U.S knew that to dispose of the mysterious girl in the polka dot dress girl, it needed to discredit them and their testimony. And, according to Chief of Detectives Robert Houghton, Serrano was the key.

"Manny Pena knew that as long as Miss Serrano stuck to her story, no amount of independent evidence would, in itself, serve to dispel the 'polka-dot-dress girl' fever, which had by now, in the press and public mind, reached a high point on the thermometer of intrigue," he wrote in his 1970 book on the assassination. "She alone could put the spotted ghost to rest."[614]

---

613 Booker Griffin, interviews with Tim Tate, 1991 – 1992
614 Robert Houghton: Special Unit Senator; pp.119-20. Op. cit.

CHAPTER FIFTEEN: "ARE YOU AFRAID?"

Sandy Serrano had not been in Los Angeles very long. Born and raised in Lorain, Ohio – a steel town just outside Cleveland – she had moved to California in the spring of 1967 to find a way out of traditional mid-western blue-collar life patterns: neighbourhood bars, marriage to a local boy and watching him compete in stock car races. She was 18 when she arrived, but she had little patience with the burgeoning west coast hippy lifestyle, viewing it as dissolute and irresponsible. Instead, she lived with her aunt and uncle, worked in an insurance agency by day and attended Pasadena City College at night.

"I'd had a very mid-western upbringing and I still had very mid-western attitudes," she recalled in 2016. "I was brought up to put my cards on the table and stand my ground over things I believed in. My parents also raised me to believe that cops were to be trusted: a cop was our friend in times of need, someone to be turned to and relied on."[615]

Serrano was about to find out that the detectives of Special Unit Senator were very different from the neighbourhood police she had been brought up to trust and respect in Lorain.

---

615 Sandy Serrano-Sewell: interviews with Tim Tate 1991 – 2016

On June 8, LAPD began a campaign to discredit her, and her story about the polka dot dress girl.

Two days earlier, Cathy Sue Fulmer, a blond 19-year-old go-go dancer, had turned herself in to Los Angeles Sherriff's Department. According to Sheriff Peter Pitches, Fulmer was worried that she might be the polka dot dress girl. Her very slender grounds for believing this were that she had been at the Ambassador on June 4 and had worn a scarf with a polka dot design. LAPD pulled Serrano in to "observe" Fulmer in the main lobby of Parker Centre.

Since the dancer bore absolutely no resemblance to Serrano's description of the polka dot dress girl, this amateurish identification parade was a waste of time: Serrano began to suspect that the detectives were playing mind games with her. "You would have had to have been blind to think that was the girl – she didn't fit the description in any way."[616] [617]

LAPD's unsettling behaviour continued. On June 10, chief criminalist DeWayne Wolfer carried out sound tests at the Ambassador Hotel. Using a .22 calibre revolver he had drawn from the police evidence room, he fired a succession of shots inside the pantry, while another officer recorded the sound levels on the outside stairway where Serrano had been sitting. The ostensible purpose was to establish whether the noise of Kennedy's assassination could have carried that far. The real aim was to portray Serrano as having lied in her throwaway recollection of hearing "six shots, six backfires".

The tests duly showed that "it would have been impossible for Serrano to have heard the pantry's gunshots. The sound-level meter indicated a ½ decibel change when the test shots were

---

616 *Ibid.*
617 In an odd, and tragic, postscript, in April 1969 Cathy Fulmer was found dead in a Los Angeles motel room. An inquest determined she had committed suicide with an overdose of Seconal tablets.

fired. The minimum sound-level change discernible by a person with normal hearing is 2 decibels."[618]

But LAPD knew that Serrano had never claimed to have heard the sound of gunfire. Her statement had made very clear that she was describing a car backfiring – a point she emphatically repeated to the FBI when it challenged her with the results of Wolfer's sound tests that same day. "Serrano said she had never heard a gunshot in her life and never claimed she had heard gunshots, but had described what she heard as six backfires, four or five of which were close together..."[619]

The FBI seemed equally keen to unsettle Serrano. After presenting her with the evidence of the specious sound tests, its agent demanded to know why she had not told NBC's Sander Vanocur about the girl and the two men going up the stairway prior to the shooting.

"It was pointed out to her the fact that she claimed one of the men going up the stairs was Sirhan Sirhan was the most significant part of the incident described by her," the Bureau's Agent reported. "Serrano stated that she could not explain why and accused those present of lying to her and trying to trick her ... Serrano stated she was very upset, could not continue and requested to be taken home."[620]

This criticism conveniently ignored the fact that when Vanocur interviewed Serrano live at 1:30am, no images of Sirhan's face had yet been broadcast or published – and thus she would have had no reason to mention – at that moment – the other young man she'd seen with the girl prior to the shooting.

---

618 Summary report of the Los Angeles Police Department Investigation of the Senator Robert Kennedy Assassination, p.414. California State Archives.

619 FBI file: "Interviews"; p.306. California State Archives.

620 *Ibid.*

Ten days later LAPD summoned Serrano to Parker Centre to undergo a polygraph examination. She had agreed to take the test, but wanted her aunt to be with her throughout, and so it was 9pm when the two women were ushered into Polygraph Room B and introduced to the examiner, Sgt. Hank Hernandez.

Hernandez' polygraph tests involved asking a series of questions while his machine recorded variations in blood pressure, pulse and respiration via a cable strapped around the subject's chest. In theory, a deceptive answer would show up as 'spike' on a rolling sheet of graph paper. After dismissing Serrano's nervousness about the reliability of polygraphs, Hernandez asked her a series of anodyne questions to gain a base level for her physiological reactions. Then, contrary to their agreement, he told her aunt to leave the room.

He began the test by asking Serrano whether she had told the truth about seeing a girl in the polka dot dress who said 'We have shot Kennedy', and whether she had ever lied to the police or the FBI. Serrano answered 'yes' to the polka dot dress questions, and 'no' to those which asked if she had lied. After this, Hernandez paused to review the results. While doing so he asked:

"HERNANDEZ: Are you afraid right now, Sandra? ... Are you afraid?

SERRANO: No ... I'm not afraid, I just don't like it.

HERNANDEZ: No, no, you're afraid. You're afraid."

This odd exchange set the tone for what was to follow. Polygraphs are meant to be conducted in an atmosphere of complete calm: anything that disturbs this can affect the reliability of the test. But over the next two hours, as a tape recorder ran, Hernandez subjected Serrano to a prolonged and, at times, brutal verbal assault.[621] He began by invoking Kennedy's wife and children.

---

621 When this tape was handed over to California State Archives in 1988 it bore the inscription "Do Not transcribe".

"The family of Senator Kennedy... they'll never know, until people come forward and are truthful with this thing... they won't be able to rest... Because they don't know. And they want to find out what happened to their father, the kids do. Ethel wants to find out what happened to her husband... don't you have any sentiment for them?"[622]

Then Hernandez repeated the polygraph test using some of the same questions about the polka dot dress girl. This, alone, was unusual: polygraph protocol allows for key questions to be asked only once (for the obvious reason that two sets of answers could, potentially, produce two differing results). But what followed was worse. The detective once again began hectoring and shouting at Serrano:

"HERNANDEZ: Ok. Here's the thing. You're an intelligent young girl. You know that for some reason this was made up. Now let me tell you this. I've talked to 19 girls... Some of the girls made up stories because they wanted publicity... some of the girls made up stories because they thought they could get something of value, money or something...

"There's only two out of the 19 girls that I've talked to that I really sincerely [believe] did it not for publicity, not for monetary value, not for their own personal gain, but because they were sorry about what happened and they loved Senator Kennedy. And I think that you're one of these girls...

"I think you owe it to Senator Kennedy, the late Senator Kennedy, to come forth, be a woman about this... You don't know and I don't know whether he's a witness right now in this room watching what we're doing in here. Don't shame his death by keeping this thing up... This is a very serious thing.

SERRANO: I seen those people!

---

622 Transcript of Sandy Serrano polygraph interview, June 20, 1969. "Special Unit Senator", Vol.94, p.257- 273 California State Archives.

HERNANDEZ: No, no, no, no, Sandy. Remember what I told you about that. You can't say you saw something when you didn't see it … Look … I can explain this to the investigators where you don't even have to talk to them and they won't talk to you … I can guarantee that nobody will ask you one more question about this but I want you to be able to go home and rest. I don't know if you're sleeping well at night or not …

"But I know that as you get older, one of these days you're gonna be a mother, you're gonna have kids and you know that you can't live a life of shame, knowing what you're doing right now is wrong. … Please, in the name of Kennedy … you know that this is wrong …

SERRANO: I know what I saw! … I remember seeing the girl!

HERNANDEZ: No, no. I'm talking about what you have told here about seeing a person tell you 'We have shot Kennedy'. And that's wrong.

SERRANO: That's what she said.

HERNANDEZ: No, it isn't Sandy … Lookit, lookit, I love this man! And you're shaming … if he can't even –

SERRANO: Don't shout at me.

HERNANDEZ: Well I'm trying not to shout, but … if you love this man, the least you owe him is the courtesy of letting him rest in peace, and he can't rest …"[623]

And so it continued. For more than an hour, Hernandez continued to bully the 20-year-old girl in front of him, calling her a liar, insisting that she never saw or heard a girl in a polka dot dress saying 'We shot Kennedy', and demanding that she change her testimony. Throughout, Serrano refused to submit. And so Hernandez once again – in the middle of a highly emotional tirade – insisted on repeating the polygraph test, before beginning a new round of hectoring.

---

623 *Ibid.*

But the most remarkable aspect of the tape is not Hernandez's brutal intimidation of a young and already-scared woman. Nor is it Serrano's resistance to his demands that she recant. Instead, it was a boast he made to her about his expertise as a polygraph examiner.

"I have been called to South America, to Vietnam and Europe and I have administered tests. The last test I administered was to the dictator in Caracas, Venezuela. He was a big man, a dictator ... this is when there was a transition in the government of Venezuela and that's where President Betancourt came in ... there was a great thing involved over there and I tested the gentleman."[624]

What was a detective sergeant, ostensibly employed by Los Angeles Police Department, doing administering polygraph tests in countries halfway across the world? The Venezuelan dictator who Hernandez claimed to have tested was Marcos Pérez Jiménez, removed from power in a coup in 1958 and allowed to settle in America, before being extradited back to Caracas. LAPD had no official involvement in any aspect of his case – though the US government most certainly did. If Hernandez was telling the truth about his resumé, he can only have been working for either the US State Department or a branch of America's intelligence services.

At the conclusion of the polygraph session – and despite reducing her to tears – the most the detective had pressured Serrano into admitting was that she was "confused", and that her statements had been blown out of proportion. But Hernandez wasn't finished: he told her to wait in the room while he obtained a portable tape recorder to document her new statement. Quite why he needed to do this when their entire conversation was already being recorded is unclear: but the transcript shows that as Hernandez left the room, Serrano whispered "Let me out ..."[625]

---

624 *Ibid.*
625 *Ibid.*

At 10.15pm he returned. As a new tape recorder rolled, he took Serrano back over the events of June 4 – 5. As before, the most he was able to get her to admit was that she had been "messed up" – by John Ambrose, the police and the FBI. At 10.35pm Hernandez ended the interview. She later recalled: "He was trying to push me into saying I had lied, even though I hadn't. In the end I just wanted to get out of there"[626].

Two days later, LAPD formally called off its search for the polka dot dress girl and told the press that Serrano had invented the entire story. On June 23, the *Washington Post* reported: "Police Friday cancelled the all points bulletin for Miss Serrano's 'polka dot' dress girl, concluding that she had been 'overwrought'. It was learned that Miss Serrano had been invited to take a lie detector test, but at least initially, she declined."[627]

Yet there was nothing in Serrano's interviews with Hernandez to support the allegation that she had invented the polka dot dress girl story. And LAPD knew that she had willingly taken a polygraph. Despite this, Lt. Manny Pena filed an internal memo claiming that Serrano had recanted her evidence and that she admitted she had been fed the story by Vincent DiPierro.

"Miss Serrano stated that she had no knowledge of any polka dot dress until after the assassination and just prior to her being interviewed. She states that she was sitting waiting to be interviewed when she heard a kid making reference to a girl in a polka dot dress. She talked to the young man and each of them enquired of the other about the description of the dress and the girl..."[628]

There were four problems with this claim. The first was that Serrano had made no such admissions. The second was that she had reported seeing and hearing the polka dot dress girl to two

626 Sandy Serrano-Sewell: interviews with Tim Tate 1991 – 2016
627 *RFK Plots Crumble, But Rumors Persist. Washington Post*, June 23, 1968
628 [In] "Background/Conspiracy Team" Progress Report"; July 19 – August 2, 1968. Special Unit Senator, Vol.46, p.348-349. California State Archives

people – one of them, an assistant district attorney – within fifteen minutes of the shooting.

The third was that she had also reported the sighting to a nationwide television audience within 75 minutes of the assassination – just before she left the Ambassador Hotel for the police station where she met Vincent DiPierro. The fourth was that, in June 1968, DiPierro was sticking to his story.

On June 7, DiPierro had testified under oath about the girl in the polka dot dress to a Los Angeles County Grand Jury behind closed doors. Within days, transcripts of the entire Grand Jury proceeding were made available to the press.

On June 22, the day before the *Washington Post* reported the cancellation of the APB for the polka dot dress girl, DiPierro was asked by reporters whether he would recant his Grand Jury evidence about seeing her with Sirhan in the pantry. He refused to do so. "I am standing by my testimony. I can't change it. I only told what I saw. She may have been just standing next to him, but they were smiling at each other. He may have been flirting with her. I don't know".[629]

Nine days later, on July 1, Vincent DiPierro was summoned to Parker Centre for a polygraph test conducted by Sgt. Hank Hernandez; he was apparently persuaded to stop standing by his testimony and completely recant his story of the polka dot dress girl. There is no transcript of this examination, only an internal memo, written some months later by Hernandez (who had, by now, been promoted to the rank of Lieutenant).

"The purpose of the polygraph examination was to determine whether DiPierro's statements were truthful... DiPierro was very cooperative throughout... He was asked a total of 21 questions of which 7 questions were pertinent key questions relative to the issues under investigation. The results of this examination

---

629 *"RFK Probe Puzzled By Polka Dots"*; New York Daily News, June 23, 1968

indicated that DiPierro's statements about the girl standing with and looking at Sirhan were untruthful.

"His responses also indicated that he did not honestly believe that he had observed any woman wearing a polka dot dress inside the kitchen area of the Ambassador Hotel ... either before or after the Kennedy assassination."[630]

Immediately after informing him that he had failed the lie detector test, Hernandez tape-recorded a new formal interval with DiPierro. Unlike the polygraph, this was transcribed and entered in S.U.S. files. What is striking about the document is just how little the young man said: throughout the five pages, Hernandez simply told him what he did and didn't see, and DiPierro responded with a succession of one or two word agreements.

"HERNANDEZ: You indicated previously ... that you had seen a girl in a black and white polka dot dress standing next to Sirhan, the suspect in the Kennedy shooting.

DIPIERRO: Yes.

HERNANDEZ: That you saw this lady standing beside Sirhan

DIPIERRO: Yes.

HERNANDEZ: As a matter of fact, you have told me now that there was no lady that you saw standing next to Sirhan.

DIPIERRO: That's correct."[631]

Like Serrano, DiPierro tried to say that he had been confused by the dramatic events in the pantry. But Hernandez wasn't buying that: he had his own explanation and he asked DiPierro to confirm it.

---

630 Intra-Department Correspondence: Lt. E. Hernandez to Captain Hugh Brown, Commander Homicide Division, December 17, 1968. Special Unit Senator, Vol. 61; p. 201 – 202

631 *Statement of Vincent DiPierro* [transcript]: 12.52pm, July 1, 1968. Special Unit Senator, Vol. 95; p.164-169. California State Archives.

"HERNANDEZ: Now, I can appreciate what you would or could have been going through on that evening ... but I think what you have told me is that you probably got this idea about a girl in a black and white polka dot dress after you talked to Miss Sandra Serrano ... is that right?

DIPIERRO: Yes, Sir.

"HERNANDEZ: Would you tell me about that? What did she tell you that prompted you to dream up or to say that you had seen a woman behind Sirhan?

DIPIERRO: She stated that there was this girl that was wearing a polka dot dress [who] came running down, I guess it was the hallway, saying that 'we shot him' and then I did – she – you know, we started asking each other questions about the girl and evidently I went along with what she said as being a person that I imagine I saw ..."[632]

But Hernandez seems to have realised that DiPierro's description of this apparently fictional girl was too detailed for it to have been no more than second-hand information.

"HERNANDEZ: Something that is very interesting to me ... is that you described this girl in the black and white polka dot dress so well, that in my experience I believe you were describing someone that you had seen during that night -

DIPIERRO: Possibly.

HERNANDEZ: – or that might be a neighbor of yours, or somebody that you had, in fact, seen somewhere else in the hotel.

DIPIERRO: That is very possible, yes, sir."[633]

There was a reason for so blatantly feeding this suggestion to DiPierro, though it would not become apparent for several months. But for now Hernandez was satisfied. After an interview lasting just eight minutes, he announced: "Okay, Vincent.

---

632 *Ibid.*
633 *Ibid.*

I think that we are pretty well cleared up as far as the girl with the polka dot dress. Time now is 1pm and this interview is now concluded."[634]

Later that day a note was entered in SUS' files by Lt. Manny Pena: "Vincent De [sic] Pierro broken down on polka dot story".[635]

Hernandez had certainly "broken down" the young college student, but there was a glaring problem with his new testimony. As the detective noted in his subsequent memo:

"He stated that after the shooting and sometime prior to being interviewed by the police at the Ambassador Hotel, he had a conversation with a young girl who was also waiting to be interviewed (Sandra Serrano). Some of their conversation was relative to the girl in the polka dot dress. Di Pierro believes that he was influenced by Sandra Serrano and that thereafter he made statements that were publicized knowing that they were untruthful."[636]

Hernandez knew – because he had conducted both interviews – that he had persuaded Serrano to say she got the story from DiPierro, and induced DiPierro to blame Serrano for putting it into his head. Both statements could not be true. What's more, DiPierro had told the FBI that he and Serrano had not shared information about the polka dot dress.

"Di Pierro said no details about the person wearing this dress were discussed since a police officer saw them talking and warned them not to discuss the case."[637]

634 *Ibid*

635 *Daily Summary of Activity, Monday, July 1, 1968*; Special Unit Senator, Vol. 25; p.162

636 Intra-Department Correspondence: Lt. E. Hernandez to Captain Hugh Brown. *Op. cit.*

637 Interview with Vincent DiPierro, June 10, 1968. FBI Los Angeles Field Office files, X-2, Volume 8; p.70. California State Archives.

In the end LAPD got round the problem by burying Serrano's recordings and not calling her as a witness in Sirhan's trial. Because he had been so close to Bobby that he was covered in the Senator's blood, the D.A. had no choice but to call DiPierro: but because his statements about the girl in the polka dot dress had been so widely publicized, the prosecution decided to defuse the potential problem by inventing its own candidate for the mysterious woman. On the stand, DiPierro was shown photographs of a Kennedy campaign worker called Valerie Schulte. She had been at the Ambassador Hotel on the night, and had worn a dress decorated with polka dots. Schulte did not, in any way, match any of the descriptions of the polka dot dress girl sitting in LAPD's files. Not only had she been on crutches that night – the result of an earlier skiing accident – the dress she had worn was an eye-catching mixture of yellow and green, not white with blue or black dots[638].

But with DiPierro pressured into a recantation (albeit half-hearted) and Sandy Serrano publicly discredited, LA law enforcement had defused its most troublesome problem; and since the files detailing its malfeasance were then suppressed, little more would be heard of the story for the next two decades. Some researchers tried to contact Serrano, but she refused to discuss the story.

"I was aware of the attempts," she said in 2016, "but I didn't want to go through all of that again. I wanted to keep away from it, to keep my mouth shut. People phoned up and asked to speak to me, but I wouldn't: I told them I would not talk about it and just hung up."[639]

By the time the S.U.S. files and recordings were made publicly available at the California State Archives, Serrano had

---

638   *The People vs. Sirhan B. Sirhan. Evidence of Valerie Schulte, February 18, 1969.* California State Archives.

639   Sandy Serrano-Sewell: interviews with Tim Tate 1991–2016

successfully run the election campaigns for Gloria Molina, a Los Angeles City Councilwoman and one of the leading Latina politicians of the 1980s. But in 1987 a routine audit by the state Fair Political Practices Commission found irregularities in the campaign's finances.

"During the campaign my husband and I had loaned Gloria money – $10,000 for her to live on – which was against the rules. After the campaign I asked her how she was going to pay the money back and she told me to write myself cheques, to pay myself as a consultant. So I paid myself back the $10 grand. Then we had a falling out and when the auditors asked her what the cheques were about, she said she didn't know. And of course there was no paperwork showing consulting hours for me to back them up.

"The next thing I knew the DA filed charges against me for embezzlement. The DA wanted me to say Gloria had been part of a conspiracy but I wouldn't: I couldn't do it; I just couldn't drop the dime on her. I felt that she was the first Latina to be elected to the state assembly, and all our hard work would have been for nothing."[640]

In September 1990, after spending $40,000 in legal fees, Serrano entered a plea of *nolo contendere* – literally: "I do not wish to contest" – to felony charges of embezzlement.[641] This staunched the haemorrhage of money on lawyers' advice and although it required her to accept conviction, it also placed on record that she was not admitting guilt by doing so.

The story of Serrano's first criminal conviction might have been little more than a sad coda to her brief moment of fame as the prime witness to the mysterious polka dot dress girl. But

---

640 *Ibid.*
641 *Moldea's Bookkeeper Pleads No Contest; Los Angeles Times,* September 8, 1990

when, in the spring of 1991, Tim tracked her down in the hope of interviewing her for his forthcoming documentary, she gave an account of an incident which had convinced her the two issues were bound together.

Although she was not difficult to find – she had worked full-time administering a child day care centre in East Los Angeles for more than a decade – Serrano had never spoken publicly about the assassination since the night of June 4-5. Nor, she said, over coffee and on condition that the meeting was off the record, was she prepared to do so in 1991.

Her reason was simple: around the time researchers discovered the tapes of her brutal interrogation by LAPD, she had received a visit from LA law enforcement telling her that if she stayed silent her felony conviction would be quietly reduced to a much less serious misdemeanour offence. Serrano did as she was advised.

A quarter of a century later, in the summer of 2016, she finally put this story on the record, but declined to identify the officials who had made an offer she felt unable to refuse.

"I was told 'keep out of things, keep clean and in a couple of years you'll get a reduction'. And that's exactly what happened. I didn't care what motivated them: this was like 'ok – I won't have a felony conviction, it will make life easier, I won't need permission to leave the state, I won't need permission for anything'. So I kept my end of the bargain and it did get knocked down to a misdemeanour. That's what happened. But I can't tell you who [made the deal] because I promised not to."[642]

Today, Sandy Serrano maintains that the story she told LAPD, and the rest of the world, about the girl in a polka dot dress was absolutely true, and that despite LA law enforcement's attempts to bully and browbeat her into re-canting, she never backed down.

---

642 Sandy Serrano-Sewell: interviews with Tim Tate 1991 – 2016

"That was my first real experience of being suspicious of people, and feeling that all these people in authority that you're raised to believe you can trust, you can't. I had been raised to believe that people are basically good and to be proud that I lived in this country with all its freedoms. And the cops are there to protect you. And that authority was not bad. That all changed for me completely. And I still feel that today."[643]

But LAPD's actions ensured that for almost 50 years the story of the Girl in the Polka Dot Dress remained a hall of mirrors, reflecting and refracting an ever-changing kaleidoscope of claims and counter-claims. A succession of researchers had assembled a long list of possible candidates, but none had been able definitively to put a name and a face to the mysterious woman. And then, in 2017, Brad did just that.

He had traced seven of the surviving witnesses who described seeing the girl on June 4 and June 5, 1968 in – and in some cases, fleeing from – the Ambassador Hotel: at his request, Vincent DiPierro, Katie Keir, John Rodman Justice, Martin Patrusky, Juan Romero, Irene Gizzi and Sandy Serrano agreed to look at a photographic line up of possible contenders.

At the time Brad suspected Shirin Khan – one of the young women most frequently cited by other researchers – as the most probable among the candidates for the girl in the polka dot dress. He obtained pictures of Sherry Khan from the 1960s and put two of them – one of Khan at age 14 and the other of her at age 17 – into his photo line-up along with ten other photographs – a mixture of randomly-selected yearbook images from the mid to late 1960s as well as those of seemingly unlikely, but possible, suspects. One was a Ku Klux Klan member called Kathy Ainsworth who had been killed by the FBI at the end of June 1968 and whose name was sometimes raised as a candidate for the polka

---

643 *Ibid.*

dot dress girl. Although he had severe doubts about her, Brad included in his line-up two pictures of Ainsworth taken – like those of Khan – several years apart.

The second outside candidate was a woman whose family had contacted Paul Schrade in 2012, only days after she had died, but who had never been publicly associated with the case. Brad's line-up included one picture of her.

To ensure a genuine blind test, none of the twelve photographs in Brad's line-up bore any name or caption, and none of the seven witnesses who examined them in spring 2017 was in contact about them with the other six. Over the course of several weeks, each of the seven witnesses independently picked Photo No. 2 – the previously unknown woman who had died five years earlier – as the closest match to the polka dot dress girl.

Her name was Elayn Neal and she had, according to her family, lived a very curious life. She had been born Patricia Elaine Neal on November 15, 1948 in Red Bluff, California, but she had been known more often by her middle name; at some point she had legally changed its spelling to "Elayn". She attended Artesia High School in the Los Angeles suburb of Lakewood, but after her freshman year in 1962–1963, left to take care of her younger siblings while her mother worked. She fell pregnant and, in early 1966, married the child's father, Luis Molina, a 20-year-old former schoolmate, three years her elder, who had just been drafted into the U.S. Army.

When he was shipped off to Vietnam, Elayn fell into a pattern which would dominate the rest of her life. She had relationships with other boyfriends and may have worked as a prostitute. She also developed a reputation for suddenly running off without telling anyone where she had gone, often disappearing for long periods. In October 1968 she and Molina divorced.

At some point, Elayn found a waitressing job at the airport in Chino, thirty-five miles from Los Angeles in San

Bernardino County, where one of the pilots introduced her to an internationally-famous songwriter and music impresario. Jerry Neil Capehart was 20 years older than Elayn and a Korean War veteran; after the army he had managed Hollywood musical star Rosemary Clooney, as well as country singer Glen Campbell and 1950s rock star Eddie Cochran.

Capehart had also co-written two of Cochran's hits, *Summertime Blues* and *C'mon Everybody*[644]. Elayn and Capehart married in 1973 and moved to Capehart's home state of Missouri. They divorced eleven years later.[645]

Elayn Neal died, aged 63, on February 4, 2012 in the Texas Gulf Coast city of Baytown. The cause of her death was formally recorded as "cirrhosis due to chronic ethanolism" (an alternative medical term for alcoholism). Shortly afterwards, her children from the marriages to Molina and Capehart began piecing together, with help from their relatives, the scattered fragments of her life. As they did, they remembered that their mother had always seemed haunted by something, often expressing fears about being followed: but as they pooled their memories, a theme emerged – Elayn's long-running obsession with a polka dot dress she kept, stored away, and the family rows that this had caused.

Elizabeth Anne Molina Capehart Bresciano, Elayn's first child, remembered her 5'7" mother putting the polka dot dress on her to see what the much shorter daughter – not yet seven years old – looked like when wearing it. Liz remembered it as "a pretty white dress with black polka dots". She recalled later: "I guess mother thought it would be fun to put it on me. Of course,

---

644 After Cochran's untimely death in 1960, Capehart scored another hit song – *Turn Around, Look At Me*.

645 Capehart was her third husband: between 1971 to 1973 she had been married to a man named Robert W. Manson. She subsequently married for a fourth time in 1988, divorcing Steven Kentner in 1993 and finally spending the last years of her life with a live-in partner, John Hein.

it swallowed a six-year-old. I did get to do a couple of swirlies in the dress before I got tangled up. She took it off me quickly thereafter."[646]

Liz's brother, Raymond Capehart, recalled two or three occasions when his mother pulled out the polka dot dress and simply looked at it. On another, when he was five or six, Ray remembered, she had intended to wear it to a church revival meeting – a decision which had angered his father; Jerry Capehart yelled at Elayn for wanting to be seen in the dress in public. Although he was only a child when this happened, Ray remembered that day vividly because instead of going to the religious event, the couple stayed home and argued intensely all day long.[647]

Marriage to Jerry had not apparently altered Elayn's habit of unexplained disappearances. At some time in or around June 1979 – the eleventh anniversary of the Bobby Kennedy assassination – she had yet again taken off without telling anyone where she was going or what she was doing. While she was away, Capehart, apparently concerned about her intentions, explicitly told the family that Elayn had been the assassination's infamous girl in the polka dot dress. They apparently took the claim with a grain of salt: by the late 1970s, Capehart's relations with his relations were strained, and the story would seem to have quietly passed into family lore.[648]

But in the days immediately following Elayn's death, the collective recollections of her odd polka dot dress fascination, Jerry's angry outburst over her attempt to wear it in public, his provocative claim about Elayn's role as the infamous girl, and

646 Elizabeth Bresciano: interviews with Brad Johnson, April and December, 2017
647 Raymond Capehart: interviews with Brad Johnson, May and December, 2017
648 Marian Capehart Burns [sister of Jerry Capehart]; interviews with Brad Johnson, April 2017

family rumours about his mysterious associations, led Elayn's nephew, Paul Stine, to contact Schrade about his aunt's possible connection to the assassination.

Schrade alerted Brad, who eventually located relatives and photos of Elayn. Although sceptical, he nevertheless decided to include her high school yearbook photo as Girl Number Two in his 12-faces line-up. Much to his shock, this was the photo which every one of his seven Ambassador Hotel witnesses independently chose as the face most closely resembling that of the girl in the polka dot dress.

This independent identification was all the more remarkable since prior to 2017 there had never been agreement between witnesses about photographs of the girl. Irene Gizzi had never seen Elayn's picture before and had previously tended towards Ainsworth after seeing a well-publicized photo of her a few years earlier. Now, unprompted, she favoured Elayn. Sandy Serrano, who for years had refused researchers' requests to examine photos of candidates for the girl, finally agreed to look at Brad's line-up in April 2017; she, like the other witnesses, picked Elayn as the closest match to the girl she had seen at the Ambassador Hotel.[649]

None of this proves beyond all doubt that Patricia "Elayn" Neal was the girl in the polka dot dress who, as Serrano and other witnesses claimed, shouted that she and her companions had shot Bobby while fleeing the crime scene. But the unanimity of identification by the seven eyewitnesses makes Neal the prime suspect: her life and alleged involvement in the events surrounding Bobby's death should form part of a new and honest official investigation.

---

649 Serrano subsequently rowed back from this recognition. In February 2018 she re-examined the photographs and declined to confirm her previous positive identification.

There are yet other reasons – a string of odd, improbable connections – to add Elayn Neal's name to the list of possible conspirators. One of Elayn's classmates at Artesia High School in Lakewood was John Purdy Beckley III, who in the mid to late 1960s, worked as a hired hand on horse ranches across southern California. LAPD detectives interviewed Beckley about allegations that he had seen Sirhan with Jerry "The Walking Bible" Owen on more than one occasion prior to the assassination.

The claims had been made by fellow ranch workers Bill Powers and John Weatherly, and were taken up by Jonn Christian. When LAPD interviewed Beckley, on February 4, 1969, he admitted that he had met Owen, but "stated that he did not know Sirhan [and] to the best of his knowledge he had never seen Sirhan."[650] Subsequently, Christian persuaded all three men to give new statements to Vincent Bugliosi, as part of the lawyer's attempts in 1975 to force a re-opening of the investigation: Beckley at first indicated he wanted to come clean but then, according to Christian, suddenly changed his mind and disappeared to rural Missouri, allegedly in fear for his life. [651]

Johnny Beckley's connection to Elayn may have been tangential. He was a year older than she was, and like her spent only one year – as a freshman in 1962–1963 – at Artesia High. It was, however, repeatedly coincidental: while Luis Molina was away in Vietnam and Elayn and baby Elizabeth were staying with his parents in the L.A. suburb of Hawaiian Gardens, Johnny Beckley and his parents moved to a house only two blocks away from the

---

650 Report of interview with John Purdy Beckley III, February 4, 1969. Special Unit Senator, Vol. 73, p.252-253

651 William Turner and Jonn Christian: *The Assassination of Robert F. Kennedy – A Searching Look At The Conspiracy and Cover-Up*; p.244-245. Random House, 1978

Molinas. Later, Elayn spent a good portion of her final decade in Springfield, Missouri, where Beckley, too, had re-located and lived until his death in 2016.

Yet Beckley was not the only one of Elayn's acquaintances who knew Jerry Owen. The man who would become her third husband – Jerry Capehart – was an old friend of the "Walking Bible". According to Ray Capehart, the two Jerrys had a friendship which lasted into the years immediately preceding Owen's death in 1993.

"My dad [Jerry Capehart] and Jerry Owen used to hang out together in the 1970s and '80s when I was growing up," Ray recalled. "They had already known each other for many years, back in southern California, long before I was born in Missouri in 1974."[652]

In the years following Bobby's assassination, Capehart and Elayn travelled frequently between their homes in Missouri and L.A. – and, according to Ray, on occasion his father met up with Owen.

"I particularly remember, well into the 1980s, my father [Jerry Capehart], my younger brother J.J. and I having dinner with Jerry Owen after one of his traveling church services in either southwest Missouri or northwest Arkansas." [653]

Ray Capehart believes it was one of these Owen services in April 1980 – a well-publicized "Walking Bible" Baptist church revival meeting in Fayetteville, Arkansas (little more than an hour's drive from the Capehart home in Goodman, Missouri) – that his father and mother were planning to attend before Jerry abruptly cancelled the outing after Elayn tried to board the family car with her polka dot dress.

---

652 Raymond Capehart: interviews with Brad Johnson, May and December, 2017
653 Ibid.

"I remember sitting in the car, waiting for mom and dad to come out and drive us to the church event. I could hear they were having a huge fight inside the house. It eventually spilled out into the driveway. My mom came out and she had the polka dot dress on and was saying that she was going to wear it to the event.

"My dad was very angry, saying there was no way she was going to wear it. He told her either she was going to take off that dress or he was going to take it off her." Elayn stormed back into the house in tears; when she failed to return to the car, Jerry also went back inside and the atmosphere remained "pretty heated for the rest of the day."[654]

Elayn's polka dot dress disappeared sometime before her death in February 2012; her three children were unable to find it among her possessions. But their memories of it – and of its apparent importance – are clear.

There is one final reason to add Elayn Neal's name to the list of possible conspirators – a tiny fragment of unproven, yet potentially crucial, family information. According to Ray Capehart, his father worked at some point in his eventful life[655] with an agency whose name repeatedly crops up in investigations into America's three major political assassinations of the 1960s.

"My dad told me that during the 1960s he had worked for the CIA complete with his own security clearance," Ray recalled in 2017. "He never told me he was an actual CIA employee or on the CIA payroll, but definitely told me he had worked for the CIA. It was crystal clear to me, as I was growing up, that my dad had a lot of mysterious friendships and associations, and that he was

---

654 *Ibid.*

655 Capehart died in Nashville, Tennessee on June 7, 1998. As well as his career in show business, he had also worked as a marine surveyor and studied to become an attorney.

concerned about his safety. We moved around a lot, as a result. It got pretty crazy to be honest with you."[656]

But it was the nature of Jerry Capehart's alleged work with the Central Intelligence Agency which was most startling: he told his son that "he had been involved in mind control experimentation."[657]

---

656 Ray Capehart: interviews with Brad Johnson, May – December 2017.
657 *Ibid.*

CHAPTER SIXTEEN:
THE MANCHURIAN CANDIDATE

The Central Intelligence Agency features so routinely in stories of alleged conspiracies that it has become essentially the *Ur*-conspiracy: an ill-motivated, all-encompassing explanation for the majority of unexplained, or contested, *causes célèbres* since the end of the Second World War. Hollywood movies and television dramas feed this trope, re-enforcing public suspicion and with it the claims of those who promote claims of secret Agency machinations.

There is, however, an important difference between conspiracies and conspiracy theories. The latter are exercises in speculation – hypotheses drawn out from events (real or supposed). By contrast, an actual conspiracy is, at heart, no more than an agreement between two or more people to carry out an act that is, by implication, immoral or unlawful.

Genuine conspiracies happen. Watergate was a conspiracy, as was the selling of arms to Iran to generate unauthorized funding for Nicaraguan rebels – the so-called Iran-Contra Affair; Al Qaeda's attacks on New York and Washington D.C. – 9/11 – were the product of a criminal conspiracy. Whilst each of these may be still surrounded by claims and counter-claims – conspiracy theories – the established facts show that the conspiracies themselves existed.

The reason the CIA has become a cliché of post-war conspiracy allegations owes much to the fact that it factually engaged in a succession of very real conspiracies. Notably, it masterminded the 1953 coup d'état which deposed Iran's democratically-elected Prime Minister, Mohammed Mossadegh and, twenty years later, sponsored the overthrow of Chilean President, Salvadore Allende.

In 2010, attorneys acting for Sirhan filed a motion in United States District Court for the Central District of California which argued that he was "an involuntary participant" in the shooting in the Ambassador Hotel pantry because he had been "subjected to extensive and sophisticated hypno programming and mind control". This had turned him into a robot assassin – a real-life "Manchurian Candidate". The organization responsible for this, the lawyers claimed, was the Central Intelligence Agency.[658] If this seemed like the stuff of science fiction, there is unequivocal documentary evidence that in the 1950s the CIA spent years developing – and perfecting – exactly this technique. And the Agency's own records show that key aspects of the program bore strikingly similarities to the facts of Bobby's assassination.

***

The phrase "Manchurian Candidate" first entered public consciousness in 1959, when Richard Condon, a World War Two Marine Corps veteran turned advertising writer and Hollywood PR man, published his second novel.

"*The Manchurian Candidate*" was a political thriller in which the son of a prominent US political family was captured by communist forces in North Korea, then brainwashed by hypnotism in nearby Manchuria, before being sent back to the United States

---

658 Brief on the Issue of Actual Innocence, US District Court, Central California, November 20, 2011.

as the unwitting assassin of a Presidential candidate. Part of the brainwashing involved post-hypnotic programming to ensure he would forget his secret orders to kill as soon as he obeyed them.

The book tapped into the rampant anti-Communist fever of late 1950s America: it quickly became a best-seller, and Frank Sinatra bought the rights to turn it into a Hollywood movie.[659] It also reflected a widespread belief that American POWs captured during the Korean War had been brainwashed into making false confessions of war crimes.

In particular, 35 US Air Force personnel had written – and some were filmed making – statements in which they admitted dropping biological weapons on villages across Korea. When they returned to the United States, each – under threat of Court Martial – recanted these confessions. But several also reported experiencing a blank period of disorientation while being held in an area of Manchuria controlled by the Chinese Red Army. In subsequent hearings, before the House Committee on Un-American Activities in March 1958, Edward Hunter – a former intelligence officer who claimed to have invented the phrase "brainwashing" while working undercover as a journalist – alleged that Chinese communists had perfected hypnosis as a military tool, and exported it to Korea.

"The Korean War began after my discovery of brainwashing," he testified. "I found it was a strategy for the conquest of the world by communism, that it was not merely another tactic, but was the framework for the entire activity of the Communist hierarchy. ... I went to Korea, where I found that the same pattern that I had seen everywhere else was being followed by the Communists. I heard of American captured personnel

---

659 "The Manchurian Candidate" has been adapted twice for the cinema. Sinatra's version, which stuck closely to the novel, came out in 1962. Jonathan Demme's 2004 version updated the story, with the Gulf War replacing Korea as a backdrop.

broadcasting denunciations of their own country and confessing to a non-existent germ warfare in a manner and in a language that fit exactly into the brainwashing pattern that I had found in China and the rest of Asia."[660]

In reality, three years earlier a special Advisory Committee established to investigate the actions of US PoWs during the Korean War had explicitly rejected Hunter's theory. It reported to the US Secretary of Defense that "most of the prisoners were not subjected to brainwashing" and that political "ignorance" was the reason for the airmen's confessions.[661][662]

But by then the CIA was deeply committed to its own top-secret project to develop hypno-programming as a covert weapon. Throughout the 1950s and 1960s the Agency spent millions of dollars on the program, using academics from universities, doctors from hospitals and inmates from American prisons. But the details of its experiments would be kept secret for another two decades.

In January 1973, in one of his final acts as the Director of Central Intelligence (DCI), Richard Helms ordered the destruction of all records relating to what the Agency's own historians describe as one of "the CIA's most notorious operations inside the United States"[663]. The documents, contained in 152 separate

---

660 *Testimony of Edward Hunter*: House Committee on Unamerican Activities; March 13 1958

661 *POW: The Fight Continues After The Battle*; Report of The Secretary of Defense's Advisory Committee on Prisoners of War; August 1955. Library of Congress, https://www.loc.gov/rr/frd/Military_Law/pdf/POW-report.pdf

662 There is also some evidence that the US Air Force had been involved in dropping bacterial weapons on Korea. See *Dirty Little Secrets* [documentary]; Tim Tate, Al Jazeera English, March 2010.

663 CIA official history: "John McCone as Director of Central Intelligence 1961–1965" (Part 2 of 2), P.281. David Robarge, CIA History Staff, Center for Study of Intelligence. CIA Library "CREST" Archive. https://www.cia.gov/library/readingroom/document/0001262737

files, referred to three linked top-secret CIA mind control programs, bearing the cryptonyms BLUEBIRD, ARTICHOKE and MKULTRA.

Helms was a CIA lifer. During World War Two he had been an intelligence officer with the Agency's predecessor, the Office of Strategic Services (OSS). He moved over to the CIA when it was formed in 1947; two years later he was promoted to Chief of Operations for the Directorate of Plans (later re-named Directorate of Operations) – "the clandestine arm of the Central Intelligence Agency"[664]. He rose through the ranks to become the Agency's sixth DCI in June 1966, serving, according to the CIA's official history, "under two of the most complex and controversial Presidents in the nation's history – Lyndon Johnson and Richard Nixon".[665] He was, more than any Director since Allen Dulles, steeped in knowledge of the Agency's covert, and often illegal, activities.

As he prepared to leave office, fallout from the Watergate scandal lapped at Langley's doors. Two of the burglars had been contract staff for the Agency, and Nixon had "repeatedly – and unsuccessfully – tried to draw CIA into the cover-up".[666]

Against this background – and with the CIA facing the threat of Congressional investigations – Helms ordered the destruction of the files, hoping to erase all record of the Agency's mind control experiments.

In December 1974, an investigation by the New York Times alleged that the CIA had been illegally operating inside

664 "Offices of CIA: Clandestine Service": Central Intelligence Agency website. https://www.cia.gov/offices-of-cia/clandestine-service/index.html.

665 "Richard Helms as Director of Central Intelligence, 1966 – 1973". CIA History Staff; Center for The Study of Intelligence. CIA library: https://www.cia.gov/library/readingroom/document/richard-helms-director-central-intelligence-robert-m-hathaway-and-russell-jack-smith

666 Ibid

the USA[667]. The following month President Gerald Ford issued Executive Order 11828, setting up a commission of enquiry headed by Vice-President Nelson Rockefeller, and compelling the CIA to co-operate. The Agency subsequently turned over hundreds of pages of what it termed 'the family jewels'[668] – internal reports detailing any historic or current activity which violated its Charter. They contained a brief reference to a drug experimentation program codenamed MKULTRA.

"In the late 1940s, the CIA began to study the properties of certain behavior-influencing drugs (such as LSD) and how such drugs mighty be put to intelligence use. This interest was prompted by reports that the Soviet Union was experimenting with such drugs, and by speculation that the confessions induced during trials in the Soviet Union and other Soviet Bloc countries during the 1940s might have been elicited by the use of drugs or hypnosis. Great concern over Soviet and North Korean techniques in "brainwashing" continued to be manifested into the early 1950s.

"The drug program was part of a much larger CIA program to study possible means for controlling human behavior. Other studies explored the effects of radiation, electric shock, psychology, psychiatry, sociology and harassment substances."[669]

The Inquiry's final report revealed that the Agency's determination to investigate the effects of LSD on unwitting victims had caused the death of one (then unnamed) employee: under the drug's influence he had jumped out of a New York Hotel

---

667 *The Central Intelligence Agency Act, Public Law 81-110* (1947) – specifically prohibited almost all Agency operations inside the United States.

668 The 'Family Jewels' were declassified and publicly released on June 25, 2007. Viewable at The National Security Archive: http://nsarchive.gwu.edu/NSAEBB/NSAEBB222/family_jewels_full_ocr.pdf

669 *Report to the President by the Commission on CIA Activities Within the United States.*
(The Rockefeller Report); p.226. Washington D.C, June 1975.

room window.[670] But Rockefeller's investigation into the full extent of the CIA's experiments was hindered by the bonfire of files which Helms had ordered. "Unfortunately, only limited records of the testing conducted in these drug programs are now available," the report concluded. "All the records concerning the program were ordered destroyed in 1973, including 152 separate files. In addition, all persons directly involved in the early phases of the program were either out of the country and not available for interview or were deceased."[671]

The same problem also obstructed an independent Senate investigation, operating in parallel to the Rockefeller Commission. The committee, headed by Senator Frank Church, heard evidence about the CIA's covert operations, including assassination attempts on foreign leaders and plots to destabilize their governments.

But when it summoned Sidney Gottlieb, one of the heads of the mind control experimentation programme, he testified that he could not recall any details[672]. Nor could the Agency supply any documents: it told the Committee that these had all been destroyed on Helms' instructions.

However, two years later, in response to a Freedom of Information Act request, the CIA discovered a treasure trove of previously-overlooked documents. In March 1977 its lawyers wrote to John Marks, a former US State Department employee,

---

670 The victim was Frank Olsen, a scientist working on bacteriological warfare. In November 1953, the CIA covertly dosed him with LSD in a glass of orange liqueur.

671 *Report to the President by the Commission on CIA Activities Within the United States.* p.226-227

672 Gottlieb had only recently succeeded the previous Project leader, Morse Allen. He gave evidence under the pseudonym "Victor Scheider". *Interim Report of the Select Committee to Study Governmental Operations with respect to Intelligence Activities* (The Church Committee), p. 20-21. Washington D.C., November 20, 1975.

turned investigative writer, saying that the Agency had located several filing boxes containing 16,000 documents. These provided, for the first time, detailed information on three linked (and Top Secret) CIA mind control projects and the men behind them.

The programs – codenamed BLUEBIRD, ARTICHOKE and MKULTRA – involved what a Senate Committee subsequently described as an "extensive testing and experimentation program which included covert drug tests on unwitting citizens at all social levels, high and low, native Americans and foreign."[673]

But the documents also revealed that the Agency had studied, then developed, the ability to "brainwash" unwitting victims. And – however bizarre or improbable this might seem – its own memoranda described successful experiments to create a hypnoprogrammed assassin – a real life "Manchurian Candidate".[674]

A file note – labelled as a Memorandum for the Record – dated January 31, 1975 set out the history of the programs.

"One paper [internal CIA document] reflected that an Office of Security team as early as 1949–50 experimented with drugs and hypnosis under a project called BLUEBIRD. ... File information indicated that in 1952, overall responsibility for Project ARTICHOKE passed from OSI [Office of Scientific Intelligence] to the Office of Security ... The unit within the Office of Security which apparently coordinated Project ARTICHOKE activities

---

673 Senator Edward Kennedy: Project MKUltra: joint hearing before the Senate Intelligence Committee, the Subcommittee on Health and Scientific Research. August 3, 1977; 95th Congress, 1st Session.

674 The documents were supplied as paper copies to John Marks. Almost all of them are available, on a CD, from the CIA at the cost of $10, However, a private network of doctors and researchers has also placed 1,778 of the mind control experiment documents – comprising 20,000 pages – online. They are viewable at http://www.wanttoknow.info/mind_control/cia_mind_control_documents_orig/

was SRS [Security Research Team], with Mr. [REDACTED] for many years the focal point.

"Details of Office of Security involvement in individual Project ARTICHOKE operational utilizations were found in very few instances. A reference in an SRS log (1951–67) reflected, however, that SRS had been involved in the experimentation and use of hypnosis 'from the start'.

"One of the few areas where detailed information was available concerned hypnotic experimentation. A log of hypnotic experiments conducted by Office of Security personnel was created, showing that numerous (probably several hundred) experiments with hypnotism were conducted in Agency buildings, and apparently utilizing staff volunteers as subjects.

"The log reflected hypnotic experiments during 1951, 1952, and 1953. It could not be determined from available file information when the hypnotic experiments actually began or were caused to be ceased"[675].

From their inception Projects BLUEBIRD and ARTICHOKE were controlled by Morse Allen, a career intelligence officer who, in the 1930s, had rooted out suspected communists for the federal Civil Service Commission[676]. During World War Two he had served with Naval Intelligence, first investigating left-wing movements in New York, then seeing active service on Okinawa.[677] By the beginning of 1950 he was part of the CIA's Office of Security and lobbying internally for funds to study unorthodox methods of "behaviour control".

Project BLUEBIRD was signed into existence by DCI Walter Bedell Smith on April 20, 1950. Several months later an undated

---

675 *Memorandum for the Record re: Artichoke*; 31 Jan 1975. Copy in authors' possession.
676 Dissolved in 1979 and replaced by the Office of Personnel Management,
677 John Marks: The Search For The Manchurian Candidate; 1979. P.26

memo (probably written on or around January 1, 1952) set out its aims.

"SUBJECT: Special Research, Bluebird

I. General Problem

For the past several months Bluebird has been endeavoring to ascertain by research, study, instruction and some practice what value (if any) can be derived from SI [Sleep Induction] and H [Hypnotic] techniques when applied to war and specific Agency problems. These broad problems; using known SI and H Techniques, may be classified as follows:

"A. Can accurate information be obtained from willing or unwilling individuals.

"B. Can Agency-personnel (or persons or interest to this agency) be conditioned to prevent any outside power from obtaining information from them by any known means?

"C. Can we obtain control of the future activities (physical and mental) of any given individual, willing or unwilling by application of SI and H techniques?

"D. Can we prevent any outside power from gaining, control of future activities (physical and mental) of agency personnel by any known means?

"Bluebird believes that A (above) can be answered in the affirmative using SI and H techniques. Bluebird is not fully satisfied with results to date, but believes with continued work and study remarkable and profitable results can be obtained regularly.

"However, B, C, and D (above) are as yet unanswerable, although Bluebird is of the opinion that there is a worthwhile chance that all three may at some future date be answered affirmatively. This opinion is supported generally by numerous individuals having knowledge of these techniques and by much literature and intelligence in this field.

"Since an affirmative proof of B, C and D would be of incredible value to this agency, Bluebird's general problem is to get up, conduct and carry out research (practical – not theoretical) in this direction."[678]

The BLUEBIRD memo also laid out the nature and extent of this "practical" research. In addition to exploring the defensive benefits of hypnosis – using "post-H (hypnotic) suggestion" to prevent CIA agents from revealing secret information under interrogation, and discovering whether any of them had already been hypno-programmed by a hostile intelligence service – the experiments were also intended to develop an offensive capability.

"Can we create by post-H control an action contrary to an individual's basic moral principles?

"Could we seize a subject and in the space of an hour or two by post-H control have him crash an airplane, wreck a train, etc.? (Short, immediate activity)

"Can we by SI and H techniques force a subject (unwilling or otherwise) to travel long distances, commit specified acts and return to us or bring documents or materials? Can a person acting under post-H control successfully travel long distances?

"Can we "alter" a person's personality? How long will it hold?"[679]

The CIA recognized that practical research into "hypnotic techniques" was far outside the capabilities of its own staff. To fill this knowledge gap, the Agency sought out experts who were familiar the procedures.

"Through internal agency channels, Bluebird was given the name of [REDACTED] individual of [REDACTED] extraction and not a citizen of the United States who had been given certain operational security clearance. [REDACTED] was reported

678 Freedom of Information Act disclosure document MORI 140401. Viewable at http://www.wanttoknow.info/mind_control/ foia_mind_control/19520101_140401

679 Freedom of Information Act disclosure document MORI 140401. *Op. cit.*

to have done considerable work in SI and H and to have an unusual and interesting general background. [REDACTED] was also reported as being reliable, trustworthy, a known anti-Communist.

"In view of the above, and on the instructions of the Director of I&SS, [REDACTED] was brought to a safe area near headquarters and interviewed, interrogated and observed by Bluebird on 19, 20, 21 February 1951. [REDACTED's] personality, ability, and intelligence, sincerity and apparent security mindedness were impressive.

"Bluebird officers were unable to find any indications of deviousness or pro-Soviet interests during these observations. [REDACTED] only apparent obvious weaknesses were his foreign background and non-United States citizenship ...

"[REDACTED] discussed at various times his work and interest in the SI and H techniques. He claimed that most of his present work was along the lines of hypnotherapy which involves post-H suggestion, but admitted that his experience with drugs, gases, etc, in conjunction with SI and H was somewhat limited, although he was familiar with much of the literature (U.S. and foreign) in these fields.

"[REDACTED] admitted that since he had been in the U.S. he had induced H conditions in at least several hundred individuals, male and female (in all age groups). [REDACTED] demonstrated successfully some of his operating methods before the B officers on the 19th, 20th, and 21st.

"The success of this demonstration led the BLUEBIRD team to propose that this expert should be "either directly employed or contractually employed ... for specific purpose of engaging in guided research, testing, and experimentation along SI and H lines"[680].

---

680 Ibid.

It was the start of an extensive program which, over the course of the three projects' existence, would involve the CIA paying for the services of staff at "86 universities or institutions",[681] as well as 15 research facilities or private companies, 12 hospitals or clinics and 3 penal institutions.[682]

But the dubious ethics of the proposed experiments troubled some of those approached. A memo by Morse Allen, dated 11 March, 1952 recorded the unease of an un-named expert consulted one week earlier.

"It was established that he was competent, had a general interest in Artichoke[683] type of work, and appreciated the necessary secrecy involved in this type of discussion. ... "After having been given a brief resume of the Artichoke work [REDACTED] stated that whereas he was interested in the problem, he wanted it clearly understood that he felt morally opposed to the application of these techniques in so far as he personally is concerned ...

"He stated, however, that he recognised the fact that we are at war and ... that while he could not carry out such techniques as injecting drugs into an individual, he, nevertheless, felt that he could quite legitimately study the problem from a scientific point of view..."[684]

Whether because of this, or because most of the project's subjects were volunteers, the CIA documents show that many

---

681 Senator Edward Kennedy: Project MKUltra: joint hearing before the Senate Intelligence Committee, the Subcommittee on Health and Scientific Research. August 3, 1977; 95th Congress, 1st Session.

682 *Statement of Admiral Stansfield Turner, DCI*: Project MKUltra: joint hearing before the Senate Intelligence Committee, the Subcommittee on Health and Scientific Research. *Op. cit.*

683 At some point in 1952 – the CIA's documents are contradictory on the exact date – BLUEBIRD was subsumed into, or re-named ARTICHOKE.

684 Memo from Morse Allen [addressee REDACTED]: 11 March 1952. Copy in authors' possession.

of ARTICHOKE's initial attempts to master hypnosis were conducted without the use of drugs. Although other researchers conducted experiments with cannabis and – particularly – LSD, the focus of the hypno-programming team was on making the technique work and then modifying it to induce post-hypnotic amnesia. By the start of January 1953 ARTICHOKE was reporting successful field trials.

"Recently... we carried out experiments involving considerable areas in and around Washington. These experiments clearly demonstrated to a certain extent that individuals under H can move about, travel and act normal over a certain amount of time and space...

"In all of these cases, these subjects have clearly demonstrated that they can pass from a fully awake state to a deep controlled state via the telephone, via some very subtle signal that cannot be detected by other persons in the room and without the other individual being able to note the change.

"In addition, under H they have moved all over the building, passed guards, engaged in conversation, taken polygraph tests , written, drawn fully under H and have had total amnesia for the activities..."[685]

The research continued throughout 1953: each experiment was designed to test the depth and duration of the hypnosis, and the reliability of the amnesia built into the subjects. A detailed three-page memo in November reported on the success of a complex experiment during which two volunteers were hypnotized and told that, under questioning, they would conceal their knowledge of an envelope they had been given; only when their interrogator used a specified code word would the programming allow them to hand it over. After they were awakened from their

---

685 Memo dated 7 Jan 1953: Handwritten reference A/B,III,6,1. In authors' possession.

hypnotic state, the programming would have wiped all memory of the incident.

"It should be noted that … the above tests were not discussed until approximately one hour later and at this point the writer explained the test to both girls. Even with details of the action Miss [REDACTED] had no memory of the action in its entirety and Miss [REDACTED] could only remember very vaguely certain minor incidents."[686]

Experiments early the following year also established that hypno-programming could be induced remotely. A file note dated February 23 recorded that "Advanced tests were conducted and were completely successful … telephone hypnosis was obtained …"[687]

The following month ARTICHOKE researchers reported that a successfully hypnotised volunteer could be programmed to produce – but not remember producing – what it termed "automatic writing".

"The concluding experiment of the evening was one of automatic writing. [REDACTED]. Following the usual procedure in obtaining automatic writing each subject was instructed upon the placing of a pencil in their hand to write and in each instance the individual participating wrote a cryptic message…

"Subject was placed in a deep H state, her hand was dissociated and instructed when pencil was placed in her hand, hand would write. In each instance the hand did write a cryptic message. … each subject was amazed and startled [once awakened] at what she had written. In the opinion of [REDACTED] and the

---

686 "SI and H Experimentation, 17 November 1953". Handwritten reference A/B, 3,2/34. In authors' possession.

687 "SI and H Experimentation, 23 February, 1954". Handwritten reference A/B, 3,2/16. In authors' possession.

writer, the activity was entirely successful and was in no sense a 'faked' operation by the subjects themselves."[688]

One of the main concerns of Morse Allen and his team of researchers was whether a subject – whether willing or not – could be to perform an act contrary to their own interests or personal moral code. Conventional academic and scientific wisdom held that this was impossible: a memo documenting a meeting with another outside expert noted:

"[REDACTED] ... doubted that a post-hypnotic suggestion could be positively depended upon to compel a hypnotized subject to carry out an activity toward which that subject, when in an unhypnotized condition, was unalterably opposed."[689]

But Allen was unconvinced by this, and determined to test the boundaries. In January 1954 his researchers were sent to explore a "hypothetical" mission with another (un-named) expert. The memo recording their week-long discussions reveals the Agency's specific interest in creating a hypno-programmed political assassin.

"The ARTICHOKE team visited [REDACTED] during period 8 January to 15 January 1954. The purpose of the visit was to give an evaluation of a hypothetical problem, namely: Can an individual of [REDACTED] descent be made to perform an act of attempted assassination involuntarily under the influence of ARTICHOKE? The essential elements of the problem areas follows:

"As a "trigger mechanism" for a bigger project, it was proposed that an individual of [REDACTED] descent, approximately 35 years old, well educated, proficient in English and well established socially and politically in the [REDACTED] Government

---

688 "SI and H Experimentation, 23 March 1954". Handwritten reference A/B, 3,2/9. In authors' possession.
689 "Conference with [REDACTED], 22 September 1953. Handwritten reference A/B, III,6,11. In authors' possession.

be induced to perform an act, involuntarily, of attempted assassination against a prominent [REDACTED] politician or if necessary against an American official.

"The SUBJECT was formerly in [REDACTED] employ but has since terminated and is now employed with the [REDACTED] Government. According to all available information, the SUBJECT would offer no further cooperation with [REDACTED].

"Access to the SUBJECT would be extremely limited, probably limited to a single social meeting. Because the SUBJECT is a heavy drinker, it was proposed that the individual could be surreptitiously drugged, through the medium of an alcoholic cocktail at a social party, ARTICHOKE applied and the SUBJECT induced to perform the act of attempted assassination at some later date.

"All of the above was to be accomplished at one involuntary uncontrolled social meeting. After the act of attempted assassination was performed, it was assumed that the SUBJECT would be taken into custody by the [REDACTED] Government and thereby 'disposed of'."[690]

Although the memo made clear that the planning for this mission involved an identified hypno-programmed killer and an equally-specific victim, it stressed that the assassination itself was not the prime motivation: what mattered was proving the technique.

"Whether the proposed act of attempted assassination was carried out or not by the SUBJECT was of no great significance in relation to the overall project."[691]

After a week of deliberations, the ARTICHOKE team decided that "in this case" the plan would not work: access to

---

690 Three-page "Project Artichoke" Memo, January 22, 1954; handwritten reference H-B/3. In authors' possession.

691 Ibid.

the proposed "involuntary and unwitting" assassin would be too limited. But the memo concluded with a decision to implement the hypno-programmed killer scheme in other circumstances.

"The final answer was that in view of the act that successful completion of this proposed act of attempted assassination was insignificant to the overall project; to wit, whether it was even carried out or not, that under "crash conditions" and appropriate authority from Headquarters, the ARTICHOKE team would undertake the problem in spite of the operational difficulties."[692] [emphasis in original document].

Back at the CIA's Langley headquarters, Morse Allen's team carried on the hypnosis experiments with its willing volunteers, and continued to consult with its contracted experts. Some of these still maintained that it was impossible to hypno-program a "subject" to commit an act which ran against the grain of their beliefs or moral code – a position which exasperated the leaders of Project ARTICHOKE.

In May 1955, an internal memo from the Chief of Technical Branch to the Chief of the Security Research Staff titled "Hypnotism and Covert Operations", denounced the "pessimism" of these Doubting Thomases.

"I now distrust much of what is written by academic experts on hypnotism. Partly this is because many of them appear to have generalized from a very few cases; partly because much of their cautious pessimism is contradicted by Agency experimenters; but more particularly because I personally have witnessed behavior responses which respected experts have said are impossible to obtain. In no other field have I been so conscious of the mental claustrophobia of book and lecture hall knowledge...

"[REDACTED SUBJECT LINE] and some other scientists do not agree, at least in so far as the therapeutic use of narco-hypnosis

---

692 Ibid.

is concerned. But suppose that while under hypnosis a subject is told that a loved one's life is in danger from a maniac and that the only means of rescue is to shoot a person designated as the maniac? Three expert practitioners (two from universities and the Agency consultant quoted above) say that there is no doubt on the basis of their experience that in such circumstances murder would be attempted. The only requirement is that the proposal be put 'in a form and manner acceptable to the subject'".[693]

There was good reason for this confidence. The previous year Morse Allen recorded a successful experiment involving two agency secretaries: as he noted in an internal memo, it proved conclusively that it was possible to hypno-program an unwilling subject to commit an act of murder which he, or she, would be unable to recall when woken from the trance.

"On Wednesday, 10 February 1954, hypnotic experimentation and research work was continued in Building 13 ... the work proceeded as follows:

"1. A posthypnotic of the night before (pointed finger, you will sleep) was enacted. Misses [REDACTED] and [REDACTED] immediately progressed to a deep hypnotic state with no further suggestion. This was to test whether the mere carrying out of the posthypnotic would produce the state of hypnosis desired. Needless to say, it did.

"2. Miss [REDACTED] was then instructed (having previously expressed a fear of firearms in any fashion) that she would use every method at her disposal to awaken Miss [REDACTED] (now in a deep hypnotic sleep) and failing to do this, she would pick up a pistol nearby and fire it at Miss [REDACTED]. She was instructed that her rage

---

693 "Hypnotism and Covert Operations"; CIA internal memo, May 5, 1955. Handwritten reference "G". In authors' possession.

would be so great that she would not hesitate to "kill" [REDACTED] for failing to awaken.

"Miss [REDACTED] carried out these suggestions to the letter, including firing the (unloaded pneumatic pistol) gun at [REDACTED] and then proceeding to fall into a deep sleep.

"After proper suggestions were made, both were awakened and expressed complete amnesia for the entire sequence. [REDACTED] was again handed the gun, which she refused (in her awakened state) to pick up or accept from the operator. She expressed absolute denial that the foregoing sequence had happened."[694]

ARTICHOKE had worked. The CIA now knew that it could create a hypno-programmed assassin who would be unable to recall his, or her, actions. However outlandish it might seem, the "Manchurian Candidate" was not – is not – a conspiracy theory: it is conspiracy *fact*.

The question is what – if any – connection this had to Sirhan and the assassination of Bobby Kennedy.

---

[694] "Hypnotic Experiment and Research"; CIA internal memo, February 10, 1954. Handwritten reference "A/B, 3, 2/18". In authors' possession.

CHAPTER SEVENTEEN:
THE HYPNO-PROGRAMMED
ASSASSIN

On March 9, 1973, Dr. Eduard Simson appeared before a Notary Public in the northern Californian city of Salinas: the purpose of his visit was to dictate and sign a 23-page affidavit.

Simson had been a licensed psychologist for 17 years: he held degrees and post-doctoral fellowships from five prestigious universities[695], was a fellow of the American Society for Clinical Hypnosis and the International Council of Psychologists, and had worked for state medical boards in Alaska, New Jersey and California, as well as spending six years as Senior Psychologist at San Quentin State prison.

He did not swear the affidavit lightly. He specifically recorded his "reluctance" to become involved in the case of a prisoner which was then attracting controversy – and one which had already cost him his job at San Quentin. But his conscience told him he had to speak out.

---

695 Stanford, New York University, the University of Louisville, Heidelburg University, and UCAL Berkeley.

"I am appalled at the conduct of the mental health professionals involved in this case. I undertook the writing of this affidavit because I feel that it would be a disservice to the profession of psychology to let this matter rest without further review..."[696]

The case which so concerned Dr. Simson was the conviction of Sirhan Sirhan for the assassination of Bobby Kennedy. He had interviewed Sirhan extensively on Death Row, and had come to a deeply disturbing conclusion. "Sirhan's trial," he swore under oath, "was, and will be remembered, as the psychiatric blunder of the century.[697]

At the heart of this blunder, according to Dr. Simson, was hypnosis, and with it, strong indications that Sirhan had been hypno-programmed.

***

Hypnosis first appeared in American courtrooms in an 1897 criminal trial. Defence counsel in *People v. Ebanks*[698] tried to introduce the evidence of an expert hypnotist who was prepared to testify that statements made by the defendant under hypnosis proved his innocence. The trial court (and subsequently the California Supreme Court) threw out the attempt, stating that "the law of the United States does not recognize hypnotism".[699] Despite this unpromising start, over ensuing decades hypnotism was increasingly used by both prosecution and defence, with many courts taking the view that testimony resulting from hypnosis should be admissible, with warnings to be given to juries

---

696 Affidavit of Dr. Eduard Simson; March 9, 1973, Salinas, Monterey County, CA. Copy in authors' possession.

697 Affidavit of Dr. Eduard Simson; March 9, 1973, Salinas, Monterey County, CA. Copy in authors' possession.

698 117 Cal. 652, 49 P. 1049 (1897).

699 *Ibid.* at 665, 49 P. at 1053 (quoting lower court).

about its credibility.[700] By the start of Sirhan's trial in January 1969, it was an accepted, if not common, element in American jurisprudence.

Since his arrest, Sirhan had remained unable to recall any of the events in the pantry of the Ambassador Hotel. His last memory, before "waking" to find bodies piling on top of him, was of drinking coffee with an attractive girl wearing a polka dot dress. It was for this reason that defence psychiatrist, Dr. Bernard Diamond, had decided to use hypnosis as a way to break through his client's amnesia. He testified at trial on the techniques he used with Sirhan.

"It is customary to simplify the hypnotic procedure to give a post-hypnotic suggestion as to how they will be hypnotized the next time; and in this case I gave a suggestion that when I counted "five" he would go to sleep, and I gave the command, and then when I counted to "three" he would wake up."[701]

Diamond found that it was surprisingly easy to hypnotize Sirhan, and that under hypnosis he could be programmed to perform bizarre feats – including climbing the cell bars – but, when wakened, have no memory of either the actions or the hypnosis. The sessions also encompassed what the architects of Project ARTICHOKE would have recognised as "automatic writing". The psychiatrist testified that under hypnotic suggestion, Sirhan wrote similar words and disjointed sentences to those found in the notebooks in his room. But despite the deep hypnotic "trance" the psychiatrist induced, Sirhan could still not recall any details of the shooting in the pantry.

---

700 For Federal guidance see: *United States Attorneys; Criminal Resource Manual;* Pp: 287 – 294. US Department of Justice. https://www.justice. gov/usam/criminal-resource-manual

701 *"People v. Sirhan B. Sirhan";* Trial testimony of Dr. Bernard Diamond. P. 6926 of trial record. California State Archives

The interviews, both regular and under hypnosis, led to a division of opinion within Sirhan's defence team. Dr. Diamond came to believe that Sirhan had hypnotized himself prior to shooting Kennedy. But, in conjunction with lead defence counsel Grant Cooper, he advised that the best legal strategy was to present him to the jury as mentally ill – a paranoid schizophrenic – and therefore protected under California law from the death penalty.

The chief defence investigator, Robert Blair Kaiser – who sat in on many of the psychiatrist's sessions – disagreed: according to an affidavit he swore in 1997, he told his superiors that Sirhan had not programmed himself but had, by contrast, been hypno-programmed to kill by someone else – that he was a real-life "Manchurian Candidate".

"I became convinced that the hypothesis that Sirhan had been hypnotically programmed to assassinate Robert F. Kennedy was the most reasonable explanation for Sirhan's actions and statements as I had heard about and witnessed them," Kaiser swore under oath. "I communicated this viewpoint both to Dr. Diamond and to Grant Cooper, lead counsel for the defence.

"Dr. Diamond was familiar with the fact that it is possible to programme a person to commit murder without knowing what he is doing and in fact gave me a book about a famous case in Denmark where this happened. However, Dr. Diamond claimed to me that the jury would not believe that Sirhan had been hypnotically programmed to kill.

"Mr. Cooper had the same view and in fact repeatedly told me to keep quiet during defense strategy sessions in which I would raise the issue of hypnotic programming in this case...

"The rationale that the jury would not believe a defense of hypnotic programming leading to unconsciousness is absurd in this case...thus defense counsel's failure to present the hypnosis defense was absolutely not justifiable on tactical grounds."[702]

The jury's subsequent rejection of Dr. Diamond's paranoid-schizophrenia diagnosis would seem to bear out Kaiser's view of the defence strategy. It neither pursued the reasons for Sirhan's unusual susceptibility to hypnotic programming, nor saved him from being sent to Death Row at San Quentin State Prison. But it was there that a truly independent medical expert first examined Sirhan.

Dr. Eduard Simson was in charge of the prison's psychological testing program: over a six year period he assessed thousands of inmates, including those condemned to execution. In the summer of 1969 he was assigned to work with Inmate Number B-21014 – Sirhan Sirhan – by the prison's chief psychiatrist, Dr. David Schmidt. A memo from Schmidt to the prison warden noted that "Dr. Simson would be more effective working with him [Sirhan] than any other staff member".[703]

As their sessions developed, Simson discovered that Sirhan's condition did not resemble any of the conclusions contained in the evidence presented at trial. "The testimony of psychiatrists and psychologists, which I have carefully studied from trial transcripts, shows significant errors, distortions, even probable falsification of facts," he wrote in his 1973 affidavit. "The main reason for these errors rests largely on their belief that Sirhan killed Robert F. Kennedy. Their approach to examining Sirhan was highly misguided because of this preconceived notion …

"Assuming that Sirhan killed Robert F. Kennedy, an assumption, the validity of which apparently no one seriously questioned,

---

702 Declaration of Robert Blair Kaiser; People of The State of California vs. Sirhan Bishara Sirhan, June 20, 1997. *Petition for Writ of Habeas Corpus.* California State Archives.

703 Dr. David S. Schmidt: Memo to Warden L.S. Nelson. Robert F. Kennedy Assassination Archives

the mental health specialists saw their role primarily in proving what to them was a known fact, rather than in discovering the truth. Consequently, since their approach was incorrect, they related erroneous conclusions to the jury…"[704]

The very fact that Sirhan had been so easy to hypnotise also raised significant concerns in Dr. Simson's mind.

"Sirhan is not and was never a paranoid schizophrenic … Dr. Diamond is wrong in testifying that the evidence for psychosis was obtained when Sirhan was under hypnosis. The fact is, paranoid schizophrenics are almost impossible to hypnotize. They are too suspicious and do not trust anybody, including friends and relatives… Psychotics in general are among the poorest subjects for hypnosis.

"They cannot concentrate, they do not follow instructions and basically do not trust. Sirhan, however, was an unusually good hypnotic subject… The fact that Sirhan was easy to hypnotize, as testified by Dr. Diamond, proves he was not a paranoid schizophrenic (during one hypnotic experiment Dr. Diamond made Sirhan jump around, like a monkey; only good hypnotic subjects respond so readily to hypnotic suggestions)"[705]

Rather more pertinently, this susceptibility begged an obvious question: who had hypnotised Sirhan prior to the night of June 4-5, 1968? Dr. Simson wanted to continue his sessions with Sirhan to explore this. But on September 24, 1969, the psychologist was ordered to abandon his detailed examinations of Sirhan's mental state: James Park, Associate Warden at San Quentin, sent a terse memo to Dr. Simson's immediate boss, Dr. David Schmidt.

"I am concerned that Dr. Simson appears to be making a career out of seeing Sirhan," Park wrote. "I think that contact

---

704 Affidavit of Dr. Eduard Simson; March 9, 1973, Salinas, Monterey County, CA. Op. cit.
705 Affidavit of Dr. Eduard Simson; March 9, 1973, Salinas, Monterey County, CA. Op. cit.

should be limited to those [sic] strictly necessary to accomplish the official purpose of psychiatric examination and should not be grossly in excess of the services offered other condemned prisoners."[706]

Dr. Simson – only independent and properly qualified psychologist to examine Sirhan – resigned from his post in protest. He had had come to the conclusion that far from being a lone and politically-motivated assassin, Sirhan had been hypno-programmed to be present in the pantry as a distraction.

"He was put up to draw attention while experts did the work," the psychologist told a radio interviewer in 1977. "He would be easily blamed ... He was programmed to be there."[707]

In the years that followed, Dr. Simson's opinion was supported by America's leading expert on hypnosis. Dr. Herbert Spiegel was a licensed doctor and psychiatrist, Special Lecturer in Psychiatry, Columbia University, New York, and Adjunct Professor of Psychology at John Jay College of Criminal Justice, New York. He authored a series of academic papers and books on hypnosis and testified as a court-certified expert witness in numerous trials.[708] Two highly publicized events in the late 1960s established Spiegel's credentials as an independent authority on hypno-programming, and as the antithesis of an assassination conspiracy theorist.

In March 1967, New Orleans District Attorney Jim Garrison charged Clay Shaw, a Louisiana businessman, with involvement in an alleged CIA conspiracy to kill President John. F. Kennedy. Dr. Spiegel was retained as a consultant by Shaw's defence team. Partly as a result of his evidence, the jury subsequently dismissed

---

706 Memorandum from James W.L. Park to Dr. D.G. Schmidt, September 24, 1969. In authors' possession.

707 Dr. Eduard Simson. Interviewed by Mae Brussell, KLRB radio, Carmel CA. June 13, 1977.

708 Curriculum Vitae of Dr. Herbert Spiegel (1914 – 2009) http://www.marciagreenleaf.com/HS/_html/pages/main.php?pageName=cv

all the charges after just an hour's deliberation; the case severely damaged public belief in Garrison's claims of a Mafia-CIA assassination plot.

But it was an experiment conducted by Dr. Spiegel as part of Clay's defence preparation which firmly established his reputation as a non conspiracy-minded expert. At the annual meeting of the American Psychiatric Association in May 1968, and filmed by NBC television, Dr. Spiegel hypnotized a politically "left of centre" volunteer and instructed the subject that when he awoke he would "embrace a right wing ideology as his own". The hypno-programming also implanted an instruction that this right wing ideology would grow stronger inside the subject's mind each time it was challenged by others. Spiegel described the outcome of this programming in a 1997 affidavit.

"After awakening, the subject began a discussion with a journalist who was participating in the experiment. The subject soon became deeply concerned about the possibility that the news organization for whom the journalist was working was dominated [by] the communists, and began talking like a right winger... Later, I showed a film of the foregoing events to the subject, and he was completely shocked to see and hear himself making right wing statements.

"All of the foregoing was included in this film, which was designed, among other things, to demonstrate how it is possible to use hypnosis to program a suitable subject to do something at variance with his beliefs, and how a suitable subject may develop a spontaneous amnesia as a result of hypnosis about the experience of being hypnotized, of the fact that he or she has been programmed and of post-hypnotic conduct that has been hypnotically induced during the trance state."[709]

---

709 Declaration of Dr. Herbert Spiegel; People of The State of California vs. Sirhan Bishara Sirhan, June 20, 1997. *Petition for Writ of Habeas Corpus.*

Dr. Spiegel regularly used this film to undermine the reluctance of American lawyers, jurors and journalists to believe that it is possible to hypno-program someone to act against his own beliefs and moral code, and then forget he had done so.[710]

"If we get a highly hypnotizable person," he said in a filmed interview in 1992, "who is subject to the proper programming under controlled conditions and is subject to some degree of supervision, and exposed to the target within a reasonable range, it is quite possible – and even probable – that he will comply with the program and end up not being fully aware of what he's doing.

"In general, there is a spontaneous amnesia for the stimulus and the program, and sometimes if that's re-enforced by the instructions of the programmer – 'you will not remember' – the odds of the amnesia is even greater."[711]

For his June 1997 affidavit, sworn in support of a plea by Sirhan to California's Supreme Court, Dr. Spiegel reviewed all the records – tape recordings and transcripts – of Dr. Bernard Diamond's hypnosis sessions with Sirhan.

He noted that "Sirhan's reactions as described by Dr. Diamond establish that he could be 'programmed' under hypnosis to carry out even ridiculous actions in the waking state and to believe that he himself was the author of those actions without knowing that he had carried out commands in response to a signal which he had been instructed under hypnosis to recognize in the waking state ... Mr. Sirhan thus exhibited a tendency to automatically repress any conscious memory of having been hypnotized."[712]

Exhibit 104. California State Archives.

710 The film now forms part of the Columbia University Film Series. Dr. Spiegel screened it for Tim Tate during interviews with him in 1991- 1992.

711 Dr. Herbert Spiegel, interviews with Tim Tate, New York, 1991–1992

712 Declaration of Dr. Herbert Spiegel; People of The State of California vs. Sirhan Bishara Sirhan, June 20, 1997. Op. cit.

But it was the speed with which Dr. Diamond had been able to hypnotize Sirhan which most concerned Dr. Spiegel. "I share Dr. Diamond's evident suspicions that the ease with which Sirhan picked up the technique ... suggests that Sirhan had been hypnotized during a prior period of time and was familiar with the counting techniques being employed by Dr. Diamond..."[713]

And since there was no record in any of Dr. Diamond's notes or testimony of giving post-hypnotic instructions to create this amnesia, it appeared likely that Sirhan had previously been trained to do this.

"Mr. Sirhan thus exhibited a tendency to automatically repress any conscious memory of having been hypnotized. This could be consistent with the hypothesis that Sirhan had been previously instructed or trained under hypnosis to have no memory of any time that he had been placed under hypnosis and to forget any instance in which he had been in a hypnotic state."[714]

This was, of course, precisely the object of Project ARTICHOKE, and precisely the outcome Morse Allen's successful experiment of programming his female volunteer had achieved.

Dr. Speigel's affidavit also highlighted what appeared to be the key point in Dr. Diamond's hypnotic sessions: the moment that he ordered Sirhan to recall meeting the girl in the polka dot dress.

"It is noteworthy that in this exchange, Sirhan denies that someone was with him at the time of the assassination, admits that "the girl" was with him at that time and then groans and shuts down when asked to identify her ...

"One plausible interpretation of Sirhan's responses to Dr. Diamond's questions about "the girl", whom he admitted under hypnosis was with him at the time of the assassination,

713 *Ibid.*
714 *Ibid.*

would be that Sirhan was programmed not to be able to identify those who were with him at that crucial time and to groan
and shut down when pressed for information even under
hypnosis…"[715]

Dr. Spiegel's statement concluded with a seemingly-obvious
course of action to determine the truth about Sirhan's apparent
hypno-programming.

"An attempt at de-programming has never taken place in
Sirhan's case, and it is my understanding from Mr. Teeter[716]
that Mr. Sirhan is willing to undergo it and wants to recover his
memory of the events in question."[717]

The suggestion fell on deaf ears. The California Supreme
Court refused to entertain Sirhan's petition for a new trial: a
decade would pass before an attempt to "unlock" his mind
would begin.

In May 2008, his new lawyers, William Pepper and Laurie
Dusek, commissioned Dr. Daniel Brown, Associate Professor
in Psychology at Harvard Medical School, to examine Sirhan.
Dr. Brown is a world-renowned authority on hypnosis: he has
been qualified as an expert witness on "psychological assessment,
memory, memory for trauma and the effects of suggestive influence" by numerous state and federal courts, and in three separate
trials has testified for the prosecution at the International War
Crimes Tribunal in The Hague. He also wrote the standard academic textbook on hypnosis[718], as well as the current forensic
guidelines on interviewing with hypnosis.

Brown worked with Sirhan over the next eight years. He
interviewed him for more than 100 hours at three separate

---

715 *Ibid.*
716 Lawrence Teeter (1949–2005) was Sirhan's attorney from 1994.
717 Declaration of Dr. Herbert Spiegel; People of The State of California vs.
     Sirhan Bishara Sirhan, June 20, 1997. Op. cit.
718 Dr. Daniel Brown: *Hypnosis and Hypnotherapy;* Erlbaum, 1986.

prisons in California, administered a series of standard psychological tests and, with Sirhan's agreement, conducted (prison-approved) hypnosis sessions.[719]

In 2011 he filed a lengthy sworn declaration of his findings. (Given its highly detailed scientific analysis, the major sections are reproduced largely verbatim.)

"The central question Attorney Pepper asked me to render an expert opinion about is whether or not Mr. Sirhan was a subject of coercive suggestive influence that rendered his behavior at the time of the assassination of Senator Robert F. Kennedy involuntary and also made him amnesic for his behavior and role in the assassination"[720]

Dr. Brown's extensive tests revealed "actual evidence of hypnotically induced alter personality states", and allowed him to set out a precise scientific diagnosis.

"I gave Mr. Sirhan the more detailed SCID-D – a detailed structured interview for dissociative disorders – the 'gold standard' in assessment of dissociative disorders[721]. According to the SCID-D Mr. Sirhan has a major dissociative disorder, dissociative disorder not otherwise specified (DDNOS).

"In subsequent direct interviews with Mr. Sirhan I directly observed Mr. Sirhan a number of times switch into at least one distinctively different alter personality state, a personality-state that responds in a robot-like fashion upon cue and adopts the behavior of firing a gun at a firing range. The alter personality state is heretofore [sic] referred to as "range mode".

---

719 Although the prisons did not allow any electronic recording of the meetings, Dr. Brown and lawyer Laurie Dusek wrote down everything as it happened.

720 Declaration of Daniel Brown Ph.D., April 23, 2011. Exhibit in *Sirhan B. Sirhan vs. Galaza, Warden,* California District Court.

721 SCID-D is a widely used and carefully structured interview protocol, approved by the American Psychiatric Association, for diagnosing dissociative disorders.

"This altered personality state *only* occurs while Mr. Sirhan is in a hypnotic or self-hypnotic state, and *only* in response to certain cues. This state never spontaneously manifests. While in this altered personality state Mr. Sirhan shows both a loss of executive control and complete amnesia.

"The *DSM-IV* diagnostic criteria[722] for dissociative identity disorder requires the presence of at least two or more distinct alter personality states. Since only one distinct self-state was observed Mr. Sirhan does not meet the full *DSM-IV* diagnostic criteria for dissociative identity disorder. This distinctive alter personality state is cue specific and state-dependent, which is quite unlike the psychiatric condition, dissociative identity disorder, wherein alter personality states manifest spontaneously. Cue-specific/state-specific alter personality states are likely the product of coercive suggestive influence and hypnosis..."[723]

Next, Dr. Brown investigated the claim, made at his trial, that Sirhan had been in a self-induced hypnotic trance at the time of the assassination.

"Since the possibility of Mr. Sirhan being in an hypnotic or self-hypnotic trance at the time of the assassination was introduced by defense expert Dr. Diamond at Mr. Sirhan's trial, I administered a standardized assessment of hypnotizability... Given the fact that no one has ever administered a normative, standardized measure of hypnotizability to Mr. Sirhan, I thought it would be important to do so...

"I have written four textbooks on hypnosis, have taught hypnosis to over 3,000 professionals, and have hypnotized over 6,000 individuals over a 40-year professional career. Mr. Sirhan

---

722 *DSM-IV* Codes are the classification found in the Diagnostic and Statistical Manual of Mental Disorders, 4th Edition, published by the American Psychiatric Association (APA) and which includes all currently recognized mental health disorders.

723 Declaration of Daniel Brown Ph.D., April 23, 2011. Op. cit.

is one of the most hypnotizable individuals I have ever met, and the magnitude of his amnesia for his actions ... is extreme, more than I have observed in many other highly hypnotizable individuals ..."[724]

Away from the prison, Dr. Brown reviewed all the pre-trial interviews carried out under hypnosis by Dr. Bernard Diamond. Like Dr. Simson and Dr. Spiegel before him, he was concerned by what he found.

"After listening to Dr. Diamond's hypnosis audio recordings of his interviews and hypnosis with Mr. Sirhan, as an expert in suggestive influence and hypnosis, I came to the conclusion that Dr. Diamond was unduly suggestive to Mr. Sirhan, in that Dr. Diamond systematically supplied specific suggestions to Mr. Sirhan to fill in the gaps of Mr. Sirhan's memory for the day and evening of the assassination. Such interviewing methods would not meet any current standard of non-suggestive interviewing ..."[725]

After completing all the psychological tests and assessments, Dr. Brown then began to do what no other expert had attempted: to unlock – forensically and carefully – Sirhan's blocked memory of the night of Robert Kennedy's assassination. Using a combination of "free recall" and interviews under hypnosis, he enabled Sirhan to describe the hours before he arrived at the Ambassador Hotel.

After a lengthy target shooting session at the San Gabriel Valley Gun Club, Sirhan had gone to the hotel in the hope of meeting a girl. At the hotel's bar he drank four Tom Collins cocktails and returned to his car, only to realize that he was intoxicated and needed coffee before driving home. According to Dr. Brown's report, Sirhan's return to the hotel bar was the pivotal moment in all his subsequent actions.

---

724 *Ibid.*
725 *Ibid.*

"The bartender told him there was no coffee at the bar. An attractive woman with a polka dot dress was sitting at the bar talking to the bartender. She overheard Mr. Sirhan asking for coffee and she said that she knew where the coffee was.

"The woman in the polka dot dress then took Mr. Sirhan by the hand and led him to the ante-room behind the stage where Senator Kennedy... [would be] speaking. There they discovered a large silver coffee urn and cups. Mr. Sirhan recalled: 'This girl was there. She was looking for coffee, too. Then all of a sudden she say[s], 'Oh, there's coffee'. It was on the way back. We zoned in on it... a big urn... We poured the coffee... then she started to act like a lady... I made up my mind I'm going to make it with this girl tonight... she didn't lead me on... it was my job to woo her...'

"It is notable that according to Mr. Sirhan's memory, the girl in the polka dot dress leads Mr. Sirhan to find the coffee, not the other way around. While Mr. Sirhan is flirting with this girl (Mr. Sirhan went to the party to pick up a girl), they are interrupted by an official with a suit and clip board. This official tells them that they cannot stay in the anteroom for security reasons, and the official tells the girl in the polka dot dress to go into the kitchen."

Sirhan then recalled what happened next. "'All of a sudden they tell us, we have to move. This guy comes by wearing a suit... darkish hair... A big, big full face... seems like he was in charge... He wasn't wearing any uniform... wearing a suit... She acknowledges his instruction... He motions toward the pantry... I followed her. She led... I was like a little puppy after her. I wanted to go back to the mariache [sic] band... but she went straight to that pantry area... with my being so attracted to her I was just glued to her...

"'As we were coming in [to the pantry]... I'm still sleepy... very sleepy... I was flirting with her... the place was darkish... a deep place to get romantic with that girl... Then she sat up on the table facing with her back to the wall ... her thighs and legs are right here .. I am just looking at her trying to take her beauty in ... I am trying to figure out how to hit on her ... That's all I can think about ... She sat on the steam table. I was leaning. I was fascinated with her looks ... I was engrossed ... She was busty, looked like Natalie Wood. She never said much ... She was a seductress with an unspoken availability.'"

The next part of Sirhan's recollection led Dr. Brown to suspect that his actions were "an automatic behavioural response to a specific post-hypnotic cue". He reported, verbatim, what his patient remembered.

"This is what Mr. Sirhan recalled: 'All of a sudden she's looking over my head toward an area ... Then she taps me or pinches me ... It is startling ... It was like when you're stuck with a pin or pinched ... he points back over my head ... She says, 'Look, look, look.'

"'I turn around. ... There are people coming back through the doors ... I am still puzzled about what she is directing me to ... It didn't seem relevant to me ... Then, all of a sudden she gets more animated ... She put her arm on my shoulder ... Then I was back at the target range ... a flashback to the shooting range ... I thought I was at the range more than I was actually shooting at any person, let alone Bobby Kennedy ... Then everything gets blurry ... I think that's when Uecker grabbed me ...' "[726]

To a psychologist as experienced as Dr. Brown, the recollections pointed at a logical conclusion.

"Overall, if Mr. Sirhan's free recall is taken at face value, this very unusual recall does indeed suggest possible hypnotic programming of, and behavioral handling of, Mr. Sirhan to serve as a distractor for an assassination of a presidential candidate ... Mr. Sirhan's memory report is consistent with an

---

726 *Ibid.*

hypnotic programming hypothesis that strongly implies that his behavior on the night of the assassination was involuntary, and was followed by amnesia for the events ...

"In addition Mr. Sirhan's report of suddenly changing his state after being touched by the girl, and then hallucinating that he was at the firing range, is suggestive of the kind of mind control done in that era, namely training a hypnotizable subject to respond on cue to a post-hypnotic suggestion to hypnotically hallucinate being at the firing range...

"After three years of testing and interviewing Mr. Sirhan ... it is my opinion that Mr. Sirhan did not act under his own volition and knowledge or intention at the time of the assassination ... and further that the system of mind control which was imposed upon him has also made it impossible for him to recall, under hypnosis or consciously, many critical details of actions and events leading up to and at the time of the shooting in the pantry of the Ambassador Hotel."[727]

But if Dr. Brown was right – and no other expert has so thoroughly tested and assessed Sirhan – when and where did the hypno-programming take place? The psychologist's investigations pinpointed the most likely timeframe.

"Friends and family state that Mr. Sirhan underwent a fundamental personality change after a fall from a horse while racing at the Corona track in [sic] September 25, 1966. The personality change is attributed to a head injury. There is no evidence of a head injury. The emergency room hospital record shows he was treated for a superficial eye injury and discharged the same day...

"Testimony by his family and best friend establishes that Mr. Sirhan was actually missing for two weeks. The facts suggest that the horse fall was drug-induced and staged, and that Mr. Sirhan was taken to an unidentified hospital unit for two

---

727 *Ibid.*

weeks, and whatever was done to him caused a fundamental change in his personality."[728]

The parallels between Dr. Brown's authoritative findings and the details of the CIA's Operation ARTICHOKE – disclosed in its own documents – are too close to be reasonably dismissed as mere coincidence. Moreover, it appears that LAPD's detectives knew Sirhan had indeed disappeared for a significant period immediately after his accident. In 2005, Bill Jordan, a Sergeant who had worked within in Special Unit Senator, told UK *The Independent* newspaper that he and his colleagues had questioned Sirhan extensively about the missing period.

"We took him back for more than a year with some intensity – where he'd been, what he'd been doing, who he'd been seeing. But there was this 10 or 12 week gap … we could never penetrate".[729]

But if this establishes the possible timing of Sirhan's alleged hypno-programming, the questions remains: who was responsible for it? One document, contained in the 50,000 pages of S.U.S. files provides a clue. Within days of the assassination LAPD's Criminal Intelligence Division received a phone call from a man called Herb Elfman. He claimed that Sirhan belonged to a "secret hypnosis group" and suggested the detectives speak to Joan Simmons, a program planner for the local Steve Allison radio show, who "had knowledge of this".[730]

Mr. Elfman was known to the police as a regular caller; "a right wing extremist" with a propensity for denouncing the influence of sinister communist forces. Nonetheless S.U.S. dutifully followed up his lead. The same memo continued: "Officer

---

728 *Ibid.*

729 *Was Robert Kennedy killed by real Manchurian Candidate-style assassin? The Independent,* January 18, 2005.

730 File memo: Interview via phone of Joan Simmons, June 11 1968. Rampart Detective Division. SUS files Vol. 51, p.332. California State Archives.

contacted Simmons … who stated she knew nothing of a secret hypnosis group but knew a Dr. Bryant of American Institute of Hypnosis, who has been on the show."[731]

On the basis of Mr. Elfman's apparent paranoia, the police decided not to pursue any further enquiries. Had they done so, however, they would have discovered that the mysterious "Dr. Bryant" was in fact Dr. William Joseph Bryan: a man who – by his own statements – had a long history of working in hypno-programming with the CIA.

Born in 1926, Dr. William Joseph Bryan was a pioneering hypnotist and one of the founders of modern hypnotherapy. According to his own account, he had worked with, or for, the CIA's MKUltra mind control project and the US military. During the Korean War he claimed to have served as "chief of all medical survival training for the US Air Force, which meant the brainwashing section"[732]. During his time with the CIA he developed a technique he termed "hypno-conditioning" and later published widely on the military's use of psychological research[733]. In 1955 he founded the American Institute of Hypnosis and edited its academic journal.

Bryan also claimed to have been hired as a consultant on Frank Sinatra's 1962 Hollywood version of *The Manchurian Candidate*; and within hours of the Kennedy shooting he had told listeners to a Los Angeles radio station that the suspect had "probably acted under post-hypnotic suggestion"[734].

This statement, together with the Elfman/Simmons tip-off and Dr. Bryan's widely-publicised history of involvement in hypno-programming, should have led detectives to call at his

---

731 *Ibid.*
732 William J. Bryan interview on KNX-FM radio, Los Angeles. February 12, 1972.
733 *"William J. Bryan's Hypnotic State"* in: Alison Winter: *Memory. Fragments of a Modern History.* University of Chicago Press, 2012.
734 *Ray Briem Show;* KABC. June 5, 1968.

Sunset Strip offices. They did not: there is no trace in the S.U.S. files of any further reference to this "brainwashing" expert.

But there was an additional piece of circumstantial evidence which – in a properly conducted investigation – should have flagged William Bryan as a person of interest. In the early 1960s Dr. Bryan worked as a hypnotism consultant on two major murders cases for Boston 'superlawyer' F. Lee Bailey. For the most famous of these, in November 1964, he worked with Bailey's client, Albert DeSalvo. Under Bryan's hypnosis, DeSalvo duly confessed to the 13 'Boston Strangler' murders[735].

Sirhan had no known connection with Boston, F. Lee Bailey or the Strangler killings. Yet one page in his notebook – the product, according to both prosecution and defence experts, of hypnotically-induced automatic writing – contained the phrase "God help me, please help me. Salvo Di De Salvo Die S Salvo".

Sirhan had no memory of writing this. Nor, after his arrest did he appear to have any knowledge of the Boston Strangler case.[736] . Which begs the question: what caused him to scribble out the name of one of Bryan's most famous hypnosis subjects during one of his own hypnotic trances?

Dr. Herbert Spiegel strongly suspected that Dr. Bryan had hypnotized Sirhan.[737] In the early 1970s he suggested to a group of researchers, then led by journalist Jonn Christian, that they should attempt to interview the psychiatrist. From his own experience of the man, Dr. Spiegel knew Dr. Bryan was voluble, bombastic and egotistical, and thought might be persuaded to open up about his knowledge of the assassination. In June 1974 one of

---

735 Albert DeSalvo Papers; John Jay College of Criminal Justice, New York City.

736 During his first hours in custody, a fellow inmate was recorded speaking to Sirhan about the Boston Strangler. Sirhan, unaware that his cell was bugged, did not appear to recognize the case.

737 Dr. Herbert Spiegel: interviews with Tim Tate, New York, 1991–1992.

the researchers, Betsy Langman[738], interviewed Bryan on tape in his Sunset Strip office. As the recording of their meeting testifies, she found him – initially – in boastful mood.

"I am an expert in the use of hypnosis in criminal law, I sure as hell am," the tape captured him bragging. "I can hypnotize everybody in this office in five minutes.[739]

Langman then asked Dr. Bryan for a professional opinion on the feasibility of hypno-programming a subject to perform actions which ran counter to their own moral code. Once more, he was happy to offer advice.

"You have to have the person locked up physically, to have control over them; you have to use a certain amount of physical torture … and there is also the use of long-term hypnotic sugges-tion, probably drugs, whatever and so on. Under these situations, where you have all this going for you, like in a prison camp and so on, yes, you can brainwash a person to do just about anything."[740]

Then, to dispel any doubt that he was speaking from personal knowledge and expertise, he added: "What I'm speaking about are the innumerable instances we ran into when I was running the country's brainwashing and anti-brainwashing programmes."[741]

But when Langman asked about Sirhan, Dr. Bryan suddenly became much less helpful, angrily snapping "I'm not going to comment on that case because I didn't hypnotize him". He then abruptly terminated the interview.[742]

---

738 Betsy Langman, an actor turned writer, was on assignment for Harpers' Magazine.
739 William J. Bryan interview with Betsy Langman, 1974. Audio tape in authors' possession.
740 *Ibid.*
741 *Ibid.*
742 *Ibid.* Langman's subsequent article floated the possibility of Sirhan having been hypno-programmed, but made no mention of Dr. Bryan. *Sirhan's Gun*: Betsy Langman & Alexander Cockburn; Harpers' Magazine, 1974. Robert F. Kennedy Assassination Archives.

Was William Bryan the hypnotism expert who programmed Sirhan? LAPD's failure to include him in their investigations prevents a definitive answer. Nor is he available to question. On March 4, 1977 Dr. William J. Bryan was found dead in the Riviera Hotel, Las Vegas, apparently of natural causes (although no autopsy was performed). He was 51 years old and unquestionably obese, weighing in at approximately 400 pounds (28 stone or 181 kg).

However, in a curious – but undocumented – footnote to the story, Prof. Philip Melanson, head of the Robert F. Kennedy Assassination Archives at the University of Massachusetts, alleged that just before his death Dr. Bryan had been summoned to appear before the House Select Committee on Assassinations.[743] [744]

There was one other equally tantalising – and equally unproven – allegation. Jonn Christian claimed that after Dr. Bryan's sudden death he interviewed two prostitutes who claimed that the psychiatrist had been a long-term, regular customer; and that during several of their twice-weekly encounters he had confessed to programming Sirhan. The allegation proved impossible to substantiate: whilst Dr. Bryan was known to have had a disturbing sexual appetite[745], Christian – then deeply affected by alcoholism and his own rampant paranoia[746] – was unable, or unwilling, to identify his alleged informants or provide any evidence supporting their supposed claim[747] [748].

---

743 Philip Melanson. *The Robert Kennedy Assassination: New Revelations on the Conspiracy and Cover-Up, 1968–1991.* (Shapolsky, 1991)
744 Prof. Melanson died in September 2006.
745 In 1969, the California Board of Medical Examiners found him guilty of unprofessional conduct for molesting four women patients whom he had hypnotized.
746 Jonn Christian: correspondence and interviews with Tim Tate, 1991–1994.
747 Jonn Christian,: interviews with Tim Tate, 1991 – 1994
748 Christian died, a pauper and ward of the State of Oregon, in February 2001.

To be sure, none of this represents proof positive that the CIA or its contracted psychiatrists programmed Sirhan to assassinate Bobby. In the wilderness of mirrors which surround and protect intelligence agencies it can be almost impossible to determine what is truth and what is misdirection.

Yet the evidence that Sirhan was acting under the influence of hypnosis, and the parallels between his involvement in the shooting in the pantry and the Agency's extensive – and evidently successful – experiments to create a hypno-programmed "Manchurian Candidate" political assassin are clear. Coupled with all the other evidence contradicting the official version of events – the eyewitness testimony, the ballistic impossibilities and, above all, the scientific proof of a second gunman contained in the Pruszynski recording – it demands a level-headed, honest and through re-investigation of the assassination. Unfortunately, LA law enforcement has vehemently refused to order any new inquiry.

CHAPTER EIGHTEEN:
TRUTH AND JUSTICE

On Wednesday, February 10 2016, Paul Schrade left his home in Laurel Canyon, Los Angeles on a 150-mile journey to the Richard J. Donovan Correctional Facility in Otay Mesa, near San Diego. Schrade was then 91 years old, and one of the last survivors of the shooting in the pantry; for the first time since Sirhan's 1969 trial, he was about to come face to face with the man who had fired the bullet which wounded him.

Sirhan himself was 71, and had been held in a succession of prisons throughout California for 47 years. Under state law he was eligible, and indeed slated, for release in 1984, but on 14 separate occasions, parole boards had denied his requests. Schrade had spent almost all of those five decades campaigning for a new investigation into the events of June 4-5; the purpose of his journey that February morning was to appear in person before the latest hearing, and to make an emotional plea for justice.

"I am here," he told the Board, "to speak for myself, a shooting victim, and to bear witness for my friend, Bob Kennedy. Kennedy was a man of justice. But so far justice has not been served in this case. And I feel obliged as both a shooting victim and as an American to speak out about this – and to honour the memory of the greatest American I've ever known, Robert Francis Kennedy..."

* * *

The judicial road which led both men to their historic meeting had been long and tortuous. Between 1970 and 1972, Sirhan's new lawyers made a succession of appeals against his conviction and sentence, arguing variously that his trial had been procedurally unfair, that the psychiatric evidence showed he had been mentally ill at the time of the shooting, that the prosecution had reneged on the plea bargain which recognized this, and that execution was cruel and unusual punishment, outlawed by the Constitution. In June 1972 the California Supreme Court rejected each and every one of the claims and affirmed both verdict and sentence.[749]

Three years later, citing the evidence of ballistic inconsistencies and LAPD criminalist DeWayne Wolfer's incompetence which emerged from third-party law suits, Sirhan's layers filed a motion for a new trial. That, too, was denied.

Between 1974 and 1987 Paul Schrade had embarked on his own legal journey, applying to the courts for the right to see the files held under lock and key by LAPD and the FBI. After these were finally released, he and the other members of the Inquiry And Accountability Foundation, Dr. Philip Melanson and Attorney Marilyn Barrett, began preparing a formal request to the Los Angeles County Grand Jury.

The United States is one of only two nations operating under common law which uses Grand Juries (the other is Liberia) to screen criminal charges prior to indictment. Although the Fifth Amendment to the US Constitution states that "no person shall be held to answer for a capital, or otherwise heinous crime, unless

---

749   *The People vs. Sirhan Bishara Sirhan*, Crim. 14026, Super. Ct. A-233421, California Supreme Court, June 1972. Following the Court's decision that the death penalty was unconstitutional, Sirhan's sentence was commuted to life imprisonment on July 2, 1972.

on presentment or indictment of a Grand Jury", more than half of individual states have abandoned the practice. In those that retain it, Grand Juries are often dismissed as little more than the tools of the local District Attorney, because the rules proscribing what evidence he presents to them in seeking an indictment are considerably less stringent than those which apply at trial.

The California Penal Code, however, also provides for Grand Juries to operate independently of the DA and specifically requires that they "inquire into the willful or corrupt misconduct in the office of public officers of every description within the county"[750]. It was that provision which Schrade, Melanson and Barrett focused on.

The 800-page request which they submitted in March 1992 was a sober and thorough statement of the flaws in the assassination investigation as they were then known. Citing the "decisive new evidence [that] has been discovered in the LAPD's files on the case", and supplying a wealth of supporting affidavits from eyewitnesses and ballistics experts, it asserted that the police 'ignored material evidentiary leads, engaged in a concerted cover-up of its failures", destroyed or falsified "crucial evidence", in addition to "browbeating witnesses and coercing them to alter testimony".

Since this unequivocally demonstrated "willful or corrupt misconduct" the submission argued that the Grand Jury had a legal duty to order a new investigation into all aspects of the case, and to appoint a special prosecutor to oversee it.

"This is a case of paramount importance. Public confidence in the American system of justice has been undermined because of official misconduct and cover-up in the assassinations of President John F. Kennedy, Dr. Martin Luther King Jnr. and Senator Robert F. Kennedy. This Grand Jury here has the unique opportunity to create a remedy in this case and restore public

---

750   California Penal Code, Section 919(c)

confidence in our justice system. The American public deserves at least this much."[751]

The document was countersigned by an impressive array of fifty legal and criminal authorities, political leaders, journalists and artists. The American Civil Liberties Union, a Professor of Law at Georgetown University, a past-President of the American Academy of Forensic Scientists and William F. Bailey, the former FBI investigator who had observed bases of bullets inside bullet holes in the kitchen pantry within hours of the assassination, were joined by Cesar Chavez and Dolores Huerta – heroes of the Delano migrant labourers' battles – actors Martin Sheen, Ed Asner and Paul Le Mat, Academy Award-winning director Oliver Stone, writer Norman Mailer and journalists Floyd Nelson and Dan Moldea as well as one of the Watergate prosecutors and two of Bobby's closest advisors in the 1968 campaign, Frank Mankiewicz and Arthur Schlesinger. All added their signatures to the request.[752]

Two months later Grand Jury foreman George S. Ackerman sent a terse (and inaccurate) three-paragraph refusal. "The matter has been investigated several times by various agencies over the past twenty-four years. Since no new evidence has been uncovered, the Grand Jury shall not pursue the matter further."[753]

The letter infuriated the Inquiry And Accountability Foundation. Marilyn Barrett sent a detailed rebuttal of Ackerman's dismissal. "There has <u>never</u> been an investigation

---

751 *Request to the Los Angeles County Grand Jury. Schrade, Melanson, Barrett et al.* March 1992. Robert F. Kennedy Assassination Archives, University of Massachusetts Dartmouth.

752 *Signatories to Request to the Los Angeles County Grand Jury. Schrade, Melanson, Barrett et al.* March 1992. Robert F. Kennedy Assassination Archives, University of Massachusetts Dartmouth.

753 *Letter from George S. Ackerman, Foreman, Los Angeles County Grand Jury, 1991–1992, May 20, 1992.* Robert F. Kennedy Assassination Archives, University of Massachusetts Dartmouth.

conducted by any governmental or independent body regarding these questions of police misconduct," she complained. "The Grand Jury's ready dismissal of the substantial evidence of misconduct submitted is a clear violation of its legal obligation to the general public who it is appointed to serve ...

"The persons who prepared the Request did so with great care and diligence and cognizant of the official discomfort with which allegations of official improprieties in assassination cases are met. It was early on decided that no allegation would be made that could not be supported by actual evidence that could be submitted to the Grand Jury for its own review ... It is deplorable that the Grand Jury did not exercise similar care and diligence ... We shudder to anticipate the future of our democratic system when our independent Grand Jury, on whom the public relies for investigations of official misconduct, can so easily ignore such substantial evidence of official misconduct."[754]

Because Grand Juries serve only for one year, in the spring of 1993 the Inquiry And Accountability Foundation re-submitted the request to the new panel. Once again, the submission ran to 800 pages, with detailed evidence and affidavits; once again it was signed by the extensive list of attorneys, political figures, forensics experts and Hollywood glitterati.

The response this time was even more curt and dismissive than in 1992. New Foreperson, John A. Grande, sent Barrett a single paragraph, saying that the Grand Jury had "looked into the matter and has discussed it with the Los Angeles Police Department". There was no mention of what, if anything, it planned to do.[755]

---

754 *Letter from Marilyn Barrett, Attorney, to George S. Ackerman, Foreman, Los Angeles County Grand Jury, May 28, 1992.* Robert F. Kennedy Assassination Archives, University of Massachusetts Dartmouth.

755 *Letter from John A. Grande, Foreperson, Los Angeles County Grand Jury, June 22, 1993.* Robert F. Kennedy Assassination Archives, University of Massachusetts Dartmouth.

Barrett once again responded on behalf of the Foundation. After politely thanking the Grand Jury for considering the submission, she asked a series of forensic questions. Who were the LAPD officers with whom it had discussed the request? What efforts had been made to ensure that the police would no longer intimidate witnesses and destroy evidence? What disciplinary action was planned against those who had so clearly done either or both? And, on the specific facts of the case, "did the Grand Jury analyze the evidence submitted indicating that more bullets were recovered in the Kennedy assassination than the maximum of eight that could have been fired from Sirhan's gun?"[756]

Other than a vague and apparently verbal assurance that the Grand Jury would examine these questions, there is no record of any further response. As far as LA law enforcement and its judicial outposts were concerned, the case was closed.

"I don't think they ever really wanted to look at this," Barrett recalled in 2016. "We collected and submitted a huge amount of very clear evidence, but never got any indication that this had been seriously examined. We certainly never got the new official inquiry that was so obviously called for."[757]

Sirhan had run into a similarly immovable object in the form of the California Board of Prison Terms, which had the power to decide on parole. Under state law he should have been automatically entitled to release in 1984. However, in in 1981 Los Angeles District Attorney John Van de Kamp persuaded the Board to annul this right, citing testimony from a jail house snitch that Sirhan had threatened to kill Senator Edward Kennedy, should he become a future candidate for President.[758] That there was no

756 *Letter from Marilyn Barrett, Attorney, to John A. Grande, Foreperson, Los Angeles County Grand Jury, June 28, 1993.* Robert F. Kennedy Assassination Archives, University of Massachusetts Dartmouth.

757 Marilyn Barrett, Attorney. Interview with Tim Tate, 2016.

758 *Another Kennedy Death Threat; Newsweek,* August 24, 1981.

evidence other than the word of another convicted felon – which Sirhan vehemently denied – did not appear to trouble either the DA or the Board.

When, in June 1986, the Board held a hearing in Soledad Prison to consider parole, it explicitly told Sirhan and his legal team that the question rested on what threat to the general public would be posed by releasing him.

"The law and Board of Prison Terms Rules state that you are to be denied a parole date if your release would pose an unreasonable risk of danger to others"," presiding member Rudolph Castro said at the outset.[759]

However, despite evidence from the prison's own psychiatric staff that, in their view, the prisoner did not represent a threat to society, and despite Sirhan's own tearful remorse – "I want to say from the outset that I am sorry for this offense", he testified – the Board ruled against him; and it did so on explicitly political grounds.

"The motive [for the assassination] was to silence the opinion of the victim, who was a representative of the American people, who the prisoner felt was in conflict with his own political views regarding the Arab-Israeli conflict," Castro pronounced. "Three shots disenfranchised millions of people who, using the democratic process, had hopes of electing Senator Robert Kennedy as President of the United States... The panel was not impressed with the prisoner's insight nor appreciation of the enormity of his crime."[760]

The decision set the template for all future parole hearings: the magnitude of the crime for which Sirhan had been convicted outweighed the evidence that paroling him would pose no danger.

---

759 Transcript of the decision of the California Board of Prison Terms, Soledad Correctional Facility, June 26, 1985. p.3
760 *Ibid.* p.235.

At the heart of this was Sirhan's inability to recall the shooting; as he had said since his arrest, he had no memory of events between the time he drank a cup of coffee with the mysterious polka dot dress girl and the moment he 'awoke' with bodies piling on top of him. Since he could not remember shooting Bobby, successive Boards essentially determined that he could not have sufficient remorse to justify parole. It was a classic Catch 22: only if he admitted that he had intended to commit murder could he be deemed suitable for release.

The issue of whether Sirhan's amnesia was genuine or a cynical ploy prompted journalist Dan Moldea to request an interview with him in 1993. California's prison rules permitted such interviews – albeit under severely restricted conditions; Moldea, by then persuaded that Thane Cesar had not fired the fatal bullets, made contact with Sirhan's brother, Adel, and a woman named Rose Lynn Mangan, an amateur citizen-investigator who had become close to the family.[761] Between September and June the following year, and with their agreement and assistance, Moldea was taken into Corcoran State Prison, north of Los Angeles for three interviews with Sirhan

"I had to fill out some forms and give them to the prison," he recalled in 2016. "I think I revealed I was a reporter in those forms [but] I don't remember. I was treated like any other guest who was visiting an inmate. I was not allowed to bring any equipment – not even a pen. I had to scrounge up a pencil from one of the guards."

Without a notebook to record the meetings, Moldea wrote notes on the back of a prison schedule he persuaded the guards to give him. He began under the impression that Sirhan had not fired the shots which killed Bobby.

---

761 Mangan, who died in 2017, billed herself as "Sirhan's Researcher" posting on her own website a succession of closely-argued claims of his innocence.

"The first interview I was basically very sympathetic towards Sirhan; I still didn't believe he had done it, but I caught him in several discrepancies. And in the second interview I started to broach those discrepancies, and I caught him in some flat-out lies.

"And then the third interview, while Adel and I were driving up to Corcoran, I said, 'you know I'm gonna really get in his face today'. And I did. And that was really something. Sirhan was furious – really furious."[762]

Moldea has never explained what "discrepancies" and "flat out lies" Sirhan allegedly uttered in those three interviews. His 1995 book reports the story Sirhan had told ever since his arrest – that he had no memory of the shooting in the pantry, and that he became "seemingly overwrought" when Moldea challenged him, "exclaiming, 'It's so damn painful! I want to expunge all this from my mind."[763]

According to his own account, it was this outburst which caused Moldea to undergo a dramatic change of heart about Sirhan's role in the assassination. "As if I had been punched with a straight right hand," he wrote in the following paragraph, "I suddenly thought to myself, 'This fucking guy has been lying to me all along.'

"In response to Sirhan, I stated firmly 'I am not a court of law; I am not a parole board. I'm a reporter who doesn't want to be wrong. I want to know, Sirhan: Did you commit this crime? Sirhan fired right back, 'I would not want to take the blame for this crime as long as there is exculpatory evidence that I didn't do the crime. The jury was never given the opportunity to pass judgment on the evidence discovered since the trial, as well as

762 *Ibid.*
763 Dan E. Moldea, *The Killing of Robert F. Kennedy: An Investigation of Motive, Means and Opportunity*, p.302. W.W. Norton, 1995.

the inconsistencies of the firearms evidence at the trial. In view of this, no, I didn't get a fair trial.'"[764]

This reply, Moldea decided, indicated a clever strategy on Sirhan's behalf. "As long as people like me continued to put forth supposed new evidence, he still had a chance to experience freedom...As I sat there I became furious with myself for having nearly been hoodwinked by Sirhan and the bizarre circumstances of this entire case. I didn't even attempt to conceal my feelings."[765]

Following this damascene conversion, Moldea changed the thrust and direction of the last chapters of his book, dismissing as mistaken all the eyewitness and ballistic evidence he had previously set out and which he himself had gathered. To explain away the impossibility of Sirhan firing the fatal shots from behind Bobby at a distance of no more than three inches when he was, at all times several feet in front of him, the reporter posited that the dynamics of the crowd in the pantry somehow pushed and twisted Bobby into Sirhan's gun.

That there was no evidential basis for this suggestion, merely his own theorizing, did not deter Moldea from boasting subsequently that while "LAPD solved this murder with its arrest and the conviction of Sirhan...I solved this case."[766] It was a hubristic and irresponsible claim – and one on which California's Attorney General would later seize and rely.

Around the time of Moldea's final interview in Corcoran Prison, Sirhan got a new lawyer. Lawrence Teeter was a veteran civil rights attorney whose dedication to his clients' causes often led him to work free of charge. He took up Sirhan's case, *pro bono*, filing a succession of suits aimed at securing a new trial.

764 *Ibid.*
765 *Ibid*,p.303
766 Dan E. Moldea: post on his own website, June 3, 2000. http://www.moldea.com/2000june3.html

The appeals – densely argued and combative[767] – all fell on deaf ears. Between 1997 and his death in 2005, none of Teeter's requests were granted by the courts.

A new team of attorneys took up the cudgels – again working *pro bono* – in 2010. William Pepper, who had previously represented the family of Dr. Martin Luther King,[768] and Laurie Dusek began gathering evidence and witness statements for a new appeal. In October 2010, they filed a petition in federal court arguing that Sirhan was not the killer of Bobby Kennedy.

The case the lawyers advanced was detailed and thorough. It included evidence that the original lawyer counsel, Grant Cooper, had "a felony indictment hanging over him" during Sirhan's trial, which was withdrawn once the death sentence was passed.[769] "There can be no reasonable doubt," Pepper charged "that this conflict influenced, more precisely directed, Cooper's lamentable trial performance."[770] The petition also rehearsed all the ballistics and eyewitness evidence which conflicted with Corner Thomas Noguchi's autopsy report, and it included a statement made under oath by Phillip Van Praag setting out the scientific analyses of the Pruszynki recording which proved the existence of a second gunman. Dr. Daniel Brown also provided a lengthy sworn account of his memory sessions with Sirhan,

---

767 Some of Teeter's appeal documents have been digitized and placed on-line by the Mary Ferrel Foundation. They can be found at: https://www.maryferrell.org/php/showlist.php?docset=1688

768 They successfully sued a Memphis restaurant owner for involvement in a conspiracy to assassinate King. *Coretta Scott King v. Lloyd Jowers*, December 8, 1999. Viewable at: http://www.thekingcenter.org/civil-case-king-family-versus-jowers

769 Cooper was charged with having illegally received secret Grand Jury testimony in the mob-related *Friar's Club* trial.

770 *Sirhan Bishara Sirhan vs. George Galaza, Warden, et al. Petitioner's reply Brief on The Issue of Actual Innocence.* November 20, 2011. Case No. CV-00-5686-CAS (AJW), US District Court, Central District of California

and asserted his expert opinion that there was clear evidence of hypno-programming.[771]

However, the bid faced two significant problems. The first was procedural: because Sirhan had been convicted at trial, US law required his appeal to clear a very high bar. As Pepper and Dusek's brief acknowledged: "The standard of actual innocence does not simply require Petitioner to demonstrate the existence of reasonable doubt as to guilt but that he must show, in the light of all the evidence from the time of trial to the present, that the evidence is such that it is more likely than not that no juror would have voted to convict him."[772] In layman's terms, this meant a 180-degree reversal of the burden of proof: instead of the District Attorney having to prove guilt beyond reasonable doubt, Sirhan had to prove himself so unequivocally innocent that every one of the original jurors would have voted to acquit had they heard the new (or, in some case, more accurately suppressed) evidence.

The second problem was evidential, and it involved a previously unheard allegation that Sirhan had 'confessed' to the assassination. Michael McCowan had been the lead defence investigator in 1968. In the years following the trial, he had not played any public role for or against the attempts to re-open the case, but in February 1995 he gave Dan Moldea a written statement about a conversation he claimed to have had with his former client. Although signed by McCowan, the document itself was written by Moldea – hence its unusual construction as a third party report.

"During a prison visitation, McCowan tried to reconstruct the murder with Sirhan. Suddenly, in the midst of their conversation, Sirhan started to explain the moment when his eyes met Kennedy's just before he shot him. Shocked by what Sirhan

---

771 *Ibid.*
772 *Ibid.* p.7

had just admitted, McCowan asked, 'Then why, Sirhan, didn't you just shoot him between the eyes?' With no hesitation and no apparent remorse, Sirhan replied, 'Because that son of a bitch turned his head at the last second'."[773]

The allegation was incendiary and the Attorney General would cite it as clear evidence of Sirhan's guilt. There were, however, a number of difficulties with the Moldea-McCowan document. The first, and most obvious, was that the investigator's claim was hearsay: the conversation he claimed to have had was not witnessed by anyone else, nor had he raised it in any of the numerous pre-trial meetings between the defence and prosecution teams held in the judge's chambers. (As a de-facto officer of the court he had an arguable duty to disclose any directly inculpatory evidence given to him, and resign from the case.)

Added to these fundamental flaws, McCowan did not provide a date on which the confession was supposed to have occurred (thus making it almost impossible to verify). He was also a convicted felon – making his evidence at least questionable; and he had kept the alleged confession to himself throughout the decades of previous law suits.

Sirhan, unsurprisingly, denied having any such conversation with McCowan, and his brother, Munir, filed a sworn statement casting doubt on the investigator's motivation and behaviour throughout the case. "From our first introduction to Michael McCowan, his main interest was to get 'money for the defense'," Munir stated. "We were all told that unless we raised money, Sirhan was going to die..."[774]

---

773 *Michael McCowan signed statement for Dan E. Moldea,* February 25, 1995. http://www.moldea.com/McCowanLetter.html

774 *Sirhan Bishara Sirhan vs. George Galaza, Warden, et al. Declaration of Munir Sirhan.* June 24, 2011. Case No. CV-00-5686-CAS (AJW), US District Court, Central District of California

Furthermore, both the AG and the court knew that in 2011 the former investigator was seeking to monetise his past involvement in the case. Pepper had been forced to obtain an emergency injunction preventing McCowan from selling at auction four pages of scrawled notes allegedly written by Sirhan during the pre-trial period – thus making him a proven adversary. (The documents did not contain anything incriminating.)[775] Given all the circumstances, his claim that Sirhan had confessed to him, privately and alone, was – at best – legally dubious.

The California Attorney General, Kamala D. Harris, thought otherwise. She filed a robust rebuttal to Pepper and Dusek's plea, citing amongst other 'authorities', Dan Moldea and his speculative "explanation" of the contradictory eyewitness, autopsy and ballistic evidence: "Moldea thoroughly researched and refuted allegations, evidence and arguments similar to those raised by Petitioner," Harris argued. She also claimed as hard fact McCowan's entirely-unsupported claim to have heard Sirhan's confession.[776]

For the next five years Pepper and Dusek submitted every conceivable legal petition to have Sirhan's conviction – and, by extension, the assassination itself – re-examined. Each bid was met with an opposing brief from the Attorney General's office. Finally, in 2015, the lawyers ran out of road.

"This case may be the final chapter in an American tragedy," Judge Beverly Reid O'Connell wrote in a ruling dismissing the entire case. "Petitioner does not show that it is more likely than not that no juror, acting reasonably, would have found him guilty

---

775 *Sirhan Bishara Sirhan vs. George Galaza, Warden, et al. Preliminary Injunction Order.* April 25, 2011. Case No. CV-00-5686-CAS (AJW), US District Court, Central District of California

776 *Sirhan Bishara Sirhan vs. George Galaza, Warden, et al. Attorney General's Supplementary Brief Regarding Actual Innocence.* September 22, 2011. Case No. CV-00-5686-CAS (AJW), US District Court, Central District of California

beyond a reasonable doubt." O'Connell decided that the fundamental contradictions between the eyewitness testimony, showing that Sirhan was several feet in front of Bobby, and Noguchi's autopsy findings could be rejected because the "eyewitness statements paint a chaotic picture which would undoubtedly make it difficult for eyewitnesses to gauge the exact locations of the Petitioner and the Senator". For good measure, she cited the technical grounds that the contradictions could have been raised by Sirhan's original defence team at his trial.

Phillip Van Praag's sworn statement detailing his extensive analysis of the Pruszynksi recording, and the 13 shots (including double shots) he discerned within it, was also to be disregarded because it was opposed by the findings of Phillip Harrison – obtained not by way of an affidavit taken under oath, but rather by cutting and pasting the version of it contained in Mel Ayton's book – and therefore "this evidence does not meet the showing required ... for actual innocence."

The ballistics problems resulting from DeWayne Wolfer's woeful handling of exhibits were disposed of on the grounds that the 1975 panel of experts had already considered them. And as for the exhaustive psychological evidence of hypno-programming, Judge O'Connell simply pronounced herself "not persuaded" and on that basis ruled the high legal bar for actual innocence had not been cleared."[777]

With that, more than 40 years of attempts to persuade California's state and federal courts to order a new and honest investigation into Bobby's assassination were over.[778]

---

777 *Sirhan Bishara Sirhan vs. George Galaza, Warden, et al. Order Accepting the Report and Recommendation of the Magistrate Judge and Denying Petition for Writ of Habeas Corpus.* January 5, 2015. Case No. CV-00-5686-BRO (AJW), US District Court, Central District of California.

778 Pepper and Dusek appealed against the ruling: the following year judges from the 9th Circuit Court of Appeals refused to hear the case. *Sirhan*

***

The Board of Prison terms had proved equally unwilling to move beyond its 1985 decision not to grant parole; by 2016, Sirhan had lost all hope of the case being re-opened.

But Paul Schrade, whose belief that a second gunman was responsible for killing Bobby had never wavered, was determined to make one final effort. It was for that reason he set off from his home on the long journey to Otay Mesa, in San Diego County: Schrade was determined to plead with the Board in person, asking it to free the man whom he believed to be innocent of murder, even though one of Sirhan's bullets had wounded him.

"Originally Sirhan didn't want to go to that Parole Board hearing," Schrade said later. "Because every time he goes through this he gets terribly sick when he goes back to his cell, and he didn't want to go through the torture of that Board who are really cruel to him. But then he finally agreed to go because I was coming in."[779]

Schrade was not alone in his belief in Sirhan's innocence, nor in seeking to persuade the Board. Dr. Daniel Brown submitted a new declaration – again, sworn under penalty of perjury – detailing his expert advice that the prisoner had not carried out the assassination.

"Mr. Sirhan has been incarcerated for over four decades for a crime he is unlikely to have committed. Extensive psychological testing by me and others shows no evidence for any clinically significant psychiatric condition and low evidence for violence risk, combined with the new evidence that raises reasonable doubt that Mr. Sirhan was the assassin of Robert F. Kennedy…

Bishara Sirhan vs. P.D. Brazelton and Attorney General of the State of California. Order No: 15-55168, March 30, 2016

779 Paul Schrade. Interviews with Tim Tate, 2016.

"There is, in my opinion, no justifiable reason to deny his parole. Since he has spent all of his adult life in prison for a crime that he may not have committed, nor has volition about, knowledge of, nor memory for, the compassionate response would be to let Mr. Sirhan live the remainder of his life free."[780]

But it was Schrade's appearance which was most powerful. He took the Board through the essential evidence, but he also turned to speak directly to Sirhan.

"The evidence clearly shows you were not the gunman who shot Robert Kennedy. There is clear evidence of a second gunman in that kitchen pantry who shot Robert Kennedy. One of the bullets – the fatal bullet – struck Bob in the back of the head. Two bullets struck Bob literally in his back. A fourth bullet struck the back of his coat's upper right seam and passed harmlessly through his coat. I believe all four of those bullets were fired from a second gunman standing behind Bob. You were never behind Bob, nor was Bob's back ever exposed to you".

As for the fact that the prisoner in front of him had fired the shot which hit him, Schrade said simply: "Sirhan, I forgive you."[781] It was, he said later, "what Bob would have wanted me to do."[782] Bobby Kennedy's second son and namesake agreed: "I'm very proud of you, Paul," Robert F. Kennedy Jr. wrote in an email to Schrade after the parole hearing, "You did a great thing."[783] But it made no difference: for the fifteenth time in three decades, the Board of Prison Terms rejected Sirhan's application for parole.

---

780 *Declaration of Daniel Brown, Ph.D.* February 8, 2017. Copy in authors' possession.
781 Statement of Paul Schrade to the California Board of Prison terms, Richard J. Donovan Correctional Facility, Otay Mesa, San Diego; February 10, 2016.
782 Paul Schrade. Interviews with Tim Tate, 2016.
783 Robert Kennedy Jr. E-mail to Paul Schrade, February 15, 2016

CHAPTER NINETEEN:
THE LAST BEST HOPE

"**M**y father was an idealist and a pragmatist at the same time," Robert Kennedy Jnr. recalled half a century after the assassination. "[He] and his [older] brother ... saw America as the template for democracy, for civil rights, for human rights. I think they tried to change what our role, particularly in the world, was. To deploy the CIA and our military and our foreign policy not so much as historically had been the case ... but instead to advance this idealistic vision of humanity and democracy that they thought the US should really represent and promote in the world; that we had a historical mission; that we were part of something larger than ourselves and that America had a unique role in the world. To model the institutions of democracy, but also model good national behaviour."[784]

The question 'what if?' is difficult for historians, and even more so for journalists. Counter-factual history – essentially seeking to understand an alternative path of human events had a single incident not taken place – is fraught with hazards, since events never occur in isolation and simply removing one bump in the historical road does not automatically preclude the changes

784 Robert Kennedy Jnr. interview with Brad Johnson and Rob Beemer, Interesting Stuff Entertainment, Malibu, October 13, 2016

that it caused. Additionally, the speculative nature of the exercise is ineluctably coloured by the leanings – or yearnings – of those who dare to risk it.

And yet. Bobby was a man – a revolutionary – who unquestionably changed the United States in the years in which he exercised power or influence. His assassination affected that process of change and – both immediately and over the ensuing decades – diverted the road down which America then travelled.

If the violence and deaths at the Altamont Rock Festival in December 1969 symbolised the death of the cultural movement which became known as "the Woodstock Nation", the assassination of Robert Kennedy marked the end of the Sixties' *political* hope and idealism. And given the truism – both hackneyed and, by definition, true – that "when America sneezes, the rest of the world catches a cold", the events of June 4-5, 1968 in Los Angeles also had a profound effect on countries across the globe. Which is why we should ask 'what if?'

At its simplest and most parochial, would Bobby have gone on to claim the Democratic Party's nomination in the 1968 Presidential election? To beat Hubert Humphrey for the prize would require a floor fight and the support – far from guaranteed – of an overwhelming majority of delegates and power brokers at the party's Convention. And even if he triumphed in Chicago, would he have beaten the likely Republican nominee, Richard Nixon, and been elected to the Oval Office in that November's election. Paul Schrade, for one, is in no doubt.

"I think if Bob had lived he would have gone on to win the nomination. One of the things that happened that night was that he got a call from [campaign manager] Kenny O'Donnell who said he had got a call from our guys in Chicago – meaning Mayor Richard Daley – and that they were going to go with Bob. Daley was going to back him, and that would have sealed it. And after that, because of the whole movement in the country against the war in Vietnam I'm sure Bob would have beaten him [Nixon]."[785]

Paul Schrade's views are inevitably affected by his affection for, and belief in, the man he knew and campaigned for. But he is not alone. Robert Dallek, formerly Professor of History at Boston University, and one of the most diligent chroniclers of American Presidents[786] argues that despite the challenges of securing the Democratic nomination, "if RFK had lived, I think he would have won the presidency and we would have seen an earlier exit from Vietnam."[787].

Vietnam. The meat grinder which ate America's youthful soldiers as inexorably as it divided the nation they served (or, in many cases, were forced to serve). Bobby's position on Vietnam changed in the years he spent reluctantly supporting Lyndon Johnson. But by the time he entered the race for the Democratic nomination he – and the nation – knew where he stood. He had opposed the build-up of American forces in Indochina as early as 1965, and after the 1968 *Tet* offensive spoke out clearly and repeatedly against President Lyndon Johnson's policies.

Had he gone on to occupy the Oval Office, it is highly likely that the United States would not have sent more troops. By contrast, President Richard Nixon not only escalated the war – at a cost of tens, possibly hundreds, of thousands of lives – but ordered bombings and incursions into Laos and Cambodia.

Biographer and Kennedy confidante Jack Newfield argues that had Bobby been elected to the White House "we would not have suffered the criminal trauma of Watergate, the deaths

---

785 Paul Schrade: interview with Tim Tate, Los Angeles, July 2016.

786 He has published biographies of Franklin Roosevelt, Harry Truman Lyndon Johnson, John F. Kennedy, Richard Nixon and Ronald Reagan amongst many others.

787 [In] *How Robert F. Kennedy's Death Shattered the Nation.US News & World Report,* June 5, 2015.

of 27,000 more Americans in Vietnam and Cambodia...the overthrow and death of Allende in Chile, the shooting of four students at Kent State."[788] For his aide and speechwriter Peter Edelman, a Robert Kennedy Presidency would have "worked hard towards racial reconciliation and narrowing of income gaps at home...and we would have been in a different place today as a consequence."[789]

Twenty years after the assassination in Los Angeles, Adam Walinsky, one of Bobby's close assistants in the US Justice Department and the Senate believed that "Robert Kennedy was the last national leader able to command real trust from blacks and whites. Since his death we have chosen from a spectrum that offers us everything but dignity, self-respect and hope. No leader today is willing to confront the reality of violent black crime and the debilitating fear and poisonous resentment it engenders. Nor does any leader offer serious attention to the growing underclass from which the crime proceeds. We avert our eyes from the thousands of children who are dying in the projects and ghettos of every major city."[790]

In April 1992, four years after Walinsky published this assessment, Los Angeles was scarred by six days of rioting, looting, arson and death in the wake of the acquittal of four police officers for beating Rodney King, a black taxi driver. The unrest was the worst outbreak of violence in the city since the Watts riots in 1965.

A second Kennedy presidency would not, of course, have prevented this (not least because, by 1992 he would by then have been out of office for many years). But the King beating – captured on videotape – was symptomatic of a wider malaise, and

---

788 Jack Newfield: *Robert F. Kennedy – A Memoir;* p.339 Berkley Publishing, 1978

789 *RFK: American Experience.* PBS July 1, 2004

790 Adam Walinsky *Why We Search for R.F.K. New York Times,* June 5, 1988

one which might not have developed (or developed as fast) had Bobby occupied the Oval Office in the 1970s.

Dr. Joseph A. Palermo, Associate Professor of History at Sacramento State University, argues that Robert Kennedy's death led to "a rightward lurch in American politics ... and the wholesale debasing of our political discourse".[791] In stark contrast to the glib and cynical sound bites of those courting the votes of a fractured and polarized electorate today, Bobby saw the flaws in his country, and in its relationships with other nations, and spoke out against them.

"The social injustices he saw in American society and elsewhere in the world produced in him a visceral moral outrage that was palpable and real," Palermo wrote in a 2016 Huffington Post article to commemorate what would have been Bobby's 90th birthday, and to mourn what might have been.

"In today's haggard parlance they'd call it 'authenticity.' Yet RFK's hue of 'authenticity' wasn't manufactured from huddling with consultants and analyzing focus group data ... He believed the nation must stand for something other than consumerism and the pursuit of material wealth."

Robert Kennedy was no plaster saint. Like all politicians – especially those raised in wealth and privilege – he had flaws and blind spots. Yet, as his last years proved, he saw beyond the selfish battlements of entitlement and offered a vision of a kinder, better and more responsible America. In April 1968 he stood before a crowd of African-Americans immediately after the assassination of Dr. Martin Luther King and quoted Aeschylus. "Let's dedicate ourselves to what the Greeks wrote so many years ago: to tame the savageness of man and make gentle the life of this world. Let

---

791 *"Robert F. Kennedy would be 90 years old today"*; Huffington Post, November 20, 2015

us dedicated ourselves to that and say a prayer for our country and our people."

Against this backdrop, it is hard to believe that, had he lived, Robert Kennedy would not have fought against America's descent into what his biographer David Talbot terms "a dark age of clashing fundamentalisms" in which "the country is ruled by... a cult of secrecy and obedience". [792]

But it is Robert Kennedy's daughter, Kerry, who most starkly highlighted the contrast between her father's vision and the destruction by successive governments of the civil liberties for which her father fought. In August 2016 – five months before Donald Trump moved into the White House – she set this out in a letter to the *Washington Post*.

"In the name of national security, the Bush administration... engaged in domestic spying, undermined attorney-client privilege, allowed unfettered government access to... personal information of Americans accused of no crime... encouraged neighbor to spy on neighbor... targeted immigrants, demanded that 5,000 Muslim men accused of no crime 'voluntarily' report to police, detained U.S. citizens and greatly expanded the use of military tribunals in which the accused could be sentenced to death with no access to the evidence used against them. I stand by my assertion that these were not consistent with Kennedy's values." [793]

***

On December 1, 1862, one month before signing the Emancipation Proclamation, President Abraham Lincoln wrote a lengthy letter to Congress, pleading for its support. "We shall nobly save,

---

792 David Talbot. *Brothers: The Hidden History of the Kennedy Years*, p.409. Simon & Schuster, 2007
793 Kerry Kennedy: letter to the *Washington Post*, August 5, 2016

or meanly lose, the last best hope of earth ... The way is plain, peaceful, generous, just – a way which, if followed, the world will forever applaud, and God must forever bless."[794]

For many in America and across the world Bobby was the "last, best hope". His death changed the course of history and allowed the United States to be steered down a path which, fifty years later, threatens to tear it apart and threatens global stability. The events in the pantry of the Ambassador Hotel on the night of June 4-5, 1968 – the third political assassination to scar the country in less than five years – marked the end of one era and the beginning of a new, much darker age. It is for this reason – if no other – that the murder of Robert Francis Kennedy demands honest investigation.

---

794 Abraham Lincoln; letter to Congress, December 1, 1862.

AFTERWORD

J ournalists don't solve crimes: that job belongs to the police, prosecution authorities and the courts.

Our role is to investigate, locate evidence – new or overlooked – and, where that shows that the historical record is wrong or deficient, to present it with a strong recommendation for the case in question to be re-opened.

The assassination of Senator Robert F. Kennedy – a possible US Presidential nominee – on the night of June 4-5, 1968 should have been followed by an exemplary police inquiry. It wasn't. "Special Unit Senator" mounted only a simulacrum of an investigation. When examined closely, Los Angeles Police constructed the criminal equivalent of a *Potemkin* village – a Hollywood-style set whose façade concealed the truth that evidence was overlooked, destroyed or suppressed, and witnesses were ignored or intimidated into silence. After which LA law enforcement locked the whole sorry saga away, hiding their mis-deeds and incompetence behind impenetrable walls of official secrecy for two full decades.

Individually and in tandem, we have done our journalistic job for the past 25 years. We believe that the preponderance of evidence we (and others) have unearthed clearly indicates the presence of a second gunman in the Ambassador Hotel pantry – and that whilst Sirhan Sirhan wounded other people, an as-yet unidentified second shooter fired all the bullets that struck Bobby, one of which killed him.

We believe also that there are strong evidential grounds for the murder to have been the result of a conspiracy. This does not make us "conspiracy theorists": instead, we have simply unearthed the facts and held them up against the universally-accepted criteria of all criminal investigations: who had the means, the motive and the opportunity to mount such an elaborate scheme? And, in the words of all standard police operating procedure, *cui bono* – who benefitted?

On the balance of probabilities – the standard used by prosecutors to determine whether any investigation should be pursued – only a wealthy or well-established organisation would possess the resources needed. Organised crime – Bobby Kennedy's arch-enemy – fits that template, and documents in LAPD's own files show that it knew there to be evidence implicating elements within the Mafia.

Similarly, the intent, details and self-proclaimed accomplishment of the CIA's Operation ARTICHOKE, demonstrates that it, too, had the means to undertake such a deliberate political assassination. However outlandish the notions of hypnoprogramming and a "Manchurian Candidate" may seem – and they do – the Agency's own documents show that it was determined to create one and had mastered the techniques to the point of success. They also bear a remarkable similarity to the facts of the shooting in the Ambassador Hotel pantry, and to Sirhan's genuine amnesia about this.

The historical record shows, too, that there was a long and dishonourable history of co-operation between Organised Crime and the CIA, including joint attempts at political assassination. And it is also a fact that two of the key officers in Special Unit Senator had previously worked for American intelligence. Sgt. (later, Lieutenant) Hank Hernadez, LAPD's resident polygrapher, had, by his own account, administered lie detector tests to South American dictators; and Lt. Manny Pena, who was in charge of the Unit's conspiracy investigation team, was open about his previous employment with the CIA.[795]

Does this prove that the CIA and Organised Crime murdered the man who was thought by many to be on his way to the White House? No, it does not. But it does meet – and easily clear – the evidentiary threshold for legitimate suspicion; and it should unquestionably form part of a new official investigation.

There is, above all, one ineluctable imperative for such a new inquiry, and it was spelled out most clearly and calmly by Robert F. Kennedy's son and namesake. "I believe in science and evidence and pursuing existential truths and doing that fearlessly," Robert Kennedy Jr. said in a filmed interview arranged by Brad Johnson in 2016. "I think that's important for our country, it's important for democracy, it's important for everything that we value. That we make sure that we're making decisions and being honest.

"So let's look at the evidence and the science; and it appears now that the forensic evidence, the acoustic evidence, the ballistic evidence, are all inconsistent with the hypothesis that Sirhan Sirhan fired the shots that killed my father.

"If the police or the District Attorney's Office can't explain those inconsistencies, I think it's clear that we ought to have another investigation. We shouldn't just sweep this under the rug and say 'we're going to put blinders on and we're not going to continue to search for empirical truths'. That is an essential function of law enforcement agencies: follow the truth, follow the science, the evidence, and then to make judgements which are consistent with the truth.

---

795 Attorney Marilyn Barrett interviewed Pena and his family: all were proud of his work for the Agency. Marilyn Barrett: interviews with Tim Tate, 1991 – 2016.

"Whoever is in the DA's office who is making the argument that Sirhan Sirhan is guilty should be required to explain the inconsistencies between the science, the forensics, the acoustics, the ballistics and that hypothesis. If the science is inconsistent there needs to be a further investigation. If you can't square the science with Sirhan's guilt then we should find out who was guilty."

We agree. Which is why we wrote this book.

ACKNOWLEDGMENTS

Our thanks are due to a large number of individuals, as well as institutions, who have given generously of their time and helped us greatly over the years this book was researched and written.

We acknowledge with gratitude the efforts of those early investigators – both journalists and private citizens – who tried to shine light into the shadows of LAPD's Special Unit Senator. Floyd Nelson and Lillian Castellano were doughty seekers of truth from the first months after the assassination; William Turner and Jonn Christian pursued enquiries which demanded examination, at times with some cost to themselves. Likewise Ted Charach made a significant contribution: his single-minded determination unearthed important evidence which – had LA law enforcement been conducting an honest and through investigation – should have been followed-up.

Beyond them, Prof. Phillip Melanson and Gregory Stone worked tirelessly and uncovered – sometimes in conjunction with Dan E. Moldea – vital evidence; it is a source of some sadness that neither Melanson nor Stone lived long enough to see these efforts bear fruit. We're glad, however, that both Robert J. Joling and Rose Lynn Mangan did live long enough to see the first of those fruits. Each was a tireless and valuable contributor to our understanding of the case.

Marilyn Barrett's legal counsel ensured that the 1992 and 1993 requests to the Los Angles Grand Jury for a re-opening of the case were well-evidenced and rigorously-sourced. We, too, have been fortunate to have received her advice for more than 25 years.

Many witnesses to the events of June 4-5, 1968, were kind enough to speak to us over the years. Booker Griffin, Paul Sharaga, William Bailey, Sandra Serrano-Sewell and – in particular – Paul Schrade gave generously of their time and recollections. Schrade's courage and unceasing quest for truth have, to our minds, set an example which others would do well to follow.

We were also helped at key stages by those with specific areas of expertise. The late Dr. Herb Spiegel shared his extensive knowledge of hypnotism and hypno-programming; and Phil Van Praag's careful scientific analysis of the Pruszynski recording provided solid scientific proof that a second gun was fired in the Ambassador Hotel kitchen pantry.

We must also thank the staff of the California State Archives in Sacramento, and those of the Robert F. Kennedy Assassination Archives at the University of Massachusetts, Dartmouth. Both organisations patiently answered our questions and provided access to their collections.

However, the documentary evidence in the case runs to many tens of thousands of individual pages. Our task in examining these, and making the connections between the often-fragmented slices of information they contained, was made immeasurably easier by the Mary Ferrell Foundation. It has not only made copies of all the LAPD and FBI files (as well as many court documents and research papers) available online, it has ensured that these PDF files were formatted to be searchable. We, like many other researchers, owe the Foundation a major debt of gratitude.

Finally, we must place on record our appreciation of the courage with which Robert Kennedy Jr. has approached the troubling questions surrounding his father's assassination, and the uncommon dignity with which he now calls for the case to be officially re-opened.

BIBLIOGRAPHY

Mel Ayton. *The Forgotten Terrorist: Sirhan Sirhan and the Assassination of Robert F. Kennedy.* Potomac Books, 2007

John R. Bohrer. *The Revolution of Robert Kennedy.* Bloomsbury Publishing, 2016

C. David Heymann. *R.F.K.* Dutton, 1998

Robert A. Houghton. *Special Unit Senator: The Investigation of the Assassination of Senator Robert F. Kennedy.* Random House, 1970

Robert Joling & Philip van Praag. *An Open and Shut Case.* JV & Co., LLC, 2008

Robert Blair Kaiser. *"R.F.K. Must Die!"* Grove Press, 1970

Robert F. Kennedy. *The Enemy Within.* Popular Library, 1960

Robert F. Kennedy. *Robert Kennedy In His Own Words: The Unpublished Recollections of the Kennedy Years.* Bantam, 1988

Maxwell Taylor Kennedy. *Make Gentle The Life of This World: The Vision of Robert F. Kennedy.* Harcourt Brace, 1998

John Marks: The Search for The Manchurian Candidate: The CIA and Mind Control. Allen Lane, 1979

Philip H. Melanson, Ph.D. *The Robert Kennedy Assassination: New Revelations on the Conspiracy and Cover-Up.* Shapolski Publishers, 1991

Dan. E. Moldea. *The Killing of Robert F. Kennedy. An Investigation of Motive, Means and Opportunity.* W.W. Norton, 1995

Robert D. Morrow. *The Senator Must Die.* Round Table Publishing, 1988

Jack Newfield. *Robert F. Kennedy: A Memoir.* E.P. Dutton, 1969

Thomas T. Noguchi. *Coroner.* Simon & Schuster, 1982

Pierre Salinger, Edwin Guthman, Frank Makiewicz & John Seigenthaler. *"An Honorable Profession": A Tribute to Robert F. Kennedy.* Doubleday, 1968.

Arthur M. Schlesinger Jr. *Robert Kennedy and His Times.* Houghton Mifflin, 1978

David Talbot. *Brothers: The Hidden History of the Kennedy years.* Simon & Schuster, 2007

Evan Thomas. *Robert Kennedy: His Life.* Simon & Schuster, 2000.

William Turner & Jonn Christian. *The Assassination of Robert F. Kennedy: A Searching Look at the Conspiracy and Cover Up 1968–1978.* Random House, 1978

PICTURE CREDITS

All photographs from the Los Angeles Police Department Records of the Robert F. Kennedy Assassination Investigation. Courtesy of California State Archives, Sacramento.

INDEX

Lightning Source UK Ltd.
Milton Keynes UK
UKHW011445180919
350011UK00003B/701/P